Library of
Davidson College

ROMAN LAW

THE GRAY LECTURES
1966

ROMAN LAW

LINGUISTIC, SOCIAL AND PHILO-
SOPHICAL ASPECTS

DAVID DAUBE

Regius Professor of Civil Law
University of Oxford

EDINBURGH
AT THE UNIVERSITY PRESS

© David Daube 1969
Edinburgh University Press
22 George Square Edinburgh 8
North America
Aldine Publishing Company
Chicago 60606
Printed in Great Britain
at Aberdeen University Press
85224 051 1

PREFACE

These are the Gray Lectures, delivered before the Faculty of Classics at Cambridge, in 1966. Except for the inclusion of material which, for lack of time, I had to skip and, of course, the footnotes, I have left them unchanged in form and substance. My thanks are due to Peter Stein, Regius Professor of Civil Law in the University of Cambridge, for reading the typescript; and to Archie Turnbull, Secretary to the Edinburgh University Press, for his extraordinary understanding, helpfulness and efficiency in all matters pertaining to the publication.

David Daube

Berkeley, August 1968

To the memory
of my father and brother

CONTENTS

1. LINGUISTIC ASPECTS ... 1
   I. The Agent Noun ... 2
   II. The Action Noun ... 11
      A. Property ... 13
      B. Obligations ... 24
      C. Varia ... 29

2. SOCIAL ASPECTS ... 65
   I. Economic Realities ... 66
      A. Damages under the *Lex Aquilia* ... 66
      B. The Have-Nots ... 71
         1. The Horror of Intestacy ... 71
         2. The *Filiusfamilias* ... 75
   II. Roman Society ... 92
      A. Altruistic Dodges ... 92
         1. The Insolvent Debtor ... 93
         2. Slaves and Freedmen ... 94
         3. *Fideicommissa* ... 96
         4. The Undowered Bride ... 102
      B. The Protection of the Non-Tipper ... 117

3. PHILOSOPHICAL ASPECTS ... 129
   I. Standards of Liability ... 131
      A. *Dolus*, *culpa* and *casus* ... 131
      B. Differentiation in Life and Differentiation in Law ... 157
         1. Negligence ... 157
         2. Intent ... 163
   II. Reductio ad Absurdum ... 176

Index ... 195

1. LINGUISTIC ASPECTS

I. The Agent Noun. II. The Action Noun: A. Property;
B. Obligations; C. Varia

A few years ago, when I was visiting Charlottesville in Virginia, a press-interviewer asked me: 'How is it that you, as a Cambridge man, are a professor at Oxford?' I replied: 'Oh, those who are not quite good enough for Cambridge are always sent to Oxford.' Next day that appeared literally in the papers. I took a cutting with me and now, when my Oxford colleagues annoy me, I can show them black on white where they stand. However, once in a while you do remember your exiles, and I am greatly appreciative of your invitation to deliver these Lectures.

I propose today to make some observation on two linguistic phenomena, the agent noun and the action noun.

I. THE AGENT NOUN

First, for the agent noun.[1] I may bake or beg or cook or dream or see or love without being a baker, a beggar, a cook, a dreamer, a seer or a lover. That is to say, the agent noun, whether identical with the verb (cook) or formed from it by means of some ending like -er (baker from bake), often has a narrower range than the verb. This goes for Latin as well as English. The agent noun tends to be confined to the striking, it designates him who deserves to be so designated because his doing marks him, it appears to be out of the ordinary and therefore singles him out. A baker, a beggar or a cook is one who bakes, begs or cooks for a living, a dreamer dreams when he ought not to, in the middle of the road, and habitually too, a seer sees what others cannot see, a lover loves in the most important, intense and interesting way; and Latin *scriptor*, from *scribere*, signifies one who has made writing his profession, a secretary or an author.

Circumstances can make what is ordinarily ordinary, striking: in a chess match between the Perse and the School for the Blind you might divide the teams into the seers and the blind. The contrast gives the former an extra standing. Similarly, when the law looks at a person who does something, who buys, sells, borrows, lends, in that capacity, maybe as one party opposed to another, it speaks of the buyer, the vendor, the borrower, the lender. Again, a frequent application of the agent noun is where the action is introduced by some other form of the verb and then there is a reference back to the agent: A man ran after a thief; said somebody to the runner.... By the time of the reference back, the man is in special case. The agent noun would not do in the first half: there was a runner after a thief. It is the 'he ran' of the first half which, for the present story, characterizes the man sufficiently to be called

[1] Cf. my article in *Law Quarterly Review*, 62, 1946, 266ff.

The Agent Noun

'the runner' in the second.[1] In general, however, the agent noun picks out a particular remarkable division of the verb: I employ all sorts of things all the time, but it is the employment of human labour over a certain period on certain terms which makes me an employer.

It follows that if we come across a verb with an agent noun and the latter covers only a sector of the former, we must not automatically try to bring, force, the two into harmony. We must not, that is, automatically infer either that originally the agent noun must have been as wide as the verb or that the verb must have been as narrow as the noun. Yet both fallacies are common among scholars paying attention to language and, in legal history, some queer conclusions have resulted.

I shall begin with the case of the agent noun being arbitrarily inflated in order to render it coextensive with the verb.

In the sources, the noun *imperator* denotes, not anyone who gives an order, but a General. Indeed, it is mostly used of that real commander, the man who has been proclaimed General by the army itself; and, to go by the picture presented by the sources, this title borne by the leader the army has chosen precedes the more inclusive meaning General.

But now take Mommsen. He assumes[2] that, as *imperator* is derived from *imperare*, it originally embraced anyone holding

---

[1] In this function, however, the agent noun is still very close to the participle. Not much would be lost by re-formulating: said somebody to the running one. Still, if a reference back of this kind keeps recurring in the same context, it must help the development away from the participial nuance towards the proper nominal one. No doubt here is a factor (one of many – I have just mentioned another one in the text) leading to the terms buyer, vendor, *emptor*, *venditor*: a man bought a farm from his neighbour; the buyer claims that it is smaller than he was told. If this kind of discussion recurs again and again, 'buyer' moves away from 'buying one' and becomes a full noun. In several languages, these steps can sometimes be indicated by slight shifts in spelling or construction. In English, promiser is less advanced than promisor. A man promised his son a birthday present; when he forgot about it, they said to the promiser. By contrast: a man promised to contribute £1,000 to an insurance fund by 17 November; he failed to do so and the fund asks whether the promisor is liable for interest.

[2] *Römisches Staatsrecht*, vol.1, 3rd ed., 1887, 123.

the *imperium*. *Es scheint selbstverständlich*, he says, 'it seems obvious'. Rosenberg goes even further,[1] and indeed why not once the basic error is granted? He starts by declaring: *Imperator ist der Mann der imperat*, '*Imperator* is the man who *imperat*'. This would include a gentleman giving an order to a servant. He cannot, of course, seriously uphold this, so, by imperceptible steps, he goes on to anyone with *imperium* and then to a *rex*. By now, manifestly, his initial statement has become rather hollow: a *rex* is not just anyone who *imperat*. Anyhow, he admits that *freilich ist in historischer Zeit der älteste, vollste Wert des Wortes imperator verschollen*; 'to be sure (he says) in historical times the oldest, fullest value of the word *imperator* is forgotten' – it is restricted to a General.

All this is seen to be futile if the role of the agent noun is understood. It is perfectly normal for *imperator* to represent only a fraction of *imperare*, to be attached to the most impressive exercise of *imperium*. The evidence given by Mommsen and Rosenberg of traces of a pre-historical, unlimited scope is – as one would expect – forced. They refer to the Capitoline triad in the inscription of the Faliscan cooks,[2] Iuppiter, Iuno, Minerva, 'highest *imperatores*'. But surely, this triad is of good military provenance. The three are more than enough to frighten the wits out of me. There is nothing here to suggest an early indiscriminate use of the noun.

Another example of this class – the unwarranted extension of an agent noun in order to make it achieve the range of the verb – is provided by *spondere* and *sponsor*. *Spondere* means to promise, but, in the sources, *sponsor* means, not anyone who promises, but only him who promises for somebody else, a guarantor, a surety. Levy admits[3] that nowhere in extant tradition does *sponsor* denote a simple promiser. Nevertheless he thinks the word must once have been just as wide as *spondere* and, in support, quotes two texts. One of them does

---

[1] *Imperator*, in Pauly-Wissowa's *Real-Encyclopädie der classischen Altertumswissenschaft*, vol.9, pt.1, 1914, 1140.

[2] *CIL*, 11, 3078; Buecheler, *Carmina Latina Epigraphica*, vol.1, no.2, 2f.   [3] *Sponsio, fidepromissio, fideiussio*, 1907, 1f.

The Agent Noun

not contain *sponsor* at all; it mentions a *fideiussor*, and some modern authorities substitute *sponsor*.[1] The other is a suitably emended and interpreted passage in Varro – the transmitted text is corrupt.[2]

This is poor evidence, and there will never be any better. While the verb *spondere* means to promise in general, the agent noun *sponsor* describes him whose promise stands out, who promises in support of another person's promise or possibly even in the place of another person. (Which it is, in support of a promise or in the place of somebody who does not himself promise at all, depends on our view of the early role of surety. I know where I stand but shall not here stir up a hornets' nest by deciding; in either case the surety's promise is of a most notable kind.) It is he whose promise gives him a special position, he is the promiser *kat' exochen*, the *sponsor*.

The converse method of attaining smoothness, by postulating an original narrow range of the verb, is equally doomed to failure. I am glad to report that nobody so far contends that *imperare* started by signifying exclusively the giving of an order *qua* General. With regard to *spondere* and *sponsor*, however, this line of reasoning has found favour, and with far-reaching consequences. *Spondere*, the verb, it is alleged, at first occupied the same small area as *sponsor*: it meant to guarantee, to stand surety.

This thesis has many followers; and it is a major factor in a fundamental doctrine concerning the birth of contract, first set forth by Mitteis,[3] now probably the most popular view,

---

[1] D.46.3.34.1, Julian *LIV digestorum*. How the text is to be reconstructed is here quite immaterial.

[2] *L.L.* 6.69: *spondit est sponsor quidem faciat obligatur sponsus conspontus.* A widely accepted emendation makes a sentence of the first three words, thus: *qui spopondit est sponsor*. And this is interpreted as covering any *spondere*. Apart from the dubiousness of the interpretation, it is surely on the cards that the words *sponsor qui ⟨i⟩ dem faciat* or *sponsor qui ⟨i⟩ dem faciat obligatur* belong together. By the way, the word *spondit*, which the prevalent emendation turns into *spopondit*, appears earlier on in the same paragraph: *declinatum spondit*. Here some authorities, though not all, emend it into *despondet*. Maybe it ought to be left unemended in both cases.

[3] *Festschrift für Bekker*, 1907, 107ff.

the doctrine that contract starts from surety.[1] How does the thesis come to play this part? *Spondere* is used of the making of an ordinary promise (with no suretyship involved) from ancient times – always remember, the sources contain no evidence of a restricted application. Actually, this ordinary promise (with no suretyship involved) is the oldest proper contract figuring in legal references and may, therefore, be regarded as the ancestor of all subsequent contracts. Now initially, it is claimed, the verb can have been no wider than its agent noun. Hence the contract by means of an ordinary promise and, with it, all subsequent contracts must descend from the contract entered into by a surety.

Whether Mitteis's idea that contract originated in surety is right or wrong I am not here concerned with; it is based on other arguments besides this one. This one, however, is utterly unconvincing since it assumes absolute, initial agreement between a verb and its agent noun to be inevitable. Language is less simple. No reason to boggle at *spondere* having the wide sense of to promise, while *sponsor* is the label for that strange man who promises by way of assistance of another man or in his stead. If I may anticipate a little, the argument I am combating receives a further heavy blow from a fact never noticed, which I shall discuss in the second part of this Lecture – namely, that the action noun *sponsio* never once signifies surety.[2]

It is amazing, incidentally, with what tenacity a beloved doctrine is carried on even when the props go one after another. Prior to the discovery of the new Gaius fragments in 1933, the advocates of the surety root of contract placed the surety phase – that primary phase when there was as yet only a promise to be liable for somebody else's debt – in the period of the XII Tables. The new fragments show that the law of that time already knew the straightforward promise to pay oneself and be liable oneself, *spondere* and *sponsio* in the wide, ordinary sense. This has, however, shaken few believers; the postulated stage

---

[1] See, e.g. Jolowicz, *Historical Introduction to Roman Law*, 2nd ed., 1954, 290f.
[2] See below, pp. 24ff.

when there was no *spondere* or *sponsio* but that of a *sponsor*, a surety, is simply dated further back. De Zulueta, for instance, still inclines to the surety root, though he does add[1]: 'However, if in the distant past *sponsio* was nothing except a method of becoming a hostage, this had ceased to be so by the time of the XII Tables.' By contrast, Levy, never really a member of this school of thought, is emphatic in pointing out the implications of the new fragments: 'Extremely questionable becomes the popular thesis that *sponsio* begins by being exclusively the acceptance of liability for others, next turns into a debtor's standing surety for himself and only in the end serves to ground debt and liability in the same person at the same time.'[2] Levy, however, we saw, in his turn assimilates *spondere* and *sponsor* by imputing the former's wide range to the latter.

There are close parallels to the relation of *spondere*, to promise, and *sponsor*, the promiser in support or in the place of somebody else – such as the Latin *actor* in the sense of advocate and English agent, from *agere*, or English factor and Italian *fattore*, from *facere*. *Agere* denotes any acting, *facere* any doing. But it is he who acts or does in another person's interest, or indeed he who acts or does while the person affected remains passively in the background, whom language promotes to the rank of *actor*-advocate, agent, factor, *fattore*.[3] Note also

[1] *The Institutes of Gaius*, vol.2, 1955, 152.

[2] *Zeitschrift der Savigny-Stiftung*, 54, 1934, Rom. Abt., 299: *Schwer in Frage gestellt sieht sich aber auch die weit verbreitete Hypothese, dass die sponsio zunächst allgemein ausschliesslich Haftungsübernahme für andere, demnächst Selbstverbürgung des Schuldners und erst zuletzt Begründung eigener Schuld und Haftung gewesen sei.*

[3] In Roman criminal law, *factor* never acquired the general sense of German *Täter* (unless we find it in the obscure D.48.3.7, Macer *II de officio praesidis*). Neither has English doer acquired it to this day (except in Germanizing academic jargon – my first series of *Gifford Lectures* at Edinburgh was inscribed 'The Deed and the Doer in the Bible'). In a few late classical or post-classical texts (post-classical according to Beseler, *Zeitschrift*, 66, 1948, 297) *factor* contrasts the person actually committing the deed with him who merely knows about it (D.29.5.1.21, Ulpian *L ad edictum*) or merely does not prevent it (D.49.16.6.8, Arrius Menander *III de re militari*). German *Täter* is, of course, derived from the noun *Tat*, not directly from the verb *tun*. In its commonest application, as denoting an offender, it palpably singles out a very notable kind of doing.

that, frequently, the man so described performs professionally. Naturally, within the compass of a verb of wide scope there may be several sectors striking enough for the agent noun to be applied. I have just adverted to *actor* in the sense of advocate, from *agere*. *Actor*, however, also signifies a player at the theatre.¹ If we adopt the reasoning of the Mitteis school in the case of *spondere* and *sponsor*, all human activity may be traced back to the stage, since *agere* must originally have been limited to the sphere of the *actor*. In reality, the noun reflects the professionalism, the artificiality, the stylized, deliberate, learned quality of the acting in question; it is these features which make of the person acting thus an *actor*, single him out from the vast realm of ordinary *agere*.

We need not, then, infer from the existence of the agent noun procurer that, in England, all aid extended to a fellow-man in obtaining his wants derives from the lowest of deals. The procurer is labelled as such because he procures a very special ware in a very special fashion and indeed makes a living by it.² But I am prepared to accept the origin of Roman contract in suretyship if my colleagues will grant me that the English contract is descended from funeral arrangements. Evidently, the undertaker must be the prototype of whoever undertakes anything. As a matter of fact, the development here is not uninteresting. The verb to undertake from the beginning embraces any kind of task. When the agent noun first appears, it singles out him who engages in a task for others – the undertaker much in the sense of its literal French translation *entrepreneur*. (Another case, therefore, somewhat comparable to *sponsor*.) Then it sticks to that particular job most readily left to a stranger, least willingly done for themselves by those principally concerned, the mourners of a near

---

[1] In English, this meaning of actor seems to have come into use later than the meaning pleader, but once established it gradually ousted the latter. Throughout this Lecture, as regards the history of English words, I am guided chiefly by the *Oxford English Dictionary*.

[2] The noun appears after Shakespeare only, in the seventeenth century. Shakespeare has the verb in this sense: *Measure for Measure*, 3.2.58, 'does she still procure?'.

The Agent Noun

relation, and thus the meaning funeral manager carries the day. Nor is this the end of the story. In colloquial speech, from this agent noun denoting the funeral manager, the verb to undertake acquires the specialized narrow sense of to direct a burial (side by side with its ordinary, general sense). Actually, it may be followed by an accusative: you may undertake a person. In literary English this sense is extremely rare. Still, *Blackwood's Magazine* of 1900 introduces a son who 'undertakes' his father. The inverted commas are in the magazine. It is not only that the usage as such is considered irregular, but in addition, in this case the normal position is reversed in that, from filial affection, a man does himself what as a rule is left to an outsider; so the verb normally in its specialized sense signifying to manage a burial for others, here refers to a burial managed by the principal mourner in person.[1]

The English contractor develops in the full light of history. In post-classical times, Latin *contractor* can mean a contracting party; it is not a frequent usage, but it is well evidenced.[2] In

[1] The Latin pair *suscipere*, *susceptor* (with the action noun *susceptio*) is relevant. The development is similar – though the funeral stage is not represented – and it certainly influenced that of to undertake, undertaker, *entreprendre*, *entrepreneur*.

[2] C.11.62.6.1, Gratianus Valentinianus et Theodosius, AD 384: certain possessions cannot be taken from the heirs of the holder or, indeed, from other *contractores*, i.e. persons who have acquired from him in some other way, chiefly purchase. In view of this text, I hesitate to accept Mommsen's emendation of C.10.2.5.pr.=*C. Theod.* 10.16.3, Valens Gratianus et Valentinianus, AD 377. An account book of a person whose goods have been confiscated shows *nomina debitorum seu contractorum*: in default of further evidence, may the authorities enforce these items? Mommsen emends *seu* into *secum*. But *seu* is in the MSS of both C. and *C. Theod*. The constitution is from the same era as that considered above. And surely, we can translate 'outstanding debts of borrowers (*debitores*) or such as had entered into other contracts (*contractores*)'. True, the rest of the constitution contemplates loans, but these might arise from purchases, tenancies, all sorts of dealings; it was quite usual to list as 'credited money' what remained unpaid, say, of a purchase price. C.5.5.8, Zeno, AD 475, is a bit different. *Contractores* here resumes the verb *contrahere* used just before: 'if unions of this kind are contracted, the contractors are to be subject to such and such consequences.' This is more in the nature of the usage described above, pp. 2f., and accordingly, this text by itself would not prove that the noun *contractor* had fully attained the sense of contracting party.

the sixteenth century the word is taken over into English, in this general sense. Subsequently, however, in the eighteenth, it gets stuck with the master-contractor, who makes the umbrella contract for all the others, the smaller participants in the affair. The general sense now becomes obsolete. Here we simply know that the narrow noun is secondary, and the verb still retains its large range.

Sir Caspar Turnstone came down the path, propelling his little nephew before him. Even so, he was not a propeller. Micawber waited for something to turn up, yet he was not a waiter. I react strongly against some ideas of our University planners, but I am not a reactor. I refrain from multiplying examples. In deference to the current emphasis on the equality of sexes, however, I give a female illustration. *Merere* or *mereri* means to earn, *meretrix*, literally, the earneress. Was the noun at one time wide, including a schoolmistress? Or was the verb narrow and there is no profit and no merit but goes back to the example set by the call-girl? In reality the noun is from the outset confined to a sector of the verb. The lady is called earneress because she makes a profession of earning, because she sets about earning in a rather special fashion, and indeed because the very fact that a woman earns is striking – there were not at the time many other ways, this kind of woman is *the* earneress.

The last point is paralleled by the English noun professional as used of a woman. For a long time this signified a *meretrix*: there was no other profession for females. Nowadays they have more openings and if you hear of a lady that she is a professional, you had better enquire before you make a date or you might find yourself landed with an estate agent or a dentist. It is in fact predictable that the earlier meaning of the noun, already obsolescent, will soon have dropped out of use.

II. THE ACTION NOUN

I now come to the action noun, in the main found with transitive verbs – expel has expulsion, terminate termination, neutralize neutralization – but also with intransitive ones, hesitate, hesitation. Nearly always the noun is later: well, it is derived from the verb. Expel exists before expulsion, hesitate before hesitation. The step of forming the noun means something; a good deal or relatively little according to circumstances, but something. To put it at its lowest, there has been some reflection on the activity in question, there is some trend towards abstraction, systematization, classification perhaps, the thing is becoming more of an institution.[1]

Take neutralization. Medieval or rather Renaissance Latin has only the verb, *neutralisare*; it occurs from the fifteenth century and signifies to favour neither. French science adopts it in the form *neutraliser* and in the sense of to render neutral, about 1600 (first appearance 1611), and it takes approximately two hundred years for the action noun, *neutralisation*, to be coined (first appearance 1797).[2] English scientists borrow the verb from their French colleagues half-way through the eighteenth century, to neutralise (first appearance 1759: 'I neutralized Spanish White by fermenting it with vinegar') and the noun some fifty years later, neutralisation (1808; Faraday employs it in 1827, 'Neutralisations are best effected with the assistance of heat'). It is by 1800, then, that the activity has become a proper, fully recognized category in science. In connection with war and international politics, the English

[1] I shall concentrate on a comparatively late group of action nouns, formed by means of a characteristic ending. My main reason is that earlier groups are too remote for the evolution from verb to noun to be readily datable. It is easily demonstrated, however, that my considerations apply to those earlier cases as well: to this day, the action noun deed, for example, suggests a higher degree of reflection, formality, institutionalization than its verb to do.

[2] For French dates I rely principally on Littré and Hatzfeld.

verb is first recorded in 1856, the noun in 1870 – both, as it happens, having regard to the Black Sea. (I was so surprised by this late entry of the concept into international relations that I checked earlier sources, for example, concerning the status of Switzerland. They invariably speak, not of to neutralise, but of recognize or guarantee the neutrality.) So though by the middle of the nineteenth century science is familiar with the noun as well as the verb, international law begins all over again with the latter and the noun represents the stage when the concept is more established, elevated to an institution in the field.[1]

This kind of development is met throughout the entire realm of language, in all areas of human engagement, in philosophy, science, politics, architecture, everywhere. Its neglect vitiates or simplifies much of the intellectual history of civilization. In fact I submit that, right across the board, if we pay it the attention it deserves, a revolutionary new picture of the unfolding of thought will emerge. Just think of the difference between a simple *aequare*,[2] to be found in Plautus, and an advanced *aequatio*[3] from Cicero on; between a simple *humare*, from Varro, or *cremare*, from Cicero, and an advanced *humatio* or *crematio*, post-Augustan; between a modest Biblical *imitari Deum* and a solemn, post-Biblical *imitatio Dei*; between *iustificare*, from Tertullian, and *iustificatio*, from Augustine. In English, between to establish, second half of fourteenth century, and establishment, slowly coming in towards the end of the fifteenth, an indispensable slogan today; between to nationalize in the sense of to bring under the nation's control, first appearing in 1836 ('Neither the Arminian System nor the Nationalizing System nor the Calvinistic System exhibits the end of the sincere Gospel'), and nationalization, 1874, significantly in an explanation of the doctrine ('Nationalization

---

[1] As an intransitive, denoting to steer a middle, undecided course (mostly used in a disparaging tone), to neutralize figures from as early as 1628. This sense, however never achieves an action noun at all.

[2] Or *appellare, concipere, contemplari, describere, donare, inducere, introducere, mittere.*   [3] *Appellatio, conceptio, contemplatio, descriptio, donatio, inductio, introductio, missio.*

The Action Noun : Property

of the land means that all the land in the country should be bought by the State'); between to transplant, before the middle of the fifteenth century, and transplantation, from the beginning of the seventeenth – or if we confine ourselves to the fashionable, surgical application, between to transplant, with reference to a tooth, 1786, and transplantation, with a wider sweep, including severed limbs as well as teeth, 1813. Just think of the insights to be gained by tracing, accounting for and evaluating such moves; by comparing the speed of progress of various concepts in a certain field; by comparing the speed of progress of various fields; and indeed by comparing, under this aspect, various languages and cultures. I shall here concentrate on Roman law, which, you will not dispute, is always in the vanguard of exploration.[1]

A. Property

Let me set out from a somewhat remote corner. It is well known that when the ancient sources refer to the appropriation of an object by seizing it, they use only the verb *occupare*, never *occupatio*[2]. At first sight this might be regarded as of no interest, a freak; but it gains in significance when we go more systematically through this branch of the law, the original modes of acquisition. *Derelinquere* in the sense of to abandon a piece of property occurs sixty times in the *Vocabularium Jurisprudentiae Romanae*[3]; *derelictio* does not occur once. (It occurs once in Cicero – in the sense of undutiful neglect, *derelictio communis utilitatis*[4]). Treasure trove is invariably spoken of as *thesaurum invenire*, never as *thesauri inventio*. Materials owned by one person being built into a house owned by another invariably as *inaedificare*, never as *inaedificatio* (a medieval word). Corn owned by one person being sown in land owned

[1] *Exploro* is Plautine (*exploratum*), *exploratio* post-Augustan.

[2] Non-technically, *occupare* is found from Plautus, *occupatio* from Cicero.

[3] Lists all occurrences of all words in the Digest, Gaius and a few other jurists; abbreviation VJR.

[4] *de Off.* 3.6.30.

by another invariably as *serere*, never as *satio*.[1] A's and B's things (say, two silver ingots) combining into one invariably as *commiscere*, never as *commixtio*. The making of a new thing with another man's materials invariably as *speciem facere*, never as *specificatio* (a medieval word).

If we had only, say, the two cases of *thesaurum invenire* and *inaedificare*, the absence of action nouns might be an accident of transmission; these cases are mentioned only a few times, so it might just have so happened that the verbs were preferred. However, in the case of *derelinquere*, the discrepancy between sixty times for the verb and nought for the noun is statistically significant; and when we find the noun missing in one after another of similar cases – *occupare, serere, commiscere, speciem facere* – then, though each case by itself would be too little represented in the texts to provide a firm basis for conclusions, the cumulative evidence is far from negligible. (I shall rely on this method a good deal: a cluster of even rare words, all pointing the same way, is as good as one frequent word.) It follows that, in this branch of the law at least, systematization had made far less headway in Roman times than would appear from our textbooks.

In several instances, to be sure, the action noun was reached; they are indeed particularly instructive. According to the legal situation, a man might acquire the fruits of an object belonging to another man either directly they are separated no matter by whom, or only if he gains control of, harvests, them.[2] In discussing the former alternative the sources use only *fructum separare*; there is no *fructus separatio*. In discussing the latter,

---

[1] The noun occurs once in the Digest (7.4.10.4, Ulpian *XVII ad Sabinum*), in the plural, denoting not a mode of acquisition, but concrete sowings which have taken place in what was originally a wood, with the result that the usufruct over the wood is extinguished by change of the object. In the language of agriculture, the farmer's activity, the nominalization of *serere* was achieved at a time when it was not yet achieved in the theory of original modes of acquisition of ownership.

[2] Of course both cases are exceptional. Mostly the owner of the principal object acquires its fruits. But suppose, for example, I am bona fide possessor of a farm, that is to say, I cultivate a farm which I honestly think is mine, though in reality, as will emerge some day, it is yours: here the law gives me the fruits coming about while I am in possession.

The Action Noun : Property

however, they use both *fructum percipere* and *fructus perceptio*. This example brings out the importance an understanding of the step from verb to noun has for appreciating the relative evolution of various institutions, how advanced or backward they are, compared with one another. *Fructus perceptio* came into being when *fructus separatio* was not yet known; the latter is a medieval coinage. Here is strong and unexpected support for Aru's thesis,[1] probable anyhow on quite different grounds, that acquisition of fruits on separation is spurious, a post-classical intrusion into the earlier texts.[2] Making a late start, this mode of acquisition did not arrive at the action noun till the Middle Ages.

Separatio, incidentally, is not uncommon in legal literature. It may denote the separation of moveables which have been mixed.[3] The noun phrase *separatio bonorum* is familiar. Strangely, only in two texts listed by VJR does *separatio* mean divorce.[4] In all these – and other – cases the more systematized, established level had clearly been attained.

A few more nouns among the original modes of acquisition are noteworthy: *ferruminatio*, from *ferruminare*, *plumbatura*, from *plumbare*, *alluvio*, from *alluere*.[5] These nouns come, the first two from an artisan's craft, the third from the science of the *agrimensores*, surveyors. (Cicero mentions[6] that disputes about *alluvio* come before the centumviral court: they involved questions traditionally considered of great communal importance.) So despite their role in the law, the three nouns are not products of an internal legal development: they grew up in other branches of civilization and were taken over, ready-made,

---

[1] *Bullettino dell'Istituto di Diritto Romano*, 45, 1938, 191ff.

[2] Typical is D.41.1.48 pr., Paul *VII ad Plautium*: 'A *bonae fidei* buyer without doubt makes the fruits his own by gaining control.... Finally, even before he gains control, as soon as they are separated from the land, they belong to the *bonae fidei* buyer.' The addition sticks out.

[3] D.9.2.27.14, 20, Ulpian *XVIII ad edictum*, 25.1.9, Ulpian *XXXVI ad Sabinum*.

[4] D.23.3.9.3, Ulpian *XXXI ad Sabinum*, 32.49.6, Ulpian *XXI ad Sabinum*.

[5] An intransitive verb.

[6] *de Orat.* 1.38.173.

by the jurists.¹ (Even so, *adplumbare* alone is represented in the sources, legal or lay; *adplumbatio*, though honoured with an entry in Pauly-Wissowa and mentioned in most major textbooks, is medieval. *Avulsio* also has no locus standi in ancient Roman law. It is a far later and rarer word than *alluvio*, attested from the elder Pliny on, but not found in the jurists. I suppose the rules about this contingency, though obviously classical,² are a later refinement to *alluvio*. It never came to a nominalization.) While in the case of *separare* and *percipere* we could gauge the relative state of progress of various legal institutions, the cases under notice give us an inkling of the comparisons which, if we are alive to the move from verb to noun and provide ourselves with sufficient material, might be possible between various provinces of endeavour – law and certain industries, law and certain crafts.

In modern expositions, *accessio* is the heading for all cases of acquisition by A of B's property as a result of the latter physically merging in A's: *alluvio*, for instance, or building on A's land with B's materials. It has long been seen that this meaning is alien to the sources. No wonder: even the verb *accedere* has not got it.³ It is noteworthy, however, that *accessio* is used by the classics technically in several other senses: in that of a subordinate object which, in certain transactions, goes with the major one⁴; in that of addition in favour of A's usucapion of his predecessor's possession or time of possession⁵; in that

---

¹ Very likely *confusio*, too, which (in addition to *confundere*) twice appears in connection with original acquisition, goes back to the language of a craft. D.6.1.23.5, Paul *XXI ad edictum*: 'Welding brings about unification (*confusionem*), soldering does not do the same'. I.2.1.27: 'If materials belonging to two owners combine, that entire object which comes into being through this combination (*confusione*). . . .' In neither text can *confusio* really be called a mode of acquisition, it is still a factual, industrial phenomenon. On *confundere* and *confusio* where right and duty merge in the same person I shall comment below, pp 37f

² G.2.71.   ³ An intransitive.

⁴ D.34.2.19.13, Ulpian *XX ad Sabinum*: if I bequeath my gold, a jewel set in gold is included.

⁵ *Accessio possessionis* or *temporis*: G.4.151, D.44.3.6.1, Africanus *IX quaestionum*, 44.3.15.1, Venuleius *V interdictorum*.

The Action Noun : Property

of the accompaniment of one obligation, thought of as the principal one, by another.[1] In all these departments, abstraction with regard to the concept in question had gone further than in that of original modes of acquisition.

I now go on to a more basic concept. The verb *acquirere* has more than a thousand entries in VJR, the noun *acquisitio* has twelve. Eleven of the latter passages are in the Digest, all interpolated,[2] the twelfth is the rubric of *Ulp. Reg.* 19. But never mind about interpolation. Even if there were twelve occurrences starting from about the middle of the second century AD, the discrepancy would be staggering. In the *Thesaurus Linguae Latinae*, apart from those twelve texts, the earliest instance of the noun is in the *Itala*. By contrast, the verb is frequent in Cicero, it is also used, for example, in the *senatusconsultum de aedificiis non diruendis*,[3] in the *Laudatio Turiae*,[4] in the edict of the curule aediles.[5] In the *Codex Theodosianus* the verb figures twenty times, in the *Post-Theodosian Novels* fifteen, the noun not once.[6]

To say that the classics preferred the verb for stylistic reasons is not enough. Style may be a contributory factor, but the phenomenon calls for a deeper explanation: it has to do with the slowness of systematizing, institutionalizing, mastery of the discipline. Beseler[7] speaks of the 'aversion of the classical jurists to the noun'. He instances *aequitas*, *captivitas*, *distinctio*, *praesumptio*, *ratihabitio*, all, he affirms, post-classical. It may be admitted that, though his criticism goes too far,[8] he has a

---

[1] G.3.126, D.44.7.44 pr., 4, Paul *LXXIV ad edictum*.

[2] Beseler, *Zeitschrift*, 52, 1932, 42.

[3] Bruns, *Fontes Iuris Romani Antiqui*, 7th ed. Gradenwitz, 1909, 200f.

[4] *Op. cit.* 323.

[5] Lenel, *Das Edictum Perpetuum*, 3rd ed., 1927, 555.

[6] Even in the rubric of *Ulp. Reg.* 19, the noun appears in the plural, signifying the various ways of acquiring (*res mancipi, nec mancipi*); it does not represent a governing notion acquisition, though, admittedly, by this time the notion may well have been current.

[7] *Zeitschrift*, 57, 1937, 15.

[8] *Distinctio*, for example, cannot be totally thrown out. On *acceptio*, which he discusses at p. 1, see below, pp. 30f.

point. But not a much stronger one than a future student of English writings who will be able to invoke an express recommendation of the Fowlers[1] to be sparing with abstract nouns and make for concrete expressions.

That the clue does not lie in mere elegance is easily proved. For one thing, the evolution from verb to noun is a universal one, reflected in lay literature as well as legal, and indeed to be found in literatures other than Latin. We just cannot put it down to a convention peculiar to the classical jurists. This is underlined by the fact that the *Codex Theodosianus* shows the same picture as the classical writings: twenty to nought (or, including the *Novels*, thirty-five to nought). No one would impute atticistic rigour to the *Codex Theodosianus*: it is a question of greater or lesser conceptual advance. For another thing, there are countless action nouns in the classics. In this Lecture, in order to make my point, I give prominence to cases where the action noun is conspicuously absent. But a glance at the dictionary will show that there was no conspiracy to avoid action nouns. One line of further research I am suggesting is precisely to find out in detail about their distribution; we have already seen that *fructus perceptio* is classical, *fructus separatio* medieval. Not infrequently it is indeed demonstrable that the classics themselves coined or took over from outside an action noun where their predecessors had been content with the verb. *Acquisitio* happens to be of post-classical Western origin (Western: it occurs in *Ulpiani Regulae* and the *Itala*); but we shall find that *fideiussio*, for instance, possibly came in at some point during the classical era. Moreover, once an action noun is in use, it may be about as frequent as the verb: *accusatio* and *appellatio* are examples.

There is in the case of *acquisitio* some strong, additional support for my approach: while *acquisitio* is late, *alienatio*, from *alienare*, goes back to the last century of the Republic. The verb is met in Plautus; the noun occurs in Cicero,[2] in

[1] *The King's English*, 3rd ed., 1930, 15.
[2] In the phrase *sacrorum alienatio*: *Orat. ad Brutum* 144, *de Leg.* 3.48. Cicero also once has *abalienatio*: *Top.* 5.28. *Abalienare* occurs in Plautus.

The Action Noun : Property

Seneca,[1] in the praetorian edict – *alienatio iudicii mutandi causa*, somebody is about to sue you for an object, so in order to thwart him you transfer it to a mighty person or to one living in another province[2] – in the jurists, in the *Codex Theodosianus*, in the *Post-Theodosian Novels*. The contrast is dramatic. No consideration of style will account for it. It must be accounted for in terms of classification, abstraction, proceeding at a different pace in different sectors of the law.

Acquisitio is late, *alienatio* early. Why? For a long time the Roman jurists[3] produced no rules – I should say, no express, formulated rules – about acquisition as such. In the main, problems of acquisition became acute in connection with litigation about an object, with the very act of acquisition being in dispute. However, what would be controverted was not acquisition as such, but a specific way of acquiring or rather, more frequently, conveying. The party denying that the other had acquired the object would say, not 'You have not acquired', but 'You have not usucaped', 'I have not mancipated to you', 'I have made no delivery to you'; and his opponent would say, 'I have used it for a full year', 'You have mancipated, delivered'. Thus the focus was all on *usucapio*, *mancipatio*, *traditio* and so forth.

By contrast, it was soon found necessary to lay down rules about alienation as such. The question of alienation arose chiefly in connection with restrictions on a man's power of disposal. Already the XII Tables knew groups restricted in a greater or less degree: women, male persons under age, lunatics, prodigals. Whatever the language of the code itself (where *alienatio* does not yet, of course, occur), magistrates and legal experts would have frequent occasion to pronounce on the position of these groups in regard to alienation in general, irrespective of any specific mode of conveyance

---

[1] In a definition of sale: *de Ben.* 5.10.1. Here also *translatio*.

[2] See Lenel, *Edictum*, 125.

[3] The Roman jurists: this is not a matter of natural law, and it would be rash to assume that, elsewhere, things might not take the opposite course, acquisition being nominalized before alienation.

resorted to. The evidence is unambiguous: about four-fifths of all texts containing *alienatio* belong here, deal with restrictions on disposal. Remember the edict I have just adverted to, concerning the transfer of a disputed object to a mighty person or one residing in another province. The way it was transferred would be totally irrelevant; the praetor was against alienation *tout court*.[1] In regard to alienation, then, there was far less in the way of a more thorough working out of the notion than in regard to acquisition. It is – we may conclude – in consequence of the very different settings of the discussions that the nominal

---

[1] Further examples. (1) The XII Tables provide (VII 12) that if an heir sells a *statuliber* (a slave manumitted 'if he pays the heir so and so much money'), the latter may pay the buyer (Bruns, 28). According to Pomponius, Aristo (a friend of the younger Pliny), in an opinion he delivered to Celsus, argued that the word 'sale' here embraced any *alienatio*: D.40.7.29, Pomponius *XVIII ad Quintum Mucium*. (2) The discussion of an edictal provision against alienation to defraud creditors, D.42.8.6.5, Ulpian *LXVI ad edictum*. (3) The discussion of a *rei vindicatio* modified by insertion of a fiction, employed where honorarian or imperial restrictions on alienation are contravened, D.50.16.28 pr., Paul *XXI ad edictum*. (Why VJR says this is the *actio Publiciana* I do not know, except that the *actio Publiciana* is also a *vindicatio* with fiction.) (4) The discussion of a problem arising out of a provision of the *lex Julia de adulteriis* forbidding alienation of *fundus dotalis*, C.5.23.1, Severus et Antoninus, AD 213. (5) The discussion of a provision of the *lex Julia de adulteriis* forbidding a woman to manumit a slave within sixty days of divorce, lest he be no longer available for questioning under torture should there be a charge of adultery. In post-classical law alienation was equally prohibited: D.40.9.14.6, Ulpian *IV de adulteriis* (see Yaron, *Revue Internationale des Droits de l'Antiquité*, 3rd ser., 2, 1955, 385). (6) The discussion of an *oratio Severi* of AD 195, forbidding a tutor to alienate urban land of the ward without consent of the praetor, D.27.9.3.1f., 5.8.7 pr., Ulpian *XXXV ad edictum*. (7) The discussion of the *actio de peculio annalis* against him who manumits or alienates a slave, D.15.2.1.5f., Ulpian *XXIX ad edictum*. (8) D.18.1.67, Pomponius *XXXIX ad Quintum Mucium*, is interesting. Originally this fragment, too, dealt with a disability: a *praedium subsignatum* – land pledged to the state – remains tied even when alienated. In the Digest, the statement is torn from its context and placed in the title *De contrahenda emptione*, with the result that a general principle emerges: throughout the private law, we are told, an object which is being alienated carries its juristic condition with it. On compilatorial generalisations of this nature see Daube, *Zeitschrift*, 76, 1959, 149ff. Note that we have to do with a 'free' text (see *ibidem*, 261ff.), a text which, by Justinian's time, was no longer otherwise applicable since the old *praediatura* was long gone.

The Action Noun : Property

stage in the case of alienation precedes by hundreds of years that in the case of acquisition.[1]

There is an illuminating corollary: *alienatio* sometimes denotes not just alienation but power of alienation. In this application, which reflects a yet further evolution of theory, the noun is often interpolated.[2] But it is represented, or at least approached, in Gaius: a ward has no power of alienation of anything without his tutor's authority.[3] In any case, no parallel signification of *acquisitio*, power of acquisition, is found either in classical or in Byzantine law. The use of *alienatio* in the sense discussed points up not only the enormously more advanced stage of this concept, but also its central area – the question of restrictions on disposal. *Alienatio* may mean the absence of a disability, the freedom to dispose.

My finding is confirmed by the synonyms of *acquirere* and *acquisitio*. The verb *parare* is very frequent, *paratio* is represented in one interpolated text.[4] *Comparare*, in the sense of to acquire, occurs two hundred times in VJR, the noun is rare and mostly interpolated.[5] Professor Lawson has recently stated[6]: 'In fact, throughout the ancient history of Roman law... where

---

[1] Even *alienatio* as a heading in an *ex professo* treatment of modes of acquisition first appears as late as *Ulp. Reg.* 19.3,7,9; e.g. *mancipatio propria species alienationis est rerum mancipi*. The rubric, it may be recalled (above, p. 17 n. 6), has *acquisitiones*.

[2] D.14.6.9.1, Ulpian *XXIX ad edictum*, 24.1.3.8, Ulpian *XXXII ad Sabinum* (Thayer, *Lex Aquilia and Gifts between Husband and Wife*, 1929, 131, in a criticism of Beseler, blunders about the *bona fide serviens*: this expression can indeed be applied to one who knows himself free), 42.8.12, Marcellus *XVIII digestorum*; see Beseler, *Zeitschrift*, 57, 1937, 3.

[3] 2.84: if you pay a ward without his tutor's authority your debt is not gone, *quia nullius rei alienatio ei sine tutore auctore concessa est*. Moreover, there is the old precedent of *datio deminutio*, Livy, 39.19.5: see below, pp. 40, 45.

[4] D.30.39.7, Ulpian *XII ad Sabinum*; see Beseler, *Zeitschrift*, 66, 1948, 342.

[5] Always according to Beseler, *Beiträge zur Kritik der römischen Rechtsquellen*, vol.5, 1931, 82f. He goes too far, however; some of the passages are surely genuine. In fact, the classical usage of the noun is, I think, interestingly confined, but there is no need here to enlarge. The situation as a whole agrees with my thesis.

[6] *Boston University Law Review*, 46, 1966, 185.

we should speak of conveyancing, the Romans spoke of acquisition.' In view of the absence or lateness of such nouns or noun phrases as *occupatio, thesauri inventio, acquisitio, comparatio*, and the classicality of *alienatio*, as also of *mancipatio, in iure cessio, traditio*, some reservation is surely needed.[1]

In passing – *mancipatio, in iure cessio* and *traditio* are indeed classical, but it is advisable not to be too sanguine even about their age. The verbs are ancient enough. *Mancipare* and *tradere* are Plautine; and though *in iure cedere* is first met in Varro, it is probably much older – we have to allow for the fact that this institution becomes progressively less prominent in classical law and is ignored by Justinian: our sources therefore present a strongly reduced picture.[2] The nouns are a different matter. When Paul says that the XII Tables confirmed *mancipatio* and *in iure cessio*[3] that does not prove that the code employed the nouns. *Mancipatio* appears in Festus, *in iure*

---

[1] The matter is infinitely complicated. It is certainly correct that in formal transactions it was usually the person acquiring who spoke or acted; see Buckland, *Festschrift Koschaker*, 1939, vol.1, 16ff. In a sense, this does mean 'emphasis ... placed on the acquisition of property even when it was acquired by an act of alienation by another person' (Lawson, l.c.). But only in a sense; the alienor, too, played a part, if only by admitting the ceremony. And it by no means follows that the Roman jurists thought of acquisition where we think of conveyance. One distinction which is noticeable when we ponder the terminology is that the 'original' modes look at the business from the point of view of the acquirer, *usucapere, occupare* and so on, the 'derivative' ones from that of the giver, *mancipare, in iure cedere, tradere*. He who bases his right on an 'original' mode will allege no transfer; it is his taking which will be controversial. He who relies on a 'derivative' mode will usually be faced, in litigation, by the person from whom he derives his right, and while he says 'You mancipated the object to me', the other will deny just this. In Jewish law, not so action-oriented, the prevailing point of view seems to be the acquirer's: *qana, qinyan*. Enough.

[2] I have little doubt, however, that *in iure cedere* is younger than *mancipare* and *tradere*. The various transactions described by *in iure cedere*, I think, went on for a long time under more specific, concrete names before this expression was coined.

[3] *Fr. Vat.* 50, Paul *I manualium: et mancipationem et in iure cessionem lex XII tabularum confirmat*. Cf. below, pp. 29f. on the case of *emptio*. Very critical about *Fr. Vat.* 50, Buckland, *Text-Book of Roman Law*, 3rd ed., Stein, 1963, 234.

The Action Noun : Property

cessio in Cicero. Very likely they existed, say, by the end of the second century BC.[1] (The same is probably true of *usucapio*, first attested in Cicero.[2]) *Traditio* as a technical term may well be a little later than that. Varro mentions *emptiones et traditiones*.[3] *Venditio traditioque* also occurs in the edict of the aediles,[4] but in a paragraph hardly part of the earliest version and quite likely added towards the end of the Republic.[5] Cicero has the noun once, in the combination *traditio nexu*, signifying *mancipatio*.[6] Otherwise we know it only from the jurists of the Empire.

Still about acquisition and transfer. *Transmittere ad heredem* and the like may be found sixty times in VJR, *transmissio* not once; nor is it found in the *Codex Theodosianus*; nor anywhere in lay literature. Its first occurrence is in a law by Justinian.[7] An enormous amount has been written in recent decades as to whether the classics ever managed to conceive of a transfer of a

---

[1] The availability of *mancipium* may have been a factor in delaying *mancipatio*: see below, p. 34 n. 4, pp. 44f.

[2] *Pro Caec.* 26.74. The form *usus capio*, with *usus* in the genitive, in *de Leg.* 1.21.55, may be meant as a reminder that the XII Tables spoke of *usus*.

[3] *R.R.* 2.6.3.

[4] Lenel, *Edictum*, 555.

[5] Lenel, 560, notices that the items which a purchaser, to succeed in *actio redhibitoria*, must restore to the seller together with the slave are listed in a different sequence in the main edict and in the pattern formula. The former places at the head compensation for damage to the slave while in the purchaser's hands (*post venditionem traditionemque*) and then such things as offspring and profit made by hiring out the slave. The formula puts offspring and profit first and compensation after. Lenel's explanation does not convince me. I think there was development. For some time, all that was expected of the purchaser was to restore the slave plus additions. Then the need for compensation in the case of damage arose, and a clause to provide for this was appended both in the main edict and in the formula. The latter remained frozen at this stage, while in the main edict a more logical order was introduced: the slave whose quality does not come up to standard may be returned, taking account, however, of such deterioration as has been caused while the purchaser was in charge, and equally offspring, profit and so on must be restored.

[6] *Top.* 5.28.

[7] C.6.30.19.1, AD 529, dealing with the transmission of the *beneficium deliberandi* to one's successors.

right – say, a transfer of ownership, *dominium*, as opposed to a transfer of the actual object; or, if they did manage, from when and how far. I shall not engage in this battle, except to observe that to discriminate between *transferre* and *translatio* would here be particularly helpful towards a more profound and accurate assessment of the development.[1]

B. Obligations

Here is a cluster of action nouns which astounded even myself: *sponsio*, from *spondere*, *fidepromissio*, from *fidepromittere*, *fideiussio*, from *fideiubere*, as designations of three kinds of surety. But do you want to know the truth about them?

Sponsio in the sense of the private law contract of surety simply does not exist, be it in legal sources, be it in lay. It always means the ordinary stipulation, formal promise, with no suretyship involved; or more precisely, that old variety of stipulation which was in use among Roman citizens only.[2] The reaction to this situation of Heumann and successive editors of his *Handlexikon* – Seckel among them – is remarkable. They badly feel the need to list the established meaning surety. So they quote for it D.1.3.1, where Papinian[3] says that *lex est . . . communis rei publicae sponsio*, 'statute is . . . the common undertaking of the state'. For making the evidence

---

[1] *Transferre* is very frequent in various senses, *translatio* occurs about a dozen times in VJR, the texts being dubious. The noun does, however, occur in the *Codex Theodosianus*. Also, I may recall, in Seneca, *de Ben.* 5.10.1, together with *alienatio* (above, p. 19 n. 1). Unquestionably the notion of transfer of property in its verbal form proceeded the systematized, institutionalized, nominal form. More I shall not say.

[2] To avoid misunderstandings – I do not, of course, mean that a surety might not avail himself of the form of stipulation called *sponsio*. In fact that form of stipulation did provide the instrument for the earliest surety. What I mean is that *sponsio* never specifically denotes the contract of surety as such, it always denotes the promise by means of *spondere* – to whatever use it is put. A man could give a *sponsio* by which he undertook delivery of a courtesan: it does not follow that *sponsio* signifies the promise of a courtesan. As it happens, no text is preserved using *sponsio* where a surety acts, but this, I suppose, is accidental: no text is preserved using *sponsio* where an *ancilla* is promised. [3] *1 definitionum*.

The Action Noun : Obligations

fit the result, this is worse than any judicial commission. Papinian's definition is a translation of Demosthenes, who (in his speech *Against Aristogeiton*) speaks of *syntheke koine*, 'a common pact'; actually, the Greek original is presented by the Digest directly after the fragment from Papinian, in D.1.3.2, from Marcian.[1] *Sponsio* is an apt rendering of *syntheke* in this context since a *lex*, like a stipulation, comes into operation by question and answer. Neither the Greek *syntheke* nor the Latin *sponsio* carries a trace of suretyship. All this apart from the fact that the statement is decidedly not concerned with private law arrangements.[2]

None the less Romanists are busy reconstructing texts as if *sponsio* did signify surety, and again and again where the Digest mentions *fideiussio*, this is declared to be a post-classical modernization and *sponsio* is substituted for it. I shall presently have surprising news about *fideiussio*. For the moment I would point out that it will not do to insert *sponsio* into the jurists.

Sponsus would be just possible. This is another action noun of *spondere* which, while it may function as a synonym of *sponsio*, denoting a formal civil promise in general, or at least a betrothal promise,[3] does also have the narrower sense of surety.[4] The word, however, is exceedingly rare. In general it

---

[1] *1 institutionum*.

[2] I have a feeling that Lewis and Short, too, are trying to find evidence for *sponsio* in a specialized sense when they register a series of treaties in Livy under a separate heading: agreement by giving surety. If by this they do mean that *sponsio* here denotes the undertaking of a *sponsor*, they are wrong. In all the texts they quote the noun is applied in the usual fashion; it refers to the undertaking of the principal contracting party, often a General. That his promise may be accompanied by further guarantees, such as the giving of hostages, or that there is the state behind him, does not affect the signification of the term. Mommsen has it right; see, e.g. *Römisches Staatsrecht*, vol.1, 247.

[3] Varro, *L.L.* 6.71, Gellius, 4.4.2, citing Servius Sulpicius Rufus, consul in 51 BC.

[4] Cicero, *ad Att.* 12.19.2 (the reading, however, is not absolutely certain), *Phaedrus*, 1,16,1 (the MSS have *sponsore* and *sponsum* is conjectured), G.4.22. The *lex Furia* discussed by Gaius dates from about 200 BC. Whether it was characterized as *de sponsu* then or, if not, from how soon after, there is no means of ascertaining.

may be assumed that if, as does happen, the appearance of *fideiussio* in a text is irreconcilable with classical law, that text must have undergone a deeper revision than the ousting of either *sponsio* or *sponsus* by *fideiussio*.[1] The older type of surety may indeed have figured, but it must have been expressed in some other fashion. The substitution of *sponsio*, a non-existent noun – non-existent in this sense – is ruled out, that of *sponsus* precarious in the extreme.

Spondere means to promise and often to promise *qua* surety. The agent noun *sponsor*, we saw, is exclusively tied to the latter, narrower sense: the surety's promise is so striking that he is the promiser *kat' exochen*. Of two action nouns, one, *sponsio*, of frequent occurrence, belongs to the general sense and no other; so the formal civil promise by means of *spondere* is an established part of the system. The other, *sponsus*, very rare, besides signifying the formal civil promise at large (or maybe its application to an engagement to be married), also has specific reference to the promise of a surety. It is – astonishingly – to this extent only that the earliest type of surety is a nominalized institution. It will be fascinating to watch how this result will be got over by those who see in *sponsio*-surety the cradle of contract.

Fidepromissio is an unmitigated artefact, not part of the real world in any sense, in any source. The *Thesaurus* has not got it. It leads a vigorous life in texts reconstructed by modern authorities who lack the insight that the road from verb to action noun tends to be arduous and may never be traversed.

---

[1] Take D.46.1.69, Tryphoninus *IX disputationum*. Lenel, Levy and others (Lenel, *Palingenesia Iuris Civilis*, 1889, vol.2, 362, Levy, *op. cit.* 4) are right in holding that the discussion, now about *fideiussio*, originally referred to a *sponsor*: there is release by lapse of a certain time from due day. But to replace (as they do) *ex fideiussione* by *ex sponsione* is impossible since *sponsio* at no time signified surety, and even *ex sponsu* would be too simple a remedy. The part from *item heres* to *agitur* which now contains *ex fideiussione* has suffered radical abbreviation. The classical author must have made it clear whether the lapse of time occurred during the actual tutor's life or after his death when the heir had entered. The consequences might differ accordingly, for instance, with regard to liability for *dolus* only or for *dolus* and negligence.

The Action Noun : Obligations

It might perhaps be argued that since *promittere* has *promissio*,[1] *fidepromittere* ought to have *fidepromissio*. The question, however, is not whether *fidepromissio* was logically or philologically possible – this I do not deny for one moment – but whether it did in fact materialize. There is no evidence whatever that it did. Queen Victoria outlived the Consort. The simple verb to live goes with life. But no book has as yet appeared: 'Queen Victoria, her life and her outlife.'

Fideiussio may date from around AD 200; hardly from long before. Gaius does not employ it. It is indeed conceivable that it was coined, or made at home in learned discussion, by Scaevola and his pupil Papinian.[2] It is not in the *Codex Theodosianus*, though the *fideiussor* is. The *Interpretatio* to the *Codex Theodosianus* has it.[3]

Considering that such is the situation regarding *sponsio*, *fidepromissio*, *fideiussio*, the complete absence of *adpromissio* is not accidental. There is no entry in the *Thesaurus*, the word is

---

[1] *Promittere* in Plautus, *promissio* from Cicero.

[2] D.34.3.28 pr., Scaevola *XVI digestorum* (in the question put to the jurist), 42.6.3 pr., Papinian *XXVII quaestionum*, 46.3.94.2f., Papinian *VIII quaestionum*, 46.3.95.3, Papinian *XXVIII quaestionum*. Earlier occurrences of the noun are extremely dubious. As for the *senatusconsultum Velleianum*, Vogt is certainly right in maintaining (*Studien zum Senatusconsultum Velleianum*, 1952, 2f.) that despite D.16.1.2.1, Ulpian *XXIX ad edictum*, the *fideiussiones* were not part of the original text. D.14.5.8, Paul *I decretorum*, describes a state of affairs as 'so to speak *fideiussio*'. By this time the concept must be fully established, but the relevant sentence does not sound Pauline. In most texts with *fideiussio* the distinction from the main debt is heavily stressed, and it would not be surprising if the noun had been coined in the course of reflection on this aspect.

[3] The difference is pronounced. E.g. *C.Theod.* 5.13, Valentinianus, Theodosius et Arcadius, AD 392, is against *sponsores et fideiussores* for a dowry's return (yes, the *sponsores* are still in the text of the constitution though no longer in the rubric of the Code), the *Interpretatio* introduces *fideiussio* (the *sponsores* are dropped, and *sponsio* in the sense of surety is of course out of the question). Note, incidentally, that *C.Theod.* 5.13 speaks of the *promissiones* of the sureties *in cavenda sponsione*: the principal promise of return is called *sponsio*, and this is guaranteed by the accessory *promissiones*. Outside Roman law proper, *fideiussio* occurs first in the *Lex Romana Visigothorum* by Alaric, of AD 506, and in Cassiodorus about Gothic law.

found in no ancient source, not even Justinian. True, the verb *adpromittere* itself is rare and has been shown to be post-classical.[1] But there is no need in this case that the verb be common for significance to attach to the absence of the noun. The cumulative evidence provided by *sponsio* and so on is fully adequate: *adpromissio* is a medieval formation.

By the same token, when we look at plurality of creditors, it is highly probable that so long as *adstipulari* was a live part of the law, it never reached nominalization. *Stipulari* is in Plautus and *stipulatio* is doubtless fairly old; it is attested from the late Republic,[2] and Cicero feels able to coin *stipulatiuncula*.[3] *Adstipulari* and *adstipulator* in the legal sense, of a subsidiary creditor added to the principal one, are extant in one jurist only, Gaius,[4] and in a very few texts from Cicero and Festus. *Adstipulatio* in this sense is not met at all prior to about AD 600. It does appear in the sense of confirmation or assent in lay literature from the elder Pliny on. Were this case isolated, we could draw no conclusion. But considering our findings in respect of *adpromissio* and so on (and also considering that the importance of contractual *adstipulari* started to decrease as early as the second century BC), it is practically certain that the absence of the action noun in the legal sense from the sources reflects its absence in fact. Apparently the *Thesaurus* finds that it ought to exist, hence accords it an entry as a technical term. But the solitary passage quoted for it, from Symmachus,[5] has

---

[1] Solazzi, *Bullettino*, 38, 1930, 1ff. He notes the absence of the action noun at p. 19. His results are approved by Buckland, *Text-Book*, 445, n.3.

[2] Gellius 4.4.2, quoting Servius.

[3] *de Orat.* 1.38.174: If you cannot advise a client as to the pitfalls which may lurk in a relatively insignificant promise, should he entrust you with an important case?

[4] 3.110ff.

[5] *Relationes ad principes*, 10.41.3. Symmachus considers it outrageous to declare a testament invalid because one of the witnesses receives a minor legacy. Among the arguments advanced by his opponents, he writes, are 'imperial rescripts setting aside the *adstipulatio* – confirmation, attestation – of one said to have furthered his own cause by his witness', *rescripta divalia quibus adstipulatio cuiusdam remota est qui suam iuvisse causam testimonio diceretur*.

The Action Noun : Varia 29

nothing to do with a subsidiary creditor; the noun means confirmation, as on the ten other occasions this writer uses the noun or the verb.

It is in a lexicographical collection of Isidore of Seville that we first come across the legal, contractual *adstipulatio*.[1] This is no accident: such treatises are apt to break through to the action noun – we are given brief comparative definitions of *stipulatio, restipulatio*,[2] *adstipulatio* and *constipulatio*, the systematizing trend is unmistakable. Significantly, the last word, *constipulatio* (presented as a species of *restipulatio*), occurs nowhere else in Latin.

C. Varia

Clearly, what is required is a thorough re-writing of the history of Roman Law – and other branches of history. In VJR as well as other dictionaries verb and action noun are often combined under the same heading, the distinction is treated as irrelevant. Yet to obtain a correct and differentiated estimate of the evolution, it is essential to note at what stage the step from verb to noun is taken. Quite a few nouns are of great antiquity, many are the result of medieval or modern preconceptions, the verb never got there while the law was alive, and the bulk lie somewhere in between.

Usus figured in the XII Tables.[3] I do not think this is true of *emptio* though it is attributed to the code by Aristo (under Trajan).[4] I would date it – and *venditio* – from the third

[1] *Differentiarum appendix* 162.

[2] Already in Cicero; also, e.g. G.4.13.

[3] See Bruns, 25.

[4] D.40.7.29.1, Pomponius *XVIII ad Quintum Mucium*: *sed verissimum est quod et Aristo Celso rescripsit, posse dari pecuniam . . . quoniam lex duodecim tabularum emptionis verbo omnem alienationem complexa videretur*. This interpretation was possible even if the XII Tables contained merely the verb *emere*. Parallels abound. The edict (Lenel, *Edictum*, 407f.) ordained *condemnatus ut pecuniam solvat*, commented upon by Paul thus: *solutionis verbum pertinet ad omnem liberationem*, D.46.3 54, Paul *LVI ad edictum*. Cf. also below, p. 33 n. 6, Jerome's introduction of *comparatio* in discussing what he regards as a wrong use of *comparare* by his opponent Rufinus.

century BC.[1] *Accusatio* is no doubt somewhat older than Cicero who provides the earliest evidence; *accusare* is Plautine. The cases of *damnatio, interrogatio* and *licitatio* look similar. Also *remissio*[2]; *remissio mercedis*, rebate of rent in tenancy, is genuinely a classical institution.[3] Also *solutio*.

I admit that in evaluating the evidence one has sometimes to follow hunches. *Satisfacere* occurs from Plautus, *satisfactio* from Cicero; I suppose the noun is somewhat earlier than Cicero. *Satisdare* and *satisdatio* both are attested only from Cicero; the noun it may be recalled, occurs in the *lex Rubria*.[4] Surely the verb at least is considerably earlier though not nearly as early as *satisfacere*. *Satisaccipere* is Plautine – it is also met in Cato – whereas *satisacceptio* occurs only in one Digest text.[5] *Satisaccipere* was clearly subjected to less institutionalization than the other two concepts, the prevalent analysis was from the angle of performance. Remember that quite a few legal verbs prefixed by *satis* never made the noun at all: *satisofferre, satispetere, satisexigere* and so forth.

Here a word about *acceptio* may be in place. Beseler says that, though it is Ciceronian, the classics made no use of it. Yet it would have been a suitable legal term for acceptance. Hence, he concludes, its absence must be due to rejection on grounds of style.[6] However, first, the classics did use it, though very

[1] Whereas Plautus has *emere*, the noun is first attested in Varro. (In the *lex agraria* of 111 BC it is due to conjecture: Bruns, 75. Leo's conjecture of *emptio* in the place of *coactio* in Plautus, *Asin.* 203 – *Plautii Comoediae*, 2nd ed., vol. 1, 1895, 611 – is arbitrary.) Still, Plautus definitely knew *coemptio*, as is proved by his use of *coemptionalis*: *Bacch.* 4.9.52. *Redimere* in the sense of to ransom is Plautine, *redemptio* is found from Livy. As for *vendere-venditio*, the verb is Plautine, the noun occurs from the *lex agraria* (Bruns, 75, 82f.) and Festus remarks on an old meaning of it (of course, he may be simply indicating that the meaning became obsolete with the decay of the censorship): *venditiones dicebantur olim censorum locationes*.

[2] *Remittere* in the sense of to forgive, to give up, *Most.* 5.2.47. *Remissio* in this sense Cicero, *In Catil.* 4.6.13.

[3] D.19.2.15.3ff., Ulpian *XXXII ad edictum*.

[4] 1.15; Bruns, 97.

[5] D.45.1.5.2, Pomponius *XXVI ad Sabinum*. Heumann-Seckel and Beseler, *Zeitschrift*, 57, 1937, 1 doubt the authenticity. I see little to quarrel with (apart from the concluding words *id est* and so on). *Acceptio* without *satis* occurs from Cicero. [6] *Loc. cit.*

The Action Noun : Varia 31

little.¹ Secondly, Cicero himself has it once only, nor is it at all common in post-classical texts. Thirdly, its tardiness is primarily explicable by the simple fact that acceptance creates relatively few problems² and, therefore, is slow in becoming an institution. We may compare the well-known phenomenon that some expositions of *traditio*, the passing of ownership, stress the requirement of the transferor's intent to transfer, while silent about the transferee's will to receive.³ The latter is rarely controversial.⁴

Abrogare and *derogare legem* may be found in Cato, *abrogatio* and *derogatio legis* from Cicero. That we do not come across the noun phrases in the classical jurists is chiefly, I assume, the result of the fact that the subject is so little discussed.⁵ *Nuncupare* goes back to the XII Tables.⁶ *Nuncupatio* is confined to post-Augustan writings. It may none the less be of Republican origin: it is part of the vocabulary of the classics in an area where they display much conservatism,⁷ and the material is not plentiful. Still the interval between verb and action noun is considerable.

Here are a few action nouns which, while classical, may well not reach back into the Republic. *Evincere* is used by Alfenus Varus,⁸ *evictio* first appears in Javolenus (who may have come upon it in the slightly earlier Plautius).⁹ *Expensum ferre* is found from Cicero, *expensilatio* once in Latin literature, in a legal anecdote of Gellius.¹⁰ We hear generally so little about

¹ Of the three entries in VJR, at least D.45.1.5.2, with *satisacceptio*, just considered, seems to me genuine.

² The case discussed by Cicero, *Top.* 8.37, is not an everyday one. The Roman general Mancinus, defeated by the Numantines, concluded a treaty; the senate repudiated it and surrendered Mancinus, but the Numantines refused to accept him. It is possible to argue, says Cicero, that he was not really surrendered, since *neque deditionem neque donationem sine acceptione intellegi posse*.

³ D.41.1.9.3, Gaius *II rerum cottidianarum*, I.2.1.40.

⁴ See Jörs, *Römisches Recht*, 3rd ed. Kunkel, 1949, 129.

⁵ *Abrogatio* is not registered in VJR, *derogatio* once: D.23.4.30, Tryphoninus *X disputationum, derogatio facta fideicommissi petitioni*. The passage is highly suspect; Beseler, *Zeitschrift*, 66, 1948, 277.

⁶ See Bruns, 25. ⁷ Look, for example, at the archaic discussion D.28.1.25, Javolenus *V posteriorum Labeonis*, where the verb is used.

⁸ D.6.1.57, *VI digestorum*. ⁹ D.21.2.60, Javolenus *II ex Plautio*. ¹⁰ 14.2.7.

this transaction that one's immediate inclination is to think this may be the top of an iceberg. The dates assume a certain importance, however, in the light of the fact that even *acceptilatio* is not evidenced prior to Gaius[1]; *acceptum referre* occurs from Cicero, *acceptum ferre* from the younger Seneca.[2]

The same passage from Gellius which supplies the only extant evidence of *expensilatio* also has the rare *obsignatio*, not in VJR,[3] indeed, first found in legal texts in two rescripts by Diocletian and Maximianus.[4] The verb is Plautine and freely used by the classical jurists. In addition, the same passage mentions *testium intercessio*, denoting the attendance of witnesses, a unique expression.[5] The accumulation of action nouns in this sentence is not accidental. Gellius tells us about his experience as a judge, when a decent man reclaimed a loan from a scoundrel. The latter denied the debt, and there was indeed no evidence apart from plaintiff's word. Defendant's advocate insisted the transaction ought to be proved *expensilatione, mensae rationibus, chirographi exhibitione, tabularum obsignatione, testium intercessione*. An impressive challenge, briefly enumerating the manifold ways to establish such a claim: lists of this kind are good soil for schematization and, hence, the action noun.

Occasionally the verb itself does not ante-date the classics. *Confundere* may denote the extinction of a right and its corresponding duty or burden by union in one person; say, I become my creditor's or debtor's heir. The earliest surviving evidence for the verb dates from around AD 100, Javolenus,[6]

---

[1] Or at most Javolenus. However, D.45.2.2 (*III ex Plautio*) is heavily revised, and the argumentation at the end of 12.4.10 (*I ex Plautio*) also shows signs of interference (see Schwarz, *Die Grundlage der Condictio im Klassischen Römischen Recht*, 1952, 196f.). It is certainly remarkable that no other first-century jurist is credited with the noun.

[2] The phrase *accepti relatio*, title of a section in Buckland's *Text-Book*, 572, is non-existent. *Fr.Vat.* 329, Papinian *II responsorum*, speaks of *acceptum vel expensum ferre*. Buckland refers to Sohm, *Institutionen*, 17th ed., Mitteis and Wenger, 1923, 477, but the noun phrase is not there employed. [3] Lewis and Short cite *P.S.*4.6.1f., but the verb alone is here used.

[4] C.4.54.7, 8.42.9, AD 286. [5] *Intercedere* from Plautus, *intercessio* as a helpful activity from Cicero. [6] D.8.6.15, *II epistularum*.

The Action Noun: Varia

for the noun, *confusio*, from some seventy-five years later, Scaevola or Florentine.[1] These dates, I guess, roughly correspond to reality. The later history is noteworthy. Till Diocletian inclusive, the rather sophisticated notion is common.[2] After him, we do not find it, either as verb or noun[3] – till it reappears again in Justinian.[4] All this may be accident, but I do not believe it is: it closely mirrors the fluctuations of jurisprudential capacity.

Post-classical action nouns. *Adnumerare* in the sense of to pay is ancient though not very frequent; it occurs in Plautus.[5] *Adnumeratio* is extremely rare. It is met in no legal source, but it is used once in Jerome's *Against Rufinus*.[6] *Adprehendere*

---

[1] D.46.3.93.2, Scaevola *singulari quaestionum publice tractatarum*, 30.116.4, Florentine *XI institutionum*. We saw above, p. 16 n. 1, that in the field of modes of acquisition, the institution *confusio* was attained at no period of Roman law.

[2] It is found in four of his rescripts: C.4.16.6 = 7.72.7, AD 294 (verb), 4.16.5, AD 294, 5.58.3, AD 294, 6.50.14, AD 293 (noun).

[3] The *Thesaurus* quotes *C.Theod.* 1.10.1, Gratianus, Valentinianus et Theodosius, of AD 381, but this is a mistake.   [4] C.6.30.22.9, AD 531 (verb).

[5] According to Beseler, the classical jurists never use the verb in a sense other than that of to count out, *zahlend übergeben*: *Zeitschrift*, 52, 1932, 39ff.

[6] 3.6. Even *adnumeratio* in the sense of reckoning, addition, inclusion, has only a single entry in the *Thesaurus*: *C.Theod.* 6.22.8.1, Theodosius et Valentinianus, AD 425. Lewis and Short give D.27.1.13, but the text is a Greek excerpt from Modestinus *IV excusationum*. Paragraph 2 towards the end speaks of *diarithmesis ton hemeron*, which Mommsen renders by *summa dierum*. The twelfth-century translation, however, has *adnumeratio dierum*; it is this translation which got into Forcellini's dictionary, from where Lewis and Short must have taken it. The passage from Jerome, by the way, has not so far, I believe, been properly understood. Jerome is criticizing Rufinus for treating *comparare* as a possible synonym of *emere*, whereas its only correct meaning (Jerome here alleges) is to join, to compare, to match. Rufinus had written to Jerome that he was gratuitously sending him a tract which, otherwise, Jerome would surely seek to buy, *comparare*. This usage, Jerome fulminates, is a barbarism: *cum comparatio aequalium sit, emptio pretii adnumeratio*, 'since *comparatio* is a matching of equal things, *emptio* the payment of a price'. That this is the point of the censure is confirmed by the continuation which dwells on another stylistic lapse. Throughout this chapter Jerome harps on Rufinus's inferiority as a philologist: 'You are bilingual, you have so much Greek and Latin that *Graeci te Latinum et Latini te Graecum putant*.' No doubt some of the criticisms are untenable, and were so at the time; but Jerome made them anyway.

is frequent in VJR, *adprehensio* does not occur in any legal source but, for example, in the *Itala*.¹ In this case, even the verb seems to become less popular with the jurists as time goes on,² so the tardiness in nominalization is not surprising. *Adprobare* in the legal senses of to approve and to show to be worthy of approval is far from common: about ten times in VJR. *Adprobatio* occurs in one interpolated passage.³ By around AD 400 the institution of *adprobatio operis* is clearly attained: Augustine, commenting on 'God saw that it was good' in Genesis 1, explains that this is *operis adprobatio secundum artem facti, quae Sapientia Dei est*.⁴ *Audire* from early on may denote to hear a case as a judge; the meaning is at least approximated in Plautus and is found in the senatusconsult *de Bacchanalibus* of 186 BC.⁵ It is amply represented in all subsequent periods.⁶ Yet *auditio* in the corresponding sense is absent not only from VJR but from all lay literature till the third century AD. It arrives in Tertullian.⁷ As far as legal sources are concerned, we find it in two rescripts jointly by Honorius and Theodosius⁸ – that is all. *Decipere*, to cheat, occurs in Plautus and is well represented in VJR; *deceptio* is not listed in VJR at all, though

---

¹ John 7.30: *nondum enim venerat hora apprehensionis*.

² Twice only in the *Codex Theodosianus*.

³ D.19.2.24 pr., Paul *XXXIV ad edictum*; the clause *quibus consequens* to the end is very badly framed.

⁴ *Civ.* 11.21. Maybe *adprobatio* was delayed by the use – however rare – of *probatio*: D.19.2.60.3, Labeo *V posteriorum a Javoleno epitomatorum*, Cicero, *pro Fonteio* 8.17 (approval by the governor of road-repairs effected by the provincials). Beseler, *Zeitschrift*, 57, 1937, 41, brackets *aut improbatio* in D.19.2.60.3, quite unjustifiably, I think. In 22.3.18.2, Ulpian *VI disputationum*, *improbatio* denotes something entirely different. It is noteworthy that *comprobare*, which starts from Plautus and is a common verb from Cicero on, about fifty-five times in VJR, makes the action noun only in a solitary statement in Cicero (*Fin.* 5.22.62) – apart from the late grammarians.

⁵ 5; Bruns, 165.

⁶ According to Beseler, *Subsiciva*, 193, 6ff., the classics avoid the sense of to accede to a request, *erhören*.

⁷ *Apol.* 9, p. 150.

⁸ *C. Theod.* 11.30.67 = C.7.62.31 pr., AD 423; *C. Theod.* 13.5.32 = C.11.6.6, AD 409.

The Action Noun: Varia

we find it in the *Codex Theodosianus*. The earliest evidence for it is the *Itala*.

Detentio, as is well known, has been endowed with its sophisticated meaning in the doctrine of possession in the past two centuries, and the same is true of *detinere* itself. The noun occurs once in the Digest, interpolated,[1] and in two constitutions by Justinian.[2] It is Western: we find it in the *Itala*. In the case of *detentare-detentatio*, even the verb is late and very rare. In the sense of to hold, it occurs in an imperial *Epistola* of AD 370/1 to the governor of Asia,[3] twice in the *Codex Theodosianus*, in constitutions from the beginning of the fifth century,[4] and once, about the same time, in Rufinus.[5] *Detentatio* is found in two interpolated texts in the Digest[6] and in two *Novels* by Justinian.[7] It is safe to conclude that the interpolations are Byzantine.

Impetrare, found in Plautus, is frequent in the jurists, in many senses; say, two hundred and fifty times in VJR. *Impetratio* takes a slow rise from Cicero. Its first appearance in legal sources is in the *Codex Theodosianus*, about ten times versus one hundred and thirty five for the verb. Even in Byzantine law, however, abstraction, institutionalization, went less far than modern expositions would suggest. *Impetratio actionis* is indeed known to this Code as well as Justinian's.[8] But *impetratio dominii*, nowadays current of a pledge

---

[1] D.43.25.1.5, Ulpian *LXXI ad edictum*. Ulpian is referring to Julian, whose statement is preserved in D.8.1.16, *XLIX digestorum*, and has *utilis petitio* instead of *detentio*. I do not believe, however, with Beseler, *Zeitschrift*, 56, 1936, 63, that *detentio* is a mere scribe's slip for *petitio*. There is an idea behind it, namely, that the pledgee is the holder of the servitude pro tem. A *utilis petitio* no longer meant much to the reviser.

[2] C.7.31.3, AD 531, 7.39.8.1, AD 529.

[3] Valentinian, Valens and Gratian, 11; Bruns, 271.

[4] 5.16.30, Arcadius, Honorius et Theodosius, AD 405, and 11.20.3, Arcadius et Honorius, AD 400.

[5] *Hist.* 5.2.7.

[6] 4.6.15.3, Ulpian *XII ad edictum*, 25.1.5 pr., Ulpian *XXXVI ad Sabinum*; Beseler, *Zeitschrift*, 56, 1936, 63.

[7] *Nov. Just.* 22.24, *Julian. Epit. Nov. Just.* 7.5.

[8] Rubric *C. Theod.* 2.3, C.2.57.

creditor's request to the court to have ownership conferred on him, is medieval: the relevant rubric in Justinian's Code reads *de iure dominii impetrando*.[1] *Sequestrare* comes from *sequester*. It occurs once in VJR, in a Byzantine interpolation,[2] and several times in the *Codex Theodosianus*. From *sequestrare*, again, comes *sequestratio*, not in VJR, though the *Codex Theodosianus* has it. The word hardly existed before the fourth century.

A number of action nouns make their first appearance in law, or at all, in Justinian. *Inhibere* in the sense of to restrain dates from the second century BC and is fairly common in the jurists, some twenty-five times in VJR, thirty in the *Codex Theodosianus*. *Inhibitio* comes up in the fourth century AD. The earliest extant legal text is a constitution by Justinian, ponderously ordaining the suppression of blasphemy and perjury in consequence of gambling losses.[3] I have already adverted to his use of *transmissio* as signifying transmission to a successor.[4] Whether or not he was the first to apply the noun in this fashion it is difficult to say. Almost certainly the expression *natalium restitutio* is his coinage. I have elsewhere written on his fascination with the elevation to freebornhood of a person born a slave – a fascination connected with his desire radically to sever Theodora, the woman he wished to marry, from her past as an actress. The making of a slave into, not just a free man, but a freeborn man, seemed to offer a legal precedent for total re-creation; and in the legislation which, inspired by Justinian, validates the union of a senator with a redeemed actress, the cleansing of the lady is avowedly based on the analogy of the grant of freebornhood. It was Justinian himself, then, who broke through from *natales restituere* to the weightier and more institutionalized *natalium restitutio*.[5]

A few medieval or modern fabrications. *Rerum amotio*. *Amovere* in the sense of *furari* is frequent in VJR, *amotio*

[1] 8.33.

[2] D.24.3.22.8, Ulpian *XXXIII ad edictum*; Cujas and Faber.

[3] C.3.43.2.2, AD 529.

[4] Above, p. 23.

[5] See Daube, *Natural Law Forum*, 12, 1967, 70ff., and *Catholic University of America Law Review*, 16, 1967, 38off.

The Action Noun : Varia

without entry,[1] nor does it occur in any sense in the *Codex Theodosianus* or *Justinianus*.[2] *Servi corruptio*, non-existent.[3] *Dedicatio in sacrum* of a thing which forms the subject of litigation, non-existent. The Roman jurists do not go beyond *dedicare*.[4] *Defamare*[5] is post-Augustan, *defamatio* medieval and helped on by *diffamatio*, which denotes principally the spreading of an ill report. Nor did the jurists ever develop the advanced *infamatio* from *infamare*,[6] though the noun does occur in lay writers from the early fourth century. *Sepulchri violatio*, non-existent.[7]

The process of nominalization may take place in successive, observable stages; the action noun may come up first in one sector of a verb, then in another, and it may take a long time before its use is general – if it ever does become general. A flood of light is thrown by these variations on the history of the area involved, and, obviously, the larger the area covered by a verb, the more chequered the history. Many of the nouns

---

[1] It means removal of rank in D.47.10.43, Gaius *III regularum*: the criminal in question will suffer *exilium aut relegationem aut ordinis amotionem*.

[2] In general, *amovere* occurs from Plautus and is fairly common, about thirty times in the *Codex Theodosianus*, *amotio* occurs from Cicero and is extremely rare, not at all in the *Codex*.

[3] *Corruptio* of corn supplies through age in *C. Theod.* 11.14.1 = C.10. 26.1.1, Valentinianus et Valens, AD 364, *corruptio usus fructus*, extinction of usufruct, in a constitution by Justinian, C.3.33.16 pr., AD 531. In general, *corrumpere* from Plautus, *corruptio* from Cicero.

[4] D.44.6.3, Gaius *VI ad legem duodecim tabularum*. *Dedicare* in general from the second century BC, *dedicatio* from Cicero, the verb eight times in VJR, fifteen times in the *Codex Theodosianus*, against no entry for the noun. In the sense of to inscribe a work to somebody, the verb comes into vogue in the first century AD – Phaedrus, the elder Pliny, Martial, Statius, Quintilian – the noun only around AD 600, with Isidore of Seville's *Dedicatio historiarum ad Sisenandum*.

[5] Usually in the form *defamatus*, but *defamari* in C.7.14.5, Diocletianus et Maximianus, AD 293.

[6] The verb figures in the late Republican edict *Ne quid infamandi causa fiat*: Lenel, *Edictum*, 401, Daube, *Atti Cong. Verona*, 1948, vol.3, 1951, 413ff.

[7] *Violatio* once only in VJR, *Coll.* 3.3.1 = D.1.6.2, Ulpian *VIII de officio proconsulis*; *turpis violatio* here envisages enforced, disgraceful practice—*si dominus in servum saevierit vel ad impudicitiam turpemque violationem compellat*.

already mentioned furnish illustrations,[1] but let me take fresh ones. There is no such institution as *confirmatio donationis* in Roman law; at the same time, in a constitution of Marcus Aurelius,[2] we do come across *confirmatio adoptionis* denoting the imperial sanction of a defective adoption.[3] *Publicatio legis* is first found in the *Codex Theodosianus*.[4] Even the verb *publicare*, in the sense to publish, is post-Augustan and extraordinarily rare.[5] By contrast, verb and noun both occur from Cicero with reference to the turning of something into public property, confiscation.

A new ghost, incidentally, has begun to haunt this area. It is now being claimed that *publicatio legis* was preceded in remote

[1] *Accessio, adprobatio, adstipulatio, amotio, cessio, comparatio, confusio, corruptio, dedicatio, derelictio, impetratio, inhibitio, intercessio, inventio, paratio, probatio, restitutio, separatio, traditio, translatio, transmissio, violatio.*

[2] D.1.7.39, Ulpian *III de officio consulis*.

[3] When Berger, *Encyclopaedic Dictionary of Roman Law*, 1953, 407, subsumes under *confirmatio donationis* (1) a gift between husband and wife confirmed in the donor's testament and (2) a gift which, though contrary to the *lex Cincia*, is enforceable if the donor dies without revoking it, there is a further objection to be raised: even the verb *confirmare* is unsuitable for case (2). The jurists do apply it to case (1) (e.g. Ulpian speaks of the *Oratio* of Severus and Caracalla *de confirmandis donationibus*, D.24.1.32.1, *XXXIII ad Sabinum*), also, for instance, to confirmation by will of a previous gift to a daughter in *potestas* (*Fr. Vat.* 256a, 294, Papinian *XII responsorum*). A gift otherwise invalid is here positively insisted on by the testator (on whose death the reason for invalidity is really gone). By contrast, a gift contrary to the *lex Cincia* is defeasible only by means of an *exceptio* against which, if it is brought by the donor's heir and the donor never revoked the gift (never revoked – not: if he re-affirmed it in his will), a *replicatio* is given: *morte Cincia removetur* (*Fr. Vat.* 259, Papinian *XII responsorum*). No room here for *confirmare*. Beseler, *Zeitschrift*, 57, 1937, 14f., observes that the classics were disinclined to employ *confirmatio*. He may be condemning too many texts however.

[4] 5.3.1, Theodosius et Valentinianus, AD 434; cf. 16.2.37, Arcadius et Honorius AD 404, with *publicatio edictorum*.

[5] It occurs in D.9.2.41 pr., Ulpian *XLI ad Sabinum*, and 47.8.2.24, Ulpian *LVI ad edictum*, both times interpolated (on 47.8.2.24 see de Ruggiero, *Bullettino*, 19, 1907, 69; in 9.2.41 pr., towards the end, the two cases of destruction and recitation are unsatisfactorily amalgamated). It denotes notification of the authorities in *C. Theod.* 4.4.4 = C.6.23.18, Arcadius et Honorius, AD 397, C.8.53.30.1, Leo, AD 459, 11.59.14, Honorius et Theodosius, AD 415.

times by *proquiritatio legis*.[1] However, the noun *proquiritatio* was born in 1940.[2] The verb is first found in Appuleius,[3] and there it is still closely linked to the simple *quiritare*, to cry for help[4]: Appuleius's adversary flaunts a letter to prove that the philosopher ensnared an honourable woman by magic. It is in Sidonius Apollinaris in the fifth century that we get *lex proquiritata*.[5] He refers to Theodosius's decree setting a time limit of thirty years to actions[6]: *ut fere decemviraliter loquar, lex de praescriptione tricennii fuerat proquiritata, cuius peremptoriis abolita rubricis lis omnis in sextum tracta quinquennium terminabatur*, 'to speak in the language of the XII Tables, a statute was promulgated concerning a thirty years' prescription, by whose decided provisions any action drawn out into six quinquennia was abolished and terminated'. From this it has long been deduced (wrongly, we shall see) that the XII Tables contained the word *proquiritare*[7]; now the further inference is drawn that they contained *legem proquiritare*; and from here to *proquiritatio legis* as an ancient Republican concept is an easy step. But, when Sidonius says that he is expressing himself in decemviral language, he has not in mind *proquiritare* at all. (Even if he had, it would still remain a pseudo-antique usage.) He has in mind the words *tricennium* and *quinquennium*. These do not figure in Theodosius's legislation but are introduced[8] in analogy to the provision of the XII Tables respecting usucapion, which by Sidonius's time was narrowly associated with prescription: *usus auctoritas fundi biennium est*.[9] Do not think I have killed a brilliant coinage. *Proquiritatio* is in for a long life.

[1] von Schwind, *Zur Frage der Publikation im römischen Recht*, 1940, 33, relying on Weiss, *Glotta*, 12, 1923, 82f.
[2] Yes, the paternity belongs to von Schwind; Weiss was still content with the verb. [3] *Apol.* ch. 82, ed. Helm, p. 90.
[4] Attested from Lucilius; originally no doubt a cry addressed to the Quirites, the co-citizens. The noun *quiritatio* is a *hapax legomenon* in Livy, 33.28. [5] *Ep.* 8.6. [6] *C. Theod.* 4.14.1 = C.7.39.3, AD 424. [7] Bruns, 40.
[8] Something of a *tour de force*: at least the *sextum quinquennium* is far-fetched.
[9] Bruns, 25. It is at this place, then, and not among *Fragmenta Incertae Sedis* that Sidonius should be noted. Whether *biennium* was actually in the code is here irrelevant: Sidonius thought it was.

Another term alleged to be an early alternative for *publicatio legis* is *renuntiatio legis*. The sequence, then, is: *proquiritatio* period of the XII Tables, *renuntiatio* from the middle of the Republic, *publicatio* I suppose from the late Republic. Well, *renuntiatio* would be conceivable from Cicero on: he has, for example, *renuntiatio suffragiorum*.[1] But surely, any confidence would be misplaced. No text has *renuntiatio legis*, no text has even *renuntiare legem*.[2] Evidently, theory in this matter progressed at a very moderate pace – and why not? I doubt whether, in my College, even yet a great deal of thought is given to the publication of our statutes.

Datio[3] has several meanings in addition to transfer, coming into use at different times and in different settings. But even in the sense of transfer the rise of this noun is very gradual. The discrepancy between the noun, rare, and the verb, frequent, is enormous. To be sure, the noun signifies transfer, or right to transfer, as early as 186 BC, in one of the senatus-consults following the Bacchanalian affair.[4] This does not mean that it was used wherever we today might do so.

I have grievously sinned in my courses on unjust enrichment (*condictio*) by teaching that, as a rule, an action on this ground was available to a person who had made to another person a *datio* which turned out unwarranted. (This is, of course, what everybody nowadays teaches.[5]) In point of fact, only the

[1] *pro Plancio*, 6.14.

[2] The doctrine is kept in life by one authority sending us to another, the sources forming a nebulous background. Von Schwind refers to Weiss; Weiss refers to Klingmüller, art. *renuntiatio* in Pauly-Wissowa IA, 1914, 600. Klingmüller does quote a series of texts, such as *Lex Malacitana*, 56f. (Bruns, 150f.), where, however, we hear of *renuntiare eum*, to proclaim a man elected.

[3] Beseler, *Zeitschrift*, 66, 1948, 273, holds that it is often interpolated.

[4] Livy, 39.19.5: see below, p. 45.

[5] Even Buckland who in his *Text-Book*, 541ff., abstains from the noun, introduced it in his lectures. Schwarz, *op. cit.*, lists *datio credendi causa* (*mutuum*), *solvendi causa* (*indebitum*), *dotis nomine*, *ob rem*, *ob causam*, *ob transactionem*, *propter condicionem*; he speaks of *gestreckte*, protractive, *datio* (where completed by *commixtio* etc. – *sit venia verbo*). Kaser, *Das Römische Privatrecht*, 1955, 496, writes: *Zum Tatbestand unserer Kondiktionsfälle gehört als Ausgangspunkt eine datio.*

The Action Noun : Varia

combination *mutui datio* is indubitably classical[1]; and *dotis datio* may be late classical, from about AD 200, though it is not above suspicion.[2] All the rest are post-classical or just not represented in the sources at all.[3] *Datio in solutum* occurs in no

---

[1] Which rather suggests that *nexi datio* in Festus 164 (quoted from Aelius Gallus) refers to obligation, not mancipation; the question is open. *Mutui datio* occurs in G. 3.90 (twice), equals D.44.7.1.2, Gaius *II aureorum*; G.3.91; D.4.4.3.4, Ulpian *XI ad edictum* (itp.); 12.1.2.1, Ulpian *XXVI ad edictum* (twice, technical as in 14.6.7.3, text interfered with); 12.1.2.2, Paul *XXVIII ad edictum* (quite established); 12.1.2.4 (interfered with); 12.1.8, Pomponius *VI ex Plautio*; 12.1.27, Ulpian *X ad edictum* (a little dubious); 14.6.7.3, Ulpian *XXIX ad edictum* (technical, cf. 12.1.2.1); 16.1.2.1, Ulpian *XXIX ad edictum* (sc. *Velleianum*, but Vogt l.c. rightly rejects *mutui dationes*, they were dodges and banned as such by the jurists, and the present text sounds as if the women were making instead of receiving the loans). *Datio pecuniae* in 14.6.3.3, Ulpian *XXIX ad edictum*, belongs here (a little dubious), though not in 35.1.57, Pomponius *IX ad Quintum Mucium*, where a slave has to give money to be free (probably itp.).

[2] It is not touched by Beseler l.c. But it is interpolated in all Digest texts: 15.1.47.6, Paul *IV ad Plautium*; 23.3.23, Ulpian *XXXV ad Sabinum*; 24.1.34, Ulpian *XLIII ad Sabinum*; 50.17.23, Ulpian *XXIX ad Sabinum. Fr. Vat.* 102, Paul *VII responsorum* maybe saves it, though it should be noted that Schulz, *Roman Legal Science*, 1946, 240, quotes this text among those in the *Fragmenta Vaticana* which are obviously revised. In any case the usage is not very technical. A *filiusfamilias* in his father's absence marries and takes a *dos*. The father, returned, does not attack the marriage. Has he thereby also consented to the *datio dotis*? This question takes up the particular act mentioned at the beginning, it does not necessarily presuppose an institution *datio dotis*.

[3] *Datio partis* in D.45.1.2.1, Paul *XII ad Sabinum*, probably itp. *Datio legati* may denote the charging of a legacy, classical (see presently, in this same footnote); in the sense of payment out of a legacy it is met only once, D.36.1.2, Celsus *XXV digestorum*, itp. (I regard *id est post legatorum dationem* as an intrusion, Beseler, *Zeitschrift*, 66, 1948, 392, cuts out the entire discussion). *Datio* of money paid by a slave to be free D.29.2.74.1, Paul *XII ad Plautium*, itp.; 35.1.57, Pomponius *IX ad Quintum Mucium*, probably itp.; 35.1.82, Callistratus *II quaestionum*, itp.; 46.3.68, Marcellus *XVI digestorum*, itp. In the last three texts, the condition to give something (not necessarily restricted to transfer proper but including, for instance, the production of accounts) is contrasted with that to do something: this comparison no doubt encouraged nominalization. In 36.1.32.2, Marcian *IX institutionum*, it is a question of *datio* by an heir to qualify, and again *dare* and *facere* are compared; *datio* is itp. No transfer, of course, is contemplated in 15.1.8, Paul *IV ad Sabinum*, where the master puts something into his slave's *peculium*; none the less *datio* is itp. Again, no transfer in the case of *datio pignoris* or *hypothecae*; 16.1.8 pr.,

Ulpian *XXIX ad edictum*, a little dubious (see Beseler, *Zeitschrift*, 56, 1936, 88f.), and 20.1.16.9, Marcian *singulari ad formulam hypothecariam*. Let us look at *datio legati, liberationis*, the charging of a legacy, testamentary grant of freedom. G.2.243. In elementary writings, action nouns are popular. D.28.5.6.4, Ulpian *IV ad Sabinum*. I do not agree with Beseler's correction (*Zeitschrift*, 66, 1948, 273) of *liberationis datio* into *liberationis*. The problem concerns revocation (ademption) and it will presently emerge that in this context *datio* was established in the classical era. The comparison of charge and revocation provoked analysis. 29.7. 14 pr., Scaevola *VIII quaestionum*, twice, in a discussion of revocation, itp. 33.5.9.2, Julian *XXXII digestorum*, again practically a contrast with revocation. Genuine, *pace* Beseler. 34.4.3.8, Ulpian *XXIV ad Sabinum*, revocation. Beseler rightly says it ought to be *ex neutro legato*. The text is interfered with, probably abbreviation. 34.4.9, Ulpian *V disputationum*, again practically the area of revocation: a pure legacy is made conditional. For Beseler, the mere provenance from the *Disputationes* is damning. 34.4.14.1, Florentine *XI institutionem*, revocation. Genuine, *pace* Beseler. This kind of statement is to be expected in an institutional work. 34.4.26 pr., Paul *IX quaestionum*, comparison with revocation, itp. 34.5.10 pr., Ulpian *VI disputationum*, contrast with revocation. From the *Disputationes*. The text is interfered with. 40.7.2.2, Ulpian *IV ad Sabinum*. Genuine, *pace* Beseler. I suppose 34.3.3.1, Ulpian *XXIII ad Sabinum*, should here be appended: a creditor on his deathbed returns an IOU to his debtor (or maybe he leaves it to him by will), the latter now has an *exceptio*, a *datio* of this kind resembling a *fideicommissum* (*liberationis*). The clause with *datio*, however, is itp. VJR takes under *datio legati* four texts which ought not to be there. *Fr. Vat.* 318, Ulpian *VIII ad edictum*, *datio cognitoris*. As this is also quoted under the right heading, it is just a slip. More serious 35.1.82, 36.1.32.3, 46.3.68, dealing with a slave who must give something to be free, not a legacy – all itp. anyway: see above earlier on in this footnote. In two texts *datio liberationis* envisages (or includes) grant of freedom *inter vivos*. D.1.1.4, Ulpian *I institutionum*. Beseler (as already Wlassak, *Zeitschrift*, 28, 1907, 4) assumes a gloss. I am not so sure: the fragment is from an elementary work. (We need not even postulate that the phrase is generalized from testamentary manumission, institutional writers of the classical period are quite capable of original systematization.) In I.1.5 pr., going back to this statement of Ulpian's, an alternative reading has *donatio*. I wonder whether this should not be preferred for I., *datio* being an assimilation to D. (though already represented in Theophilus: in fact we are given the Latin as well as the Greek, *datio libertatis, toutestin he dosis tes eleutherias*). The other text with *datio liberationis* among the living is 40.9.20, Modestinus *singulari de enucleatis casibus*. A little dubious. *Datio* signifies a grant in 37.9.1.1, Ulpian *XLI ad edictum*, *datio bonorum possessionis*, genuine. I shall not go into *datio* as denoting appointment of a person, *datio hominis* (*tutoris, cognitoris*, etc.), except to point out that, for example, *dare iudicem* occurs over forty times in VJR, *datio iudicis* in one interpolated passage, 5.1.32, Ulpian *I de officio consulis*.

The Action Noun : Varia

ancient source. In the *Codex Theodosianus dare* appears three hundred and twenty times, *datio* once – *datio libelli*.[1] *Reddere* is listed seven hundred and fifty times in VJR, *redditio* twice.[2] In neither passage does it signify re-transfer: once it stands for *redhibitio*[3] and once it refers to the return of a *pignus*.[4] May I remind you, by way of comparison, that *venditio* occurs in the *lex agraria* of 111 BC[5] – as does *deditio* from *dedere*[6] – and that *traditio* occurs in Varro and the aedilician edict.[7]

The systematizing thrust of the action noun goes on after it is in existence: it is not only a sign of advance, it in turn stimulates further refinement. Such subdivisions of concepts as

---

[1] 13.9.6 = C.11.6.5.1, Honorius et Theodosius, AD 412. *Datio libelli* also in one Digest text (twice), 5.2.7, Paul *singulari de septemviralibus*, probably itp.

[2] In general, *reddere* is found from Plautus, *redditio* from Quintilian.

[3] D.21.1.21 pr., Ulpian *I ad edictum aedilium curulium*: '*redhibitio* is called a sort of *redditio* (*quasi redditio*)'. Beseler, *Zeitschrift*, 56, 1936, 88f., admits this as genuine, hence has to reconcile it with his thesis that the classics for stylistic reasons avoided unnecessary nouns. He remarks: *hier erzwingt der Gedanke den Gebrauch des Wortes*, 'here the thought enforces the use of the word'. But this is to beg the question. I suppose he means that Ulpian, wishing closely to connect *redhibitio* with *reddere*, has to introduce *redditio*. Correct. Only there might be a million other occasions when such a thought, or a different thought, might lead to a noun: it is always some thought that does it. On the other hand, had there been a classical ban on nouns, it could have been obeyed in this case as well as elsewhere.

[4] D.16.1.8 pr., Ulpian *XXIX ad edictum*, a little dubious (see above, pp. 41f. n. 3). While *datio pignoris* for somebody else's debt is intercession, *redditio* to one's debtor is not.

[5] See above, p. 30 n. 1.

[6] Bruns, 78, 80. The verb in Naevius and Plautus.

[7] See above, p. 23. For completeness – *abdere, didere, indere, interdare, obdere, pessumdare* and *subdere* are Plautine, but none ever came by a noun. *Addere*, frequent, is found in the XII Tables (x 8: Bruns, 37) and in Plautus; *additio*, rare, first appears in Varro. *Circumdare* is Plautine, *circumdatio* attested from the *Itala*. *Condere* is found in the XII Tables (VIII 1: Bruns, 29) and in Plautus; *conditio* from the *Itala*. *Edere* occurs in Plautus, *editio* from Cicero. *Perdere* is Plautine, *perditio* comes in about AD 300. *Prodere* with reference to a putting off is adumbrated in Plautus (*Trin*. 2.2.58f.), *proditio* is employed by Cato (Festus 242); the sense of betrayal is adumbrated at the verbal stage in Ennius (Festus 229) and Terence (*Heaut*. 3.1.70), the noun in this sense occurs from Cicero.

stipulatio poenalis, possessio civilis, naturalis, are not indeed impossible at the verbal stage: one might, for example, resort to verb with adverb, *naturaliter possidere.* But often it would be difficult to express the specialization simply – as in the case of *cautio Muciana.*[1] These differentiations are smoother and incomparably more frequent once a noun is available.[2] One can apply a *Gegenprobe*, a counter-test. Take the interdict *de migrando*, forbidding a landlord to prevent his tenant, when he wishes to move, from taking with him such belongings as are not pledged for the rent.[3] How different, how much wider and more fundamental, *de migratione* would sound. The Commonwealth Immigrants Act of 1962 by its very title gives itself out as a more modest, more *ad hoc* measure than if it had been called Commonwealth Immigration Act.

From the specimens I have presented it may be seen that the action noun has a particularly good chance, on the one hand, in mechanical enumerations, elementary treatises and the like, where the addressee is to be given a readily memorizable presentation; and on the other, in probing and wide-ranging reflection. We find periods of slow growth alternating with veritable action noun explosions. A notable number of juristic action nouns derive from the last hundred and fifty years of the Republic, when the foundation for an intelligible workable legal order was being purposefully laid. Even individuals stand out: when full allowance is made for the fact that Cicero certainly did not father all the words for which his work is the earliest evidence, he does remain author of a great many. The evolution is influenced by an enormous variety of factors. Among them, the peculiar linguistic position of a concept plays a not negligible part: I have the impression that *donatio* might have been formed sooner had not *donum* been

---

[1] *Cavere* with reference to promise and security in Varro, *cautio* in Cicero but unquestionably antedating him; see below, pp. 57f.

[2] To be sure, the action noun in these cases is apt to designate the result of the action rather than the action itself. On this aspect, see below, pp. 57f.

[3] Lenel, *Edictum*, 490. In general, *migrare* Plautus, *migratio* Cicero.

The Action Noun : Varia

more or less adequate for the job[1]; *mancipium* may have delayed *mancipatio*[2]; *mutuum mutuatio*.[3]

It is partly because the action noun implies institutionalization, solidity, durability, that it is favoured where a particularly impressive utterance is wanted. It is hardly accidental that, while *aestimare, deferre, iudicare, petere* occur from Plautus, *aestimatio, delatio, iudicatio, petitio* first emerge in the *lex Acilia repetundarum* of 123 BC. *De ea re eius petitio nominisque delatio esto*, 'in this matter let there be suit for it and report of name', does sound momentous.[4] Again, a senatusconsult of 186 BC, rewarding the freedwoman Hispala Faecenia for helping to uncover the Bacchanalian conspiracy, accorded her *datio deminutio, gentis enuptio, tutoris optio*, 'power of transfer and disposal of property, of marriage outside her clan, of choice of tutor'.[5]

The praetor, it seems, is more reticent. Heavy nouns in the edict do not appear to be due to deliberate solemnity. For instance, he will not in principle admit as advocate a man found guilty of *praevaricatio*: this term is practically unavoidable, a recognized category.[6] Again, in the *actio fiduciae*, defendant is supposed to act *ut inter bonos bene agier oportet et sine fraudatione*. This is demonstrably an ordinary development of the kind I am harping on, from an earlier version with the verb. In the original, oral procedure, plaintiff requested *uti ne propter te fidemve tuam captus fraudatusve sim*.[7] By the time of the

[1] *Donare* Plautus, *donatio* Cicero, *donum* Plautus.

[2] *Mancipare* Plautus, *mancipatio* Festus, *mancipium* XII Tables (VI 1, Bruns, 25) and Plautus.

[3] *Mutuare* Caecilius and Cato, *mutuatio* Cicero (apparently personal to him), *mutuum* Plautus. One action noun may delay another: *initium*, Ennius, versus *incohatio*, Itala, *litigium* (and *lis* itself), Plautus, versus *litigatio*, Lactantius.

[4] 3; Bruns, 59. Other notable first appearances in this statute: *praevaricatio, pronuntiato, provocatio, sanctio*.

[5] Livy, 39.19.5.

[6] The crime of representing one side in court but really playing for the other. It is mentioned in the *Lex Acilia repetundarum*, Bruns, 59; also in the *Tabula Heracleensis*, 120, Bruns, 108.

[7] Lenel, *Edictum*, 291ff.

written formula, *fraudare* in this domain had become an established *fraudatio*.¹ Of course, the praetor has no hesitation to apply it elsewhere as well, as in the edict *Qui fraudationis causa latitat*.² In course of time, the jurists, who had to work out exactly what conduct fell under this provision, arrived at *latitatio*.³

Creatio is worth noting.⁴ It offers an illustration of the confluence of legislative ponderosity and systematizing trend, besides posing a little puzzle as to dates.

Creare in the sense of to elect to an office is fairly frequent in VJR, *creatio* is confined to two spurious texts. The *Thesaurus*, in a listing marked as incomplete, has five hundred entries for the verb, the oldest being the *lex agraria* of 111 BC⁵, compared with a complete list of seven for the noun.⁶ Of these seven, one is from Cicero, the other six are much later. The *Thesaurus* as usual is unaware of even non-controversial interpolations in the Digest and, accordingly, assumes that

---

¹ The noun is already met in Plautus, *Asin.* 257.

² Lenel, *Edictum*, 415: hiding from creditors.

³ D.42.4.7.5,7,9, Ulpian *LIX ad edictum*. The noun is already used by Quintilian, 7.2.46, of hiding as an indication of guilt, in a passage which briefly recapitulates what a preceding chapter expounds by means of the verb *latere*, 5.10.45. Cicero, quoted by Ulpian, D.42.4.7.4, defined *latitare* as *turpis occultatio sui*. Beseler, *Zeitschrift*, 66, 1948, 337, points out that there is no other entry for *occultatio* in VJR; which, he says, corroborates his view of the gulf between Cicero, noun-loving, and the classics, noun-hating. The appearance of *latitatio* in the latter, however, should serve as a warning that we must not exaggerate; not to mention the fact that *occultatio* is missing also from post-classical law. On the other hand, it is indicative of the prevalent insensitivity to the difference between verb and noun that Heumann-Seckel list four texts under *occultatio sui*, though only the one which quotes Cicero has the noun phrase.

⁴ It is a sheer fluke that in learned literature it is not quite so prominent as, say, *acquisitio*, *denegatio*, *editio* and has no place, for example, in the Index to Mommsen's *Staatsrecht*. It has an article, however, by Brassloff, in Pauly-Wissowa (vol.4, 1901, 1686ff.) and an entry in Berger's *Encyclopædic Dictionary*, 417.

⁵ 53; Bruns, 82.

⁶ True, it fails to register the rubrics of C.10.68 and 10.70. By the time of Justinian, *creatio* is evidently a technical notion. Significantly, the text of the constitutions under these rubrics does not contain the noun.

The Action Noun : Varia

the earliest of the six is a fragment assigned to Papinian, about AD 200.[1] In reality, the first occurrence of *creatio* in the sense of election, after that passage from Cicero, is probably an enactment of Anthemius, of AD 468: 'The Divine Majesty and Our election have entrusted the full power of the Empire to Our son.'[2]

With regard to dating, obviously, if it were not for the isolated use by Cicero, the conclusion would be that verb and action noun are separated by some six hundred years. Cicero however, does contain the noun. At first sight, we might become uneasy about all the other instances of a huge time-lag in the sources: there could always be a sporadic earlier occurrence of the noun, only the evidence is lost. Well, even suppose it were so, all that would follow is that the evolution towards the action noun was more gradual, irregular.

But it is not likely. In fact, Cicero's introduction of *creatio* strongly militates in favour of my approach. The word figures in his *de Legibus*[3]: *Creatio magistratuum, iudicia populi, iussa vetita, quom suffragio sciscentur, optumatibus nota, plebi libera sunto*, 'Let the creation of magistrates, the verdicts in popular trials, positive and negative laws, as they are resolved on by ballot, be known to the nobles, free to the commoners'. Between 138 and 106 BC a series of statutes concerning voting tablets, the *leges tabellariae*, had for these three votes – the election of a magistrate, the sentence in a trial and the passing of legislation – replaced the open, oral vote by the secret, written one. Cicero would have all votes divulged to the optumates though kept from the plebs.[4] What is relevant for us

---

[1] D.26.7.39.6, *V responsorum*. In classical law, you do not 'create' a tutor; even the verb would be out of place. The other text is 48.14.1 pr., Modestinus *II de poenis*, asserting that the *lex Julia de ambitu* is out of date since 'the creation' of magistrates is now dependent on the care of the Emperor and not on the favour of the people. Albertario is surely right (*Bullettino* 33, 1923, 52) in holding this Byzantine. Should he be wrong, however, then this is the earliest *creatio* (apart from Cicero): Modestinus is among the very latest classics, a pupil of Ulpian's.

[2] *Nov. Anth.* 3.1.   [3] 3.3.10.

[4] See Mommsen, *Römisches Staatsrecht*, vol.3, pt. 1, 3rd ed., 1886, 404ff., Costa, *Cicerone Giureconsulto*, vol.1, 1927, 314ff.

is that in this work he avowedly resorts to formal, pompous language.[1] Moreover, as he sees himself as the author of the ideal constitution, he does give the electoral act more of an established, institutionalized place than it would ordinarily enjoy: his in any case pronounced inclination to systematization is here under a particular stimulus.[2] Hence *creatio* instead of *creare*.

The case brings out well what is implied in the advance from verb to action noun. For very special reasons Cicero is here far ahead of his time. I would say that if, by mischance, this passage were among the missing chapters of *De Legibus*, not only would it not affect the overall picture of linguistic development: even the view we should form of the relation of *creare* and *creatio* would remain basically – basically – correct.

To infiltrate the action noun into a stratum where it had not yet matured is a grave distortion of intellectual history. Conversely, when we do find it at a remarkably early date the presumption is that the institution was endowed with a particular status – even if (as happens) it has lost it by the time our main sources begin to run. *Ambitio*, from *ambire*, *auctio*, from *augere*, and *manus iniectio*, from *manum inicere*, are all of them old and all of them retain their standing in later periods.[3] It is different with *captio*, from *capere*, and *consultatio*, from *consultare*. While they figure among the extraordinarily small number of nouns in Plautus, signifying deception (*captio*) and deliberation as to a marriage or the like (*consultatio*),[4] they are distinctly less conspicuous in the literature of the Empire; or more precisely, in the case of *consultatio*, the ancient meaning has become rare. Evidently, the two phenomena played a greater role in archaic law and custom. Both *indicare* and

---

[1] 2.7.18: *Sunt certa legum verba ... quo plus auctoritatis habeant, paulo antiquiora quam hic sermo est.*

[2] A certain pomposity also is a general characteristic of his. He employs *testificari* and *testificatio* instead of *testari* and *testatio*; he may well be the author of *testificatio*.

[3] Though the unlawful kind of *ambitio* comes to be preferably expressed by *ambitus*; cf. below, Second Lecture, p. 126 n. 2.

[4] In Terence, *Hec.* 650, the meaning is very similar: deliberation whether to take a wife back.

The Action Noun: Varia

indicatio are used by Plautus of the naming of the price in the food-market. Neither is found in this sense in the classical jurists. From lay writers it may be seen that the usage continued, though the noun is uncommon. Here is an institution which, clearly important in early times, might have been taken up in earnest by the jurists, but was not.[1]

However, I believe we must distinguish. The action noun, we saw, is suitable for ceremonious, authoritative pronouncements. By the same token, it can be used to provoke mirth. Even today, an intricate pseudo-scholarly or bureaucratic monster may raise a smile: subdepartmentalization. At a time when action nouns are few and far between, here is a great opportunity for entertainers. I believe that a large proportion of action nouns in Plautus are dragged in for a joke, many even invented by him: these latter obviously reflect no established notions.

Listen to this angry, forbidding question: *Quid tibi, malum, hic ante aedes clamitatiost?*[2] This kind of address is frequent in Plautus. Another example: *Quid tibi interpellatio aut in consilium huc accessio est?*[3] It is generally held that such was everyday speech.[4] That may be so: in which case Plautus is showing up the ponderousness of people in these situations.[5] The Epilogue of the *Captives* presents an accumulation of action nouns: *neque subigitationes neque amatio nec suppositio nec circumductio*.[6] Of these, *suppositio* was surely current. It is met in three other plays of Plautus, and we know that the sub-

---

[1] *Indicatio* occurs in one interpolated text, D.19.1.13.3, Ulpian *XXXII ad edictum* (see Beseler, *Zeitschrift*, 66, 1948, 320). It denotes the statement by a seller of a slave who is a thief that the slave is reliable. If, as is very doubtful, this application of the noun comes down from the market term, we have before us one of the numerous cases of pre-classical language re-emerging (in a modified sense) in post-classical jurisprudence.

[2] *Most.* 6.   [3] *Trin.* 709.

[4] Lorenz, *Mostellaria*, 2nd ed., 1883, 45f.

[5] Another possibility, I suppose, is that the phrasing *quid tibi* etc. goes back to some most formal occasion and is being brought down into ordinary encounters in the comedy. It should be noted that *clamitatio* and *interpellatio* occur nowhere else in Plautus, and *accessio* only in another such exclamation, *Tru.* 258: *Quid tibi ad hasce accessio aedis est prope?*

[6] 1030f.

stitution of a false child was a prominent theme in antiquity. *Subigitatio* and *circumductio* recur nowhere else in Plautus. *Amatio* is indeed an exclusively Plautine word. He is fond of it, employing it in five comedies. Probably he made it up; indubitably whoever made it up meant it to be suggestive and amusing. Another accumulation in the *Stichus*: *cavillationes, adsentatiunculae, periuriatiunculae*.[1] *Conduplicatio* and *congeminatio* signify embrace in the *Poenulus*, surely artificial formations at the time.[2] When poor Sceledanus continues his watch, his words are weighty and ridiculous: *certumst nunc observationi operam dare*.[3] Mock-firmity is conveyed by a line in the *Poenulus*: *ita negotium institutumst, non datur cessatio*.[4] Admittedly, it is not always possible to be confident whether a noun is to strike the public as unusual or not.[5]

The fact that an action noun is the product of the Middle Ages or even more recent times does not make it any less interesting, to me at any rate. Only we must get things straight, both for the previous phase and for the new one. I have pointed out a fair number of such cases.[6] The first step is negative: not

---

[1] 228f. *Adsentatiuncula* and *periuriatiuncula* nowhere else in Plautus. *Cavillatio* recurs in *Tru.* 685, where there is punning on it; see Enk, *Truculentus*, vol.2, 1953, 156. Another accumulation in the pimp's list of his mistakes, *Rud.* 502: *quid mihi scelesto tibi erat auscultatio, quidve hinc abitio quidve in navem ascensio?* The nouns nowhere else in Plautus.

[2] 1297: *sed quid hoc est? quid est? quid hoc est? quid ego video? quo modo? quid hoc est conduplicationis? quae haec est congeminatio?* (cf. *Pseud.* 1245, *corpora conduplicant*). The nouns of course nowhere else in Plautus, neither has he *duplicatio* or *geminatio*. He must be the inventor.

[3] *Mil. Glor.* 485. *Observatio* nowhere else in Plautus.

[4] 925. *Cessatio* nowhere else in Plautus.

[5] *Coactio* in *Asin.* 203 is probably not by itself funny (on Leo's emendation, see above, p. 30 n. 1). *Altercatio* in *Au.* 486 is hardly a fresh coinage, though perhaps meant here to sound slightly pompous. Nor, I daresay, is *velitatio* in *As.* 307 and *Rud.* 525 due to Plautus; whoever coined it, though, intended it to sound elaborate.

[6] *Adpromissio, accessio, amotio, confirmatio, corruptio, datio, dedicatio, defamatio, derelictio, fidepromissio, inaedificatio, inventio, occupatio, proquiritatio, publicatio, renuntiatio, satio, separatio, specificatio, sponsio, violatio* are all medieval or modern, altogether or in one of the senses attributed to them.

The Action Noun : Varia

to project them back into the Roman law from the XII Tables to Justinian. But there remains a second, constructive task: to discover exactly when and why they were wanted, since, at certain moments. Some grew out of the continuing practice of Roman law, some are the work of students. Whether in one category or the other, they are illuminating as to the state of thought behind them.

Let me exemplify by a sizeable group of modern creations which is curiously revealing. *Denegatio actionis* may serve as typical. The noun *denegatio* occurs in no ancient legal source in any sense, and the earliest lay evidence is Servius on Virgil, about AD 400.[1] That the jurists do not speak of *denegatio actionis*, only of *denegare actionem*, was actually seen by Wlassak,[2] but this has not diminished the popularity of the noun phrase. The latter is not merely the result of the scholar's urge to bring the material before him up to his own standard of systematization. It appeals to the nineteenth- and twentieth-century admiration for strength. The noun phrase is more powerful. How sombre-splendid the sound of *damnatio memoriae*. Vittinghoff, who knows that it is modern, and even establishes a rather pedestrian meaning for *damnare memoriam*, immediately substitutes *abolitio memoriae*.[3] But *damnatio memoriae, abolitio memoriae, rescissio actorum* are all Wagnerian images; only the verbal constructions are found in the texts.[4] Similarly with *laudatio auctoris, nominatio auctoris, editio actionis*.[5]

These elevations are not without consequences: the way you speak of a thing influences your ideas about it. For example Pliny writes to Trajan[6] about litigation *de natalibus restituendis*, cases where a man is alleged to be wrongly considered a slave

[1] The verb is found from Plautus. *Negatio*, too, is missing from VJR.

[2] *Festgabe Pfaff*, 1910, 45, now reprinted: *Labeo*, 13, 1967, 262.

[3] *Der Staatsfeind in der römischen Kaiserzeit*, 1936, 12f., 47, 64ff.

[4] *Rescissio* altogether only four times in VJR, always, it appears, interpolated: Beseler, *Zeitschrift*, 56, 1936, 31.

[5] *Editiones* (without *actionum*) occurs in one interpolated passage, D.2.13.1.2, Ulpian *IV ad edictum*.

[6] *Ep.* 10. 72. See articles quoted above, p. 36, n. 5.

or a freedman: he was really born free, and the object of the suit is to get this native freedom restored. According to the prevalent interpretation, however, Pliny is referring to the grant of freebornhood to persons of servile birth. This is an anachronism, such grants were not yet made in that period, and even later they were made by the Emperor, not a proconsul. When we ask how it is that so gross a misunderstanding is universally shared, the answer must include (among other factors) the noun phrase *natalium restitutio* regularly used by those who discuss Pliny. The phrase, I may recall, is first met in an enactment by Justinian, where it does signify a grant of freebornhood: he thinks of Theodora's redemption as comparable to it. Pliny, however, soberly puts *natales restituere*. The momentous-sounding *natalium restitutio* is far more likely than a modest *de natalibus restituendis* to conjure up in the historian's mind the discretionary promotion to freebornhood by an act of state. Again, the commanding *denegatio actionis* not only makes you feel good, it also leads you on in a certain direction. It has been depicted as flowing from the *königliche, später prätorische Machtvollkommenheit*, 'the royal, subsequently praetorian omnipotence'.[1] Whether this is right or wrong – *denegare actionem*, which alone appears in the sources, implies less institutionalization and less majesty than the noun phrase and, proceeding from it, one is bound to be more hesitant.

The achievement or non-achievement of the action noun is no less significant in non-legal areas of culture than in law: nor is it a peculiarly Roman phenomenon. Biblical law knows the verb *shamar*, to guard, to keep, *custodire*, but it is only in post-Biblical law that we get *shemira*, *custodia*. The verb *ya'ash*, to despair, is found in the Old Testament and in Tannaitic sources; *ye'ush*, abandonment of property, is an Amoraic institution.[2] Greek *katecho*, to hold, and *tithemi*, to set, are met in Homer and Hesiod, *katoche* from Herodotus, *thesis* from

---

[1] Broggini, *Zeitschrift*, 79, 1962, 384.

[2] *Ḥazaqa* in the technical sense of prescriptive acquisition is post-Biblical. Levy, *Wörterbuch über die Talmudim und Midraschim*, 2nd ed., vol.2, 1924, 30, regards the Hiphil *heḥeziq* in this sense as derived from the noun – surely that is unlikely.

The Action Noun: Varia

Pindar; *lytroo*, to release for ransom, occurs in Plato, *lytrosis* first appears in the *Septuagint*. While *verpfänden* is Middle-High-German and *übereignen* sixteenth century, *Verpfändung* and *Übereignung* are both seventeenth. An English example: to bail – to begin with used in the French shape, *bailler* – precedes by a considerable time its action noun bailment, which latter comes in only in the seventeenth century.

In English law, the position is indeed complicated by the interplay with Latin and French or Norman-French. Still, it is perfectly possible to investigate it from the point of view from which I have looked at Roman law, and just as vital for a proper appreciation. After all, at Rome, in many cases, the history of a concept is influenced by a Greek precursor, though I have refrained from expatiating on this aspect. Here are a few English illustrations of how borrowing may upset the normal sequence verb – action noun. The noun cession was taken over into legal language before the verb to cede, compensation before to compensate,[1] inhibition before to inhibit, naturalization before to naturalize.[2] In another case, extradition, the noun alone was imported from French, 1839, the verb to extradite being made up twenty-five years later (what philologists call a back-formation). In fact, in French itself, which had only *tradition* but no corresponding verb *trader*,[3] the noun *extradition* came first and *extrader* a little later (both second half of eighteenth century).

To peep outside the law, *maṣa'*, to find, and its passive *nimṣa'*, to be found, to exist, are common in the Old Testament; the noun *meṣi'a*, denoting the act of finding or the object found, is Talmudic, the noun *meṣi'uth*, existence, is medieval. Similarly, the Old Testament again and again reminds us of how the children of Israel went forth from Egypt and how God brought them forth, *yaṣa'*, *hoṣi'*, *mimmiṣraim*. The noun

---

[1] Though to compense – now obsolete – was adopted about the same time as compensation: this may have delayed to compensate.

[2] Though with reference to adaptation of a practice, the verb considerably precedes the noun.

[3] I am discounting here the far earlier *trahison* and *trahir*.

phrase *yeṣi'ath miṣraim*, the exodus from Egypt, is post-Biblical.[1] It may be indebted to the Greek noun *exodos*, which occurs in the *Septuagint*, the *Apocrypha*, the *Epistle to the Hebrews*,[2] Philo and Josephus. Again, the Old Testament knows people that hate without cause, *sone'e ḥinnam*.[3] It is in post-Biblical ethics that hatred without cause, *sin'ath ḥinnam*, becomes an important category.[4] Both the Old Testament and the New have to imitate, follow after, become like, an exemplary figure, God, Christ: *mimeisthai, akolouthein, homoiousthai*. The nominalization is confined to subsequent elaborations of the Scriptures. In the case of the Old Testament the time lag is big. Our first evidence of the action noun is Philo, writing in Greek and obviously influenced by Platonic philosophy. He uses *mimema* and *exomoiosis*. There is a far shorter interval in the case of the New Testament: here expositors like Clement, from the outset, had the noun ready at hand in Greek literature. One might indeed differentiate further and inquire which of the various suitable nouns is preferred in any given period or milieu. Again, it would be interesting to go into the growth of these concepts in Greek and find out by what steps the Platonic action nouns were reached.

That there is a substantial difference between the stage of a mere *imitari Deum* or *Christum* and that where one may speak of *imitatio Dei* or *Christi* is surely undeniable. Actually, German scholars deplore the lack in English of a noun from to follow after. In German there are nouns both from *nachahmen*, to imitate, namely *Nachahmung*, and from *nachfolgen*, to follow after, namely, *Nachfolge*. As English forms a noun only from

---

[1] See Daube, *The Exodus Pattern in the Bible*, 1963, 33f.: 'It marks a decisive step from thinking about that event in concrete terms towards a historical-theological concept. Awareness of the step is indicated by the fact that, though the Old Testament offers several nouns which might have done, a new one was chosen'.

[2] 11.22.

[3] Ps. 35.19, 69.4: 'they that hate me without cause are more than the hairs of mine head.'

[4] E.g. *Babylonian Shabbath* 32b, *Yoma* 9b, *Authorised Daily Prayer Book*, ed. by Singer, 1891, 261. See below, Second Lecture, p. 119.

The Action Noun : Varia

to imitate, imitation, English scholars tend to make this do for *Nachfolge* as well as *Nachahmung*. Which, the Germans rightly maintain, leads to serious muddle. Seeing that English has two perfectly good different verbs for the two nuances, this is a remarkable tribute to the importance of the action noun. It is not without irony that, while it is absolutely correct that the ideas of following after a person and imitating a person must be kept apart, the introduction of the noun *Nachfolge* is none the less a falsification of the beginnings of Christian thought on the subject – more so than the noun *Nachahmung*, imitation. The Greek for the latter, *mimema* or *mimesis*, is met, though not in the Bible, yet in such ancient writers as Philo and Clement. The Greek for the former, *akolouthia, akolouthema, akolouthesis*, does not in this context appear in the earlier theological authorities at all.

Needless to say, different languages offer different facilities – some better, some poorer – for creating an action noun or, maybe, finding a substitute. In English, in an extraordinary number of cases, the action noun is simply the infinitive substantivized – a make from to make,[1] a pull from to pull.[2] A language's potential in this respect is in itself a pointer to the mode of thinking in that civilization, and, I ought to add, at that moment, for we come across amazing expansions and contractions. It is essential not to neglect the particular historical circumstances of a language. When one crosses over from Latin to Greek, one's first impression is that the latter took far less time in equipping itself with a full complement of action nouns; and by and large that may be the truth. Some allowance, however, must be made for the fact that the earliest major works in Greek preserved to us – Homer, Hesiod, Aeschylus and so on – in many respects reflect a more advanced stage than their Latin counterparts. The development which, at Rome, takes place under our eyes, in Greece largely

---

[1] The verb ninth century, the noun fourteenth.

[2] The verb about AD 1000, the noun three-hundred years later. We must, of course, be careful. The verb to man (first half of twelfth century) is derived from the noun man (first half of ninth).

lies back of the sources. Anyhow, what is called for is nothing less than a complete overhaul, within each civilization, of the histories of its several territories, law, philosophy, religion, science, paying attention to the progression from the verbal phase to the nominal. Then will follow a comparison of these several areas. Then a comparison of the various civilizations.

I must confess, however, that in dwelling on the move from verb to action noun I have presented only the basic, roughest distinction. A fuller study would have to take note of subtler gradations. Even within the action noun there are significant shadings. In legal Latin, especially, an action noun sometimes denotes not the activity as such but the right to undertake it. I mentioned earlier on *alienatio* and *datio deminutio* in the sense not of disposal but of power of disposal.[1] *Testamenti factio* may denote the power to make a will; Cicero has it,[2] and it is common among the jurists. Indeed, in course of time, the expression so much recedes from the actual making of a will and concentrates on the capacity in this connection that post-classical idiom extends it to the right to take under a will – whence the *testamenti factio passiva* from the late Middle Ages.[3]

It is probable that, as a rule at least, this meaning, the power to act, is secondary compared with the act itself. In the case of *alienatio* the evidence definitely points this way, the meaning power of alienation not being attested before Gaius. Similarly, *factio* denotes conduct in Plautus,[4] and *testamenti factio* the actual making of a will in a statement of the late Republican jurist Aelius Gallus.[5] In the case of *datio*, the assumption that

---

[1] Above, pp. 21, 40, 45.

[2] *Top.* 50, *Ep. ad Fam.* 7.21.

[3] Krüger, *Zeitschrift*, 53, 1933, 505ff. *Electio, nominatio, optio* may signify the right to elect, nominate, choose. English option and choice also may mean the power.

[4] *Quae haec factio est?*, 'What sort of conduct is this?': *Bacch.* 843, *Rudens* 1371.

[5] Festus 165: *nexum est, ut ait Gallus Aelius, quodcumque per aes et libram geritur . . , quo in genere sunt haec, testamenti factio, nexi datio, nexi liberatio.*

The Action Noun: Varia

it meant transfer before it meant power to transfer is an act of faith, but I am prepared to make it.[1]

Another nuance to be considered is the action noun in the sense of the result of the activity. Performance, from to perform, may mean not only a doing ('Besides her walking and other actual performances, what have you heard her say?'[2]), but also a piece of work ('He published lives of Saints and other performances'[3]). Once again, we can formulate a presumption: the reference to the activity antedates that to its result.[4] Admittedly there are exceptions. But the main trend is clear enough, and of no small relevance to a grasp of the history of concepts.

Three Latin specimens. *Aratio*, from *arare*, must have signified the result of ploughing, a plot farmed, before Plautus, since he uses it – and, indeed, *aratiuncula* – in a transferred, obscene sense.[5] As on a previous occasion, we find agriculture in the forefront of terminological evolution. *Cautio*, from *cavere*, is first attested by Cicero.[6] But already

---

[1] In the senatusconsult of 186 BC, above, pp. 40, 45, the meaning is power to transfer; and in the *lex agraria* of 111 BC, 33, 35, the meaning is power (and duty) to set up a court and judges.   [2] *Macbeth*, 5.1.13.

[3] Garrow, *History and Antiquities of Croydon*, 59.

[4] To perform fourteenth century, performance as activity fifteenth, as the result sixteenth. The step from activity to result is found even with action nouns formed by means of the suffix -ing. Clearing denotes the action from the late fourteenth century, while the sense of a piece cleared in a forest is American (New York) frontier speech around 1800: 'There was what in the language of the country was called a *clearing*, and all the usual improvements of a new settlement' (Cooper, *The Pioneers*, 1823, 5, with *clearing* in italics. The action is supposed to take place towards the end of the eighteenth century). The noun holding occurs from the first half of the thirteenth century; it denotes tenure of land from the first half of the fifteenth; and land held in tenure from the first half of the seventeenth. Here, too, there are exceptions to the sequence activity – result, but some are apparent rather than real. Building has the sense of edifice (late thirteenth century) before that of erecting one (late fourteenth). But, then, the earlier sense may derive from the (now obsolete) intransitive usage of to build, i.e. to build in the sense of to reside – as dwelling derives from to dwell.

[5] *Truc.* 148f.: *aratio* of a boy, *aratiuncula* of a girl. The verb is used obscenely in *Truc.* 149, *Asin.* 874. cf. *Antony and Cleopatra*, 2.2.227f.: 'Royal wench, she made great Caesar lay his sword to bed, he ploughed her and she cropt.'   [6] See above, p. 44 nn. 1f.

here it may signify not only the contract but also the instrument.[1] Which agrees with what one would suspect from other considerations – that the term as denoting the contract was established well before that date. *Possessio*, from *possidere*, already in the *lex agraria* of 111 BC signifies both the possessing of land[2] and land in possession.[3] The latter usage is combated in a definition of the term by Aelius Gallus, at the end of the Republic,[4] and even Labeo's definition, at the beginning of the Empire, till sticks to the possessing.[5]

Three English examples. Satisfaction. Latin *satisfactio* is confined to the active meaning, what a debtor or offender performs. It comes into English (via French) around 1300; and it is only in the second half of the fifteenth century that we find it expressing a state of mind of the recipient – 'the greatest richesse is satisfaction of the heart.'[6] Exhibition, in the sense of displaying to the public, occurs from the second half of the seventeenth century; in the sense of articles displayed from around 1800.[7] Inhibition – Latin *inhibitio* is invariably active, a check. So was English inhibition from the second half of the fourteenth century to quite recently. In the late nineteenth century psychology availed itself of the word, to describe a check on thought or action by the unconscious will. Popular speech is now about to turn it into a state; something like unaccountable disinclination.[8]

[1] *Ep. ad Fam.* 7.18.1.   [2] E.g. 16, Bruns, 76.

[3] E.g. 9, 93, Bruns, 75, 88. This meaning is also found in Festus, 241: *possessiones appellantur agri*, 'possessions are such and such fields'.

[4] Festus, 233: *possessio est ut definit Gallus Aelius usus quidem agri aut aedificii, non ipse fundus aut ager*, 'possession is the use of a field or building, not the farm or field itself'.

[5] D.41.2.1 pr., Paul *LIV ad edictum*: *possessio appellata est, ut et Labeo ait, a sedibus quasi positio, quia naturaliter tenetur ab eo qui ei insistit, quam Graeci katochen dicunt*.

[6] Anthony Woodville, Earl Rivers, *Dictes and Sayings of the Philosophers*, 7, a translation of the French version of a Latin work. The development in French is quite similar.

[7] The noun show signifies the action from 1300, the passive side from two-hundred years later. As a synonym of exhibition in the sense of display on a large scale it dates only from the first half of the nineteenth century.

[8] I could go on indefinitely. So much so that it may be well to note that many action nouns have kept to the action – demolition, for instance,

beautification, fumigation. Here are a few more examples of action and result. (1) Publication in the sense of issuing a book occurs from the second half of the sixteenth century, in that of a book published from the second half of the eighteenth. (2) Revision denotes the action from the early seventeenth century, the product from the mid-nineteenth. (3) Plantation in the active sense occurs from the mid-fifteenth century, in that of the result from the mid-sixteenth. (4) Vegetation signifies the process from the second half of the sixteenth century, concrete plants some two-hundred years later. The noun, incidentally, was taken over from French before the verb. French *végéter* figures from the fourteenth century, *végétation* from the sixteenth; English vegetation from the sixteenth, to vegetate from the early seventeenth. (5) Coalition did not reach the sense of united parties till the mid-nineteenth century, 'government by coalition', 1866. Up to then it meant the process of uniting, 'towards a coalition', 1715. Latin *coalescere*, to grow together, is common of the uniting of men in the historians, Sallust, Livy, Tacitus. *Coalitus*, rare, occurs from about 300, always with reference to the process. Neither *coalescentia* nor *coalitio* is found in ancient Latin, but the latter appears in the Middle Ages, still signifying the process: *coalitionem instituentes*. In English, to coalesce and coalescence are launched simultaneously by sixteenth-century medicine, referring to the process. Coalition follows in the seventeenth, going outside science, but still denoting a growing together. To coalesce and coalescence first enter politics in the second half of the eighteenth century, 'coalescing parties' 1783, 'Fox's party will propose a coalescence' 1788. Coalition in this field is earlier: 'an essay towards a coalition of parties' 1715. And it outlasts the other two which have become obsolete. A verb to coalite, however, derived from coalition (a back-formation) about 1735, barely made it through the eighteenth century. (French *coaliser* has endured.) Chesney, *A True Reformer*, vol.3, 1873, 99, distinguishes coalition, as an alliance from expediency, from coalescence, a genuine union in a crisis: 'not a coalition in any sense, rather a Constitutional Coalescence'. But he has his tongue in his cheek. (6) *Démoraliser* is a term of the French revolution, meaning to corrupt, and *démoralisation*, the act of corruption, is barely younger; though, significantly, the verb was admitted by the Académie in 1798, the noun in 1878. The verb was Englished as early as 1793: Noah Webster himself coined to demoralise. The noun first appears in Southey, 1809. In the sense of to destroy the stamina, English uses the verb from the middle of the nineteenth century. A little later, demoralization may signify a state as well as the action: 'his army (the Turkish commander's) is in a state of utter demoralisation and disorganisation', *Daily News*, 5 November 1877. (7) No discernible gap separates the sense of action and that of result, e.g. in the cases of afforestation and generation. *Afforestare* is used in medieval Latin from the thirteenth century, to afforest appears in the early sixteenth, afforestation a hundred years later – denoting both the act of afforesting and the resultant state. Generation comes into English from Latin and French in the late fourteenth century, with a large variety of meanings acquired in the course of a long previous history. The verb to generate is adopted from Latin in the second half of the sixteenth century: French has no *générer*, only *engendrer*. (8) Anyone wishing for examples of inordinately chequered development might pursue the fortunes of institution and representation from Cicero to the present day.

Forgetting about these subtler differentiations – the English action noun, like the Latin, has periods of gradual advance as well as moments of proliferation: the Renaissance belongs to the latter. Formal language favours it. To cancel dates from before the middle of the fifteenth century, but it is a statute of 1535 which introduces the noun: 'The said Chancellor shall have power to make cancellation of such leases and letters patents.'[1] In worship, 'we make supplications',[2] and we praise God who stirred up 'the mind of Henry Chichele, for the relief of the distressed and the increase of learning and godliness'.[3] English satirists are no less alive than their Roman forerunners to the opportunities offered them by this style wigged, robed or gaitered. Primers, lists of definitions, glossaries are fertile soil for the action noun today as they were at Rome, and we must now add advertisements and the like. Journalists seem generally attracted by its crisp and systematizing character.[4] As at Rome, the nominalization may affect only a sector of the verb. To electrify is first attested in a letter by Benjamin Franklin, 1747, electrification in the *Philosophical Transactions* 1748. Four years later Chesterfield uses the verb in a transferred sense: 'You will not be so agreeably electrified as at Mannheim'. But even today, one could not speak of the electrification of Professor Daube by the appearance of Marlene Dietrich at his lecture.[5]

[1] Act 27, *Henry VIII*, xxvii. *Cancellare* is not used by the classics according to Beseler, *Zeitschrift*, 56, 1936, 32; *cancellatio* is exclusively technical of the fixing of boundaries.

[2] The noun was taken over into English (late fourteenth century) before the verb (early fifteenth).

[3] To relieve in this sense from 1375, relief from 1400; to increase early fourteenth century, the noun late fourteenth.

[4] To subsidise in the sense of to support by grants goes back to the first half of the nineteenth century, subsidization is first met in the *Daily Chronicle* of January 1, 1907. While getting this Lecture ready for publication, I found the noun in an editorial of the *Daily Californian* of February 22, 1967, p. 1, discussing a letter from a professor. The letter is reproduced on p. 13: it speaks of subsidising, not subsidization.

[5] Wrong. From the *Supplement* to the *Oxford Dictionary* I see that since the last quarter of the nineteenth century electrification has indeed been employed figuratively; e.g. 'her electrification by Mr Belport's proposal'. I doubt, however, whether this usage is represented in good writers.

The Action Noun : Varia

Frequently the emergence of the noun illumines what goes on in that province. To fraternize, early seventeenth century; 'they gave the kiss of fraternisation to negros' 1792, French revolution and Wilberforce. To mechanize, second half of seventeenth century; the noun 1839, in a complaint by Sterling about 'the mechanization of the mind'. To enlight, tenth century, and to enlighten, late fourteenth; Milton and Butler first use the verb of instruction, and it is at the same time that there enters the noun enlightenment, which later, in the second half of the nineteenth century, becomes a rendering of *Aufklärung*. To measure, fourteenth century; measurement starts in architecture in the middle of the eighteenth. The work of Gärtner and Darwin is reflected in to hybridize 1845, immediately followed by hybridization in 1851.[1] To disinfect, seventeenth century; 'On the influence of oxygen in the process of disinfection' 1803, Andrew Duncan, Professor of Medicine at Edinburgh. To atomize, in the sense of to reduce to tiny particles, occurs before the middle of the nineteenth century; atomization marks the introduction in the seventies of that century of the therapeutic inhalation of a spray. To motorize in the sense of to furnish with a motor 1918, motorization 1929, mostly with reference to a collective.[2]

By now so many English verbs have action nouns that the birthrate is low. In another sense, however, the growth is more rapid than ever: a new verb usually gets its noun with hardly any delay – which means that the existence of the noun is correspondingly less significant. Even so, nominalization is far from universal. To botanize as an intransitive is second

[1] There was a craze: 'By the acquisition of this species, a new field for the hybridist is thrown open' 1849. The notion of mongrel also received a fresh impetus from Darwin. To mongrelize 1629, mongrelization 1889.

[2] But at least in facetious speech the verb is coming to be applied to a person: 'Are you motorized?', meaning 'Have you your car with you?'. The noun contraception is not, of course, derived from a verb. Actually, contraceptive seems slightly earlier, end of last century, based on conceptive, mid-seventeenth century. Then, in the first quarter of the present century, contraception was coined, thought of as the opposite to conception. I guess that when the verb arrives (back-formation), it will be not to contraceive but to contracept, sounding less passive, more energetic, a bit like to intercept.

half of eighteenth century – 'they will botanize charmingly'[1] – and as a transitive a hundred years later – 'to botanize the islands thoroughly' – yet it has not come to botanization. Again, though many of us commute between the town where we reside and that where we work, to the best of my knowledge the phenomenon is not yet described as commutation. In this case, however, it is a safe bet that we shall see the noun before long in some planning report or sociological monograph. I have not the heart to withhold from you the history of this concept, more zigzag than one might expect. The verb *commutare*, to change, to exchange, occurs in Plautus, *commutatio* in Cicero. English takes them over in the sixteenth century: to commutate or commute and commutation. They are frequently used where it is a question of, say, substituting a down payment of 100 for twelve annual instalments of 10. In the second half of the last century American railways introduced reduced fares for passengers doing the same journey every day and buying a ticket for a fortnight or a month. In consideration of the undertaking of regular travel a lower price was substituted for what the several journeys would normally come to. Hence the name of such a ticket: commutation ticket. There was indeed deliberate emphasis on this aspect, deliberately weighty, formal nomenclature, since it was this quid pro quo, the undertaking of multiple travel for a reduction, which exempted the ticket from a law prohibiting alterations in fares. The holder of a commutation ticket was at first called a commutation passenger. Soon, however, he became a commuter, and the verb to commute accordingly came to denote this kind of travel. In course of time the connection with cheap tickets evaporated; thus what remains in the States as well as English-speaking countries to which the usage has spread is the daily displacement. Note that even now it must in principle be a move between two towns, i.e. railway stations. Within the same town, however great the distance between home and

---

[1] Not so charming: 'Philosopher!– a fingering slave, One that would peep and botanize Upon his mother's grave'. Wordsworth, *A Poet's Epitaph*, 19, 1799–1800.

office, one rarely speaks of commuting. So we have *commutare* first, then *commutatio*; in the nineteenth century the commutation ticket in the sense of substitution ticket; then to commute signifying to travel on such a ticket – and I trust you appreciate my broadmindedness in ending with a case where the verb follows the action noun, instead of the other way round; finally to commute signifying to travel routine-wise from home to office and back. Or not quite finally, for the action noun to this meaning is yet to come, and is sure to come. For the moment I suggest commutation for dinner to our respective Colleges.

2. SOCIAL ASPECTS

1. Economic Realities: A. Damages under the *Lex Aquilia*; B. The Have-Nots (1) The Horror of Intestacy (2) The *Filiusfamilias*. II. Roman Society: A. Altruistic Dodges (1) The Insolvent Debtor (2) Slaves and Freedmen (3) Fideicommissa (4) The Undowered Bride B. The Protection of the Non-Tipper.

There is no doubt that the Romanists of today are more alive to social and economic questions than their predecessors of fifty years ago.[1] Even so, the systematic coherence and conceptual smoothness of the law they are concerned with are so seductive that the temptation to forget about the rugged realities behind the façade is far greater for them than, for instance, for an English legal historian. I shall devote the first and major part of this Lecture to some typical illustrations of this danger. In the second part I propose to point out a few remarkable consequences of the close-knit character of the upper class at Rome, and in particular to call attention to an area of legislation and jurisdiction which almost deserves a name of its own.

[1] See, e.g. Kelly, *Roman Litigation*, 1966.

I. ECONOMIC REALITIES

A. Damages under the *Lex Aquilia*

Damage to property was regulated by the first and third chapters of the *lex Aquilia*, from the middle of the Republic. The first chapter ordained that a man who killed another man's slave or *pecus* – ox, cow, horse – should pay the highest value in the past year; whether the killing was deliberate or merely from negligence made no difference.[1] The original scope of the third chapter is controversial. What is agreed is that, in classical and later law, it covered all damage not falling under chapter one, hence the injuring (without killing) of a slave or *pecus* and the destruction as well as the damaging of an inanimate object or an animal not *pecus*, a dog, a cat, a chicken. And, of course, again whether deliberate or just negligent.

Now where a man merely injures (as opposed to killing) another man's slave or *pecus*, or merely damages (as opposed to destroying) another man's inanimate property or dog, one would expect him to have to pay not the full value but only the difference between that and the reduced value after interference; plus expenses for cure, repair and the like. This is indeed what in the opinion of some scholars, myself included, classical and later law did make him liable for under the third chapter; and I have written several studies tracing in detail the not uninteresting route by which the sensible, generally applicable solution was reached.[2] However, the prevalent view is different. It is – believe it or not – that once you damaged somebody's slave, beast or inanimate object, however partially, you had to pay him the full value. Remember that it is not

---

[1] Though one could plead justification, the statute speaking of killing *iniuria*; see, e.g. D.9.2.4 pr. (Gaius *VII ad edictum provinciale*) and 5 pr. (Ulpian *XVIII ad edictum*) on self-defence.

[2] See, above all, *Studi Solazzi*, 1948, 93ff.

Economic Realities : the Lex Aquilia

primarily a case of criminal wrongdoing: negligence sufficed. Schulz writes as follows[1]: 'If a thing only suffered deterioration and was not completely destroyed, the offender had to pay the full value of the thing. Thus the penalty was the same when a dog was killed and when he was only wounded.'

At one time I was tempted to publish an article acknowledging the error of my ways and describing how, by at last embracing the reigning doctrine, I had a veil removed from my eyes and many perplexing facts never before understood had become explicable to me. Take, for a start, the disturbingly large number of names Romans used to bear: Gaius Octavius Tidius Tossianus Lucius Javolenus Priscus – that is what a jurist was called. The reason, we now realize, is that children inevitably passed through countless families. There is no child that does not at some time or other scratch a letter or two, or even four, on the wall of a house. At Rome, on the basis of the prevalent view, the father would have to pay for the entire estate – not just the house, but the grounds as well. Damage worth threepence, estate worth 25,000 pounds: he had to pay 25,000 pounds – unless, indeed, he was prepared to surrender the child to the owner. In most cases he would not be able to afford not to surrender. Let it not be said that *de minimis non curat lex*. A scratch is not a *minimum* if any damage however slight is to be made good by paying the total value of the thing; a scratch, under such a rule, is worth what the thing is worth. Some texts tell us expressly that the third chapter applies even where there is absolutely no diminution in the value of the slave – who was, say, bumped into – but medical costs were incurred.[2] So we must clearly not invoke *de minimis*. According to the current doctrine the owner was entitled to the full price of his healthy slave. If it was my child who knocked against him, I would be a fool not to hand over the child rather than paying, since, on the one hand, sooner or

[1] *Classical Roman Law*, 1954, 590. At least he has the courage of his conviction. Quite a few authors hedge.

[2] D.9.2.45.1, Paul *X ad Sabinum*, and the – hardly intact – second half of D.9.2.27.17 (cf. *Coll.* 2.4.1), Ulpian *XVIII ad edictum*; see Rotondi, *Scritti Giuridici*, vol.2, 1922, 458, 476.

later I should have to part with the child owing to this Aquilian liability in any case, and on the other, I should keep receiving other people's children instead. Children, unless totally disabled, were never more than transient members of a family: Gaius Octavius Tidius and so on, and so on.

Another feature of Roman life that had always puzzled me is the inordinate amount of lending and borrowing carried on. Now I see: it was so common because there was really no private property. If I negligently turn round on my swivel-chair and your slave falls and sprains his ankle, or let us even suppose he loses a tooth, I must pay for him in full. If he is one of a performing troop of twelve you keep together, I must pay the full value of the whole troop though he goes on performing: I should have to do that if I killed him, so I must do it also in the case of partial damage.[1] If he happens to be instituted heir by a friend of yours, I guess I pay for the inheritance as well. Moreover, if I defend the action, I pay double.[2] That in a society governed by this kind of regulation nobody will be rich or poor for long is evident.

That – at first sight – most paradoxical arrangement of Roman procedure, that the judges were laymen, is finally accounted for: they did not need to know the law because it did not matter. Nothing mattered when all material life became a joke through the third chapter of this statute, which equated damaging with destruction. Ah, there was one difference, which made the regulation even more playful: the first chapter spoke of the highest value in the past year; the third, in the past month. Accordingly, if you ran over your neighbour's cow and she perished, you paid, say, 250 pounds, highest value in the past year; if she only got a bit lame, you paid a mere 235, highest value in the past month. Remember that for inanimate objects and animals not *pecus*, always the past month alone was considered. Thus, if you dropped some cigarette ash in my orchard and the orchard, with the summer house on it, went up in flames, you paid 15,000 pounds even if

[1] G.3.212, referring to killing.
[2] G.3.216, D.9.2.27.24, Paul *XXII ad edictum*.

Economic Realities : the Lex Aquilia

three months before it would have come to 16,000. And also, of course, if the ash did nothing beyond scorching a branch with a few apple blossoms – damage amounting to half a crown – you paid 15,000 not 16,000.[1]

The magistrates of the Republic were anxious to intimate to their people – and maybe they had posterity in mind as well – that the Aquilian edifice was not due to ineptitude but was set up with tongue in cheek. So they issued a series of edicts which demonstrated that the Roman mind was perfectly capable of conceiving of compensation adjusted to the loss inflicted. An edict by the praetor dealt with things thrown from a dwelling into the road and damaging your belongings – your clothes, a slave of yours, a dog of yours. The householder's liability was strictly in accordance with the harm in the individual case: he had to pay you a double indemnification. If a free man was hit, a clear distinction was drawn between death and lesser harm: in the former case a considerable fixed sum was payable, in the latter an amount equitable in the circumstances.[2] The aediles promulgated an edict exactly analogous, concerning the case where you kept a wild animal by the wayside and it attacked property or a free man: double indemnification for damage to property, varying with the actual harm done, a fixed sum in the event of a free man's death, an equitable amount in the event of injury to a free man.[3] These edicts go back to pre-classical times: Servius knew them.[4] It is obvious that the way the jurists operated the third chapter of the *lex Aquilia* was a real hoax. Doubtless some results were found particularly amusing. If I allowed my bear to escape and he broke a finger of your slave or a leg of your dog, a careful calculation was made of any permanent deterioration as well as your expenses, say, 10 pounds in the case of the slave, 5

[1] G.3.210, 218. If, however, it was a freshly planted tree which had not yet taken root, you paid for the tree: 1 to 2 pounds, G.2.74. Law was fun.

[2] Lenel, *Edictum*, 173f.

[3] Lenel, *Edictum*, 566. Why 50,000 sesterces for death in the praetor's edict *de his qui deiecerint* and 20,000 in the aedilician edict *de feris* I am not going to discuss.

[4] Or the former at least: D.9.3.5.12, Ulpian *XXIII ad edictum*.

shillings in that of the dog, and, by way of warning to keep better guard over a dangerous animal, the edict made me pay twice that figure, 20 pounds for the slave, 10 shillings for the dog. By contrast, if I inadvertently let slip a case I was carrying and it broke a finger of your slave or a leg of your dog, under the *lex Aquilia* I had to pay the total price of slave or dog, say, 300 pounds for the slave, 3 pounds for the dog – for, as Schulz says, 'the penalty was the same when a dog was killed and when he was only wounded'. It certainly paid to keep a bear rather than carry a load.

Such, then, is the outline of the article I once planned but never got around to. To return from this wonderland of Lewis Carroll – I hold that there are numerous texts in flagrant conflict with the prevalent doctrine. Moreover, not a single one raises any of the problems which would flow from such a weird regulation. This latter point is admitted even by its advocates. Surely, in this case, the argument from silence is overwhelming. Again, quite a few decisions are concerned with the accurate distribution of borderline cases between the first chapter and the third: for example, one which lays down that if I injure your slave and, though the wound in itself is not fatal, he dies from neglect, I am liable only under chapter 3.[1] Would these scrupulous distinctions really be meaningful if it were only a question whether I pay the highest value in the past year or in the past month?[2]

Buckland did notice the waste of resources which must take place under the system assumed by the current view: there would be no inducement whatever for a person who had caused some slight damage not to finish the job.[3] This result would indeed be inevitable; and to make a brief re-entry into

[1] D.9.2.30.4, Paul *XXII ad edictum*.

[2] In fact, even the first chapter was not carried to unreasonable extremes. If you kill my slave while it is open to me to acquire an inheritance through him, you will have to pay me its value; but if you kill him after I have acquired it through him, you need not pay for it – though, strictly, *quanti in eo anno plurimi fuerit* ought to include it. G.3.212: *antequam cerneret*. Cf. de Zulueta, *The Institutes of Gaius*, vol.2, 1953, 211.

[3] *Text-Book*, 586.

Economic Realities: the Have-Nots

the world of Alice – the many fires at Rome should no longer surprise us. If my chariot ran into a corner of your house, doing 7/6 worth of damage, I might just as well get a can of petrol and have the pleasure of seeing the whole building go up in a glorious blaze, since I must pay for it anyway. No difference between a tiny blemish and radical elimination, nor – that was the beauty of it – between inadvertence and malice. The law discouraged half-measures.

But even apart from this particular consequence, my submission is that no economy could go on for a fortnight with the regulation ascribed to the Romans by the orthodox school; maybe it would not be viable for one day. Gerke has attacked my dissent in *Studia et Documenta Historiae et Juris*,[1] charging: *Er verkennt das pönale Element der Klage*, 'he fails to appreciate the penal side of the action'. Some penal side!

B. The Have-Nots

1. *The Horror of Intestacy*. I now want to say something about a major cause of historical distortion: failure to take account of the have-nots. They are apt to be forgotten because the sources, the legal ones in particular, concentrate on the haves; it is they who occupy the centre of the stage while the have-nots appear on the fringe, as delinquents or the like. Scholars too readily identify with the viewpoint fed to them.

A glaring example is the horror of intestacy attributed to the Romans.[2] The colourful expression is Maine's.[3] His thesis is taken over by one author after another: at Rome, not only when it was still a small community, but long after it had expanded into an Empire, it was an exception for a man not to make a will.[4] Far-reaching conclusions are drawn regarding the make-up of the Roman psyche, eager to dominate its individual sphere even beyond death. Indeed, the most

[1] 23, 1957, 79.
[2] See my article in *Tulane Law Review*, 39, 1965, 253ff.
[3] *Ancient Law*, new ed. Pollock, 1920, 233.
[4] E.g. Costa, *Cicerone Giureconsulto*, vol.I, 1927, 215.

terrible curse (Maine alleges) one Roman could utter against another was to wish on him that he should die without leaving a will.

A moment's reflection on the economic realities should reveal the fantastic nature of this universally held theory. Take the stretch of 250 BC to AD 250. Why or how would the poor chaps who slept under the bridges of the Tiber make a will? They had nothing to make a will about, nor the wherewithal to engage the cheapest lawyer to draw it up. The current misconception is due to the enormous role played by wills in the legal writings. But these writings reflect the doings of a tiny fraction of the population. Actually, I am convinced that even among the haves will-making was no commoner than it was, say, in Victorian England. Certainly the have-nots, the vast majority of citizens, were right out of it.

The view I am combating is bolstered up by evidence which, on closer inspection, turns out to be worthless. Let me present the three chief arguments.

The first is that the XII Tables designate a person who has made no will by the negative word *intestatus*,[1] hence this must be an exception. The conclusion, however, is far from cogent. The primary function of a word is to call attention to the striking, the uncommon. At the early stage of legal Latin in the time of the XII Tables, the likelihood is that a word for to make a will, *testari*, is coined precisely because the act is anything but ordinary. There is, then, a positive label, *testatus*, attaching to that remarkable figure who has made a will, which leaves the negative *intestatus* for the usual case.[2] When we

---

[1] V 4, Bruns, 23: *si intestato moritur*.

[2] To be sure, the negative itself comes into use where the negative situation starts being remarkable or for some special reason requires extra consideration. To begin with, *confiteri* is a notable act and *confessus* designates him who has acted in this notable fashion. Much later, *inconfessus* is coined, when (in certain circles and on certain occasions at least) it is unusual not to have confessed. *Damnare* is manifestly a rare act, *damnatus* signifies a person affected by this rare act; and it never becomes an ordinary thing. *Indemnatus* is an epithet objectively applicable to the vast majority of people in all periods; but, as a historical fact, it is coined to describe the case where this quality acquires special importance, namely, where a person is charged with a crime but not (yet) sentenced in due form. Cf. below, p. 102, on the case of *indotata*.

Economic Realities: the Horror of Intestacy 73

call the world unredeemed, it does not follow that redemption is an everyday affair. What implications the prevalent argument has as to the conduct of the young Roman ladies, considering the term *virgo intacta*, I need not spell out. Incidentally I often hear Englishmen observe with pride that their language has no equivalent to the German *Schadenfreude*. The pride might be misplaced: maybe the emotion is too common here to attract notice and call for a term whereas the Germans are so sweet that if, on a rare occasion, it does occur, it stands out. Anyhow this argument from *intestatus* is no good at all.

The next piece of evidence is a statement by old Cato that he made three mistakes in his life[1]: he told a secret to his wife,[2] he paid for a boat when he could have walked it, and he spent an entire day *adiathetos* – which is translated 'without a will'. To base on such an utterance by an eccentric one's estimate of the *mores* among, say, the tailors or carpenters or even the bankers of Rome is surely indefensible. The same Cato, let me remind you, remarked[3] that he never made love to his wife except during a thunderstorm. Are we to generalize this too? Why not? There is, however, another little flaw in the argument under consideration: *adiathetos* does not mean 'without a will' at all, it means 'without serious, planned work'. As we know from Cicero, Cato preached the principle that a statesman ought to make constructive, rational use of his free time as well as his hours of official business.[4] So one of the three sins he committed in the course of his life is that he once spent a day without being purposefully engaged; his statement has not the remotest connection with wills. To be sure, there are plenty of references to the importance of wills. Cicero sees a proof of the immortality of the soul in man's concern about what will happen after his death, a concern shown in 'the procreation of

---

[1] Plutarch, *Parallel Lives, Cato Maior*, 9.6.

[2] On the advisability of this course opinion was divided. Nicostratus holds that a husband keeps nothing from his wife but communes with her as with another self: Stobaeus, *Floril.* ed. Meineke, vol. 3, 1856, 69f.

[3] Plutarch, *Cato Maior*, 17.7.

[4] *pro Plancio*, 27.66; see Nicolai, *Saeculum*, 14, 1963, 215.

children, the propagation of the name, the adoption of sons, the care taken about wills, the very burial monuments and epitaphs'.[1] But the end gives him away as speaking for his class. Paupers may procreate, because that costs nothing, but wills and monuments are a different matter. This second argument, then, for the horror of intestacy goes the way of the first.

We thus come to the third, which is the one that inspired Maine to coin this phrase. In one of Plautus's comedies the lover wants to summon a captain to court. For this, some formality before witnesses is required, called *antestari*, but the captain refuses to cooperate. The young man shouts at him 'live unsummoned, unattested, then, *intestatus vivito*, I can go through the formality with somebody else'.[2] There is also a very obscene *double entendre* which Plautus's audience apparently loved, for it recurs several times in his work,[3] but which is not fit for an audience like you. Maine, it is clear, did not suspect it. For him, and all the many writers on the subject following him, here is evidence that there was no more fearful curse in Latin than to say to a man he should die without a will. The passage has absolutely nothing to do with a will. The enraged lover is not a bit interested in the ultimate destiny of the captain's property, such as it is, nor could that wretch care less. 'Go to blazes',[4] that is what it means, 'live unattested (and without testicles)'.

In the forties BC the number of recipients of free grain in the

---

[1] *Tusc. Disp.* 1.14.31: *procreatio liberorum, propagatio nominis, adoptiones filiorum, testamentorum diligentia, ipsa sepulchrorum monumenta, elogia.*

[2] *Curculio*, 621ff. The someone else is the willing Curculio. It is also possible to interpret 'may you live without being able to call witnesses when you need them' or 'may you live incapable of being called as witness, infamous'; see my article quoted above. My thesis is quite unaffected: none of the renderings conceivable can be brought into association with a will. I now much prefer the translation proposed in the text, which seems to me simplest and most in accordance with the situation. Moreover, it would fit also in *Curculio*, 695, where the pimp objects to being dragged off for punishment *indemnatus atque intestatus*, 'unsentenced and unsummoned'.

[3] Once more in the same play, *Curculio*, 30, another time in *Miles Glor.* 1417.

[4] *Iuppiter te perdat.*

Economic Realities: the Filiusfamilias 75

city of Rome was 320,000; as only adult males were eligible, the figure does not include women and children in this class. On the other hand, ancient historians tell us that 'well-to-do residents were presumably not numerically significant'.[1] In these circumstances, if there were anything in the orthodox view, the normal Roman will should run: 'Let my three sons Titius, Maevius and Sempronius be my heirs. I leave them my entire possessions, consisting of the shirt and the sandals I am wearing, in equal parts, with a usufruct for my widow for life.' But not one will of this kind has come to light anywhere in the Empire. The most modest wills extant at least involve a house or something of comparable value.[2] The younger Pliny, in a letter, tells a friend about one Domitius Tullus who appeared to be the kind of man that would leave his estate to worthless flatterers; but, surprisingly, he distributed it dutifully among deserving relations, thus refuting 'the general notion that wills mirror people's mentality'.[3] Well, well. Domitius Tullus was a multi-millionaire. Wills mirror the mentality of the well-to-do, others do not make them. The have-nots are invisible: *die im Dunkeln sieht man nicht*. But they do exist and a history of law which discounts them is apt to go wrong.

2. *The Filiusfamilias* A fundamental Roman institution, the complete incapacity of a *filiusfamilias* to own property, can be adequately explained only by bearing in mind the have-nots. If you were a Roman citizen and your *paterfamilias* was alive, you could not own anything.[4] Age or rank made no difference. Suppose the head of a family was ninety, his two sons seventy-five and seventy, their sons between sixty and fifty-five, the sons of these in their forties and thirties, and the great-great-grandsons in their twenties, none of them except the ninety-

[1] Brunt, *Past and Present*, 35, 1966, 8f.
[2] Except for the *testamentum porcelli*: below, pp. 77ff. This is not to deny that, say, among a panicked army there may be an outbreak of will-making: see Caesar, *Bell. Gall.* 1. 39.
[3] *Ep.* 8.18: *quod creditur vulgo, testamenta hominum speculum esse morum.*
[4] Buckland, *Text-Book*, 280.

year-old Head owned a penny. If the seventy-five-year-old senator or the forty-year-old General or the twenty-year-old student wanted to buy a bar of chocolate, he had to ask the *senex* for the money. This is really quite extraordinary. Had it been so only in very early times, in the fifth and fourth centuries BC, when Rome was a compact settlement of peasants and craftsmen, it would be understandable. But it was still the law in the time of Caesar or Hadrian, when Rome was the capital of the Western world and full of foreigners under no such restraints. An adult Greek or Jew could buy, sell, borrow, lend, keep horses, go to the pictures, send flowers to his lady, even if his father or grandfather was still around. His Roman contemporary was unable to do any of these things unless he succeeded either in persuading the old man to support him or in finding somebody willing to extend credit to him in the hope that he would outlive his elders and eventually, when a *paterfamilias* himself, settle his debts with the addition of a generous bounty. From Constantine onwards, in the fourth century AD, the system was dismantled. Mostly the books (if they are interested in social or economic aspects at all) ask why this happened. The foremost question to put is surely how the system could go on for so long.

From a cursory reading of the literature one might gain the impression that already Augustus carried out a radical reform; but this is definitely not the case. He ordained that a *filiusfamilias* serving in the army might dispose by last will of what he had acquired by way of soldier's stipend and booty.[1] Obviously, this affected only a tiny group and even that only in a marginal way. So long as a soldier managed to escape death, in practice, whatever the law, stipend and booty had always been his. Even before the Augustan decree no *paterfamilias* could run after his son or grandson fighting the Pannonians on the Danube if he took his pay, as well as the ring taken from a slain enemy, to the local beauty queen. When in the early Empire this camp property, *peculium castrense*, was officially recognized as freely available to the soldier, that was no more

[1] I.2.12 pr.

Economic Realities : the Filiusfamilias 77

than legalization of an inevitable state of affairs. Augustus did go just a little further: a *filiusfamilias*-soldier was to be able to make a valid will about stipend and booty.[1] We can imagine how his popularity with the troops increased when he took the line that the last wishes of one who fell in battle should be given effect, and his possessions go to the comrade or girl he named. But remember that a *filiusfamilias* lost this privilege as soon as he left the service: prior to Hadrian, a *filiusfamilias*-veteran had no property to leave, and even if he had made a will in the army, it lapsed, since everything was now again fully in his father's or grandfather's hands. It cannot be said that Augustus's measure had the slightest impact on the position of a *filiusfamilias* in general.

There is preserved a *testamentum porcelli*, a will of a piglet,[2] which has been neglected by Romanists because it infringes most of the rules about the drawing up of a will and therefore looks devoid of legal interest. But it is a will of a soldier – the piglet is about to perish under the butcher's knife – and a soldier's will was exempt from formalities.[3] Indeed, the piglet is evidently disposing of his *peculium castrense*: his father is still alive and actually among the beneficiaries.[4] St Jerome, around

[1] The legal recognition of *peculium castrense* in the *filiusfamilias*-soldier's lifetime was undoubtedly speeded up by this measure of Augustus concerning disposal *mortis causa*.

[2] Brilliantly edited by Haupt, *Opuscula*, vol.2, 1876, 175ff., now easily accessible in Buecheler, *Petronii Saturae*, 6th ed., Heraeus, 1922, 346f.

[3] G.2.114. A sketchy history in D.29.1.1 pr., Ulpian *XLV ad edictum*. Institution of several persons as heirs *certarumrerum* is admitted in D.29.1.17 pr., Gaius *XV ad edictum provinciale*.

[4] Examples in the Digest of fathers as beneficiaries in this case: D.29.1.17.3, Gaius *XI ad edictum pronvinciale*, 49.17.17.1, Papinian *II definitionum*, 49.17.20, Paul *singulari ad regulam Catonianam*. Juvenal, 16.51ff. counts it among the privileges of soldiers that 'they alone have the right to make a will in the father's lifetime, for it has been decided that what is obtained by military labour should not be included in the bulk of the property whose absolute control is with the father'. He goes on to introduce a decrepit father legacy-hunting, courting his successful soldier-son with a view to inheriting his valuable decorations. It is noteworthy that the piglet, though doing something in his will for father, mother and sister, makes no mention of a wife: in the first two centuries of the Principate soldiers could not marry.

AD 400, knew this will[1]; it was concocted, we learn from him, by Thracians[2] – Thracians were prominent in the Roman armies. The will, then, is prior to Jerome, considerably prior since it was a popular joke by his time. The *terminus post quem* is Augustus's concession of will-making in respect of the *peculium castrense*. The piglet is on active service, so the will might – though it need not – ante-date Hadrian, who extended the concession to veterans. On the other hand, the piglet seems to dispose not only of what he acquired while a soldier but also of objects given him for the purpose of service when he joined up: exactly from when such objects were recognized as part of the *peculium castrense* we cannot say.[3]

As there is no translation into a modern language, let me read it to you.

"M. Grunter Hyena the piglet has made this will. As I cannot write myself,[4] I have dictated it.[5] Butcher the cook said: 'Come here, destroyer of the house, digger up of the soil, runaway, piglet, and today I take your life.' Hyena the piglet said: 'If I have done anything, if I have sinned in any way, if I have broken some little vases with my feet, I petition you, master cook, I ask my life, grant it to the petitioner.' Butcher

---

[1] In the Preface to ch. 12 of his *Commentary on Isaiah* he observes that more people appreciate light stories than Plato; the *testamentum porcelli* is recited by crowds of laughing schoolboys; as for himself, he is content with the praise of the superior few. In *Against Rufinus*, 1.17 he is running down Rufinus's Latin style (cf. above, First Lecture, p. 33 n. 6); of course, he remarks, there are the simple multitudes who enjoy the unlearned and nonsensical, such as the *testamentum porcelli*. Editors of the *testamentum* and others (Friedlaender, *Sittengeschichte Roms*, 9th ed., Wissowa, vol.1, 1919, 177) have concluded that the will is the work of schoolboys. This does not follow at all. The imagery smacks of the barrack-room. I see no reason not to take Jerome's *Bessorum* seriously: see the next footnote. It matters little.

[2] *Bessi*, a leading Thracian tribe. See also below, p. 81 n. 1, on *Tergeste*, Triest.

[3] Fully recognized, for example, in D.49.17.11, Macer *II de re militari*; Macer wrote in the first half of the third century. See Jörs, ed. Kunkel, 291f.

[4] *Potui* as a present, I cannot, occurs again further on, *in cuius votum interesse non potui*; see below, p. 80 n. 1.

[5] Dictation of a military will, e.g. in D.29.1.40 pr., Paul *XI responsorum*.

Economic Realities : the Filiusfamilias 79

the cook said: 'Come here, boy, hand me the knife from the kitchen[1] in order that I may make a bloody end of this piglet.'[2] The piglet is seized by the assistants, led off on the fifteenth day before the first of the Herbal Month,[3] when herbage is plentiful, in the consulship of Roastingtin and Peppersauce. And as he saw that he was going to die, he asked for an hour's reprieve and petitioned the cook in order to be able to make a will. He called for his parents,[4] in order to apportion to them[5] something from his provisions. He declares: 'To my father Hoggy Lardy I give and bequeath to be given 30 pecks of acorn, and to my mother Reverend Sow I give and bequeath to be given 40 pecks of bearded wheat,[6] and to my sister

[1] On *cocina* instead of *coquina* see next footnote but one.

[2] I would not press details. Lest it be argued, however, that the piglet seems to be executed by his commander for his military crimes rather than killed in battle, and what about the right to make a will in such circumstances?, I draw attention to D.29.1.11 pr., Ulpian *XLV ad edictum*: 'Those soldiers who are sentenced to death for a military crime may make a will only in respect of *bona castrensia*.' The passage may have suffered interference, but I think the gist is classical.

[3] Haupt says there is no trace anywhere of *kalendae lucerninae*: it is just facetious. This is correct, but at least the approximate meaning of *lucerninae* can, I think, be established. I connect it with English lucerne in the sense of clover (or something like it), which is known from the seventeenth century, and French *luzerne*, known from the sixteenth, apparently most at home then in the Provence and Languedoc. The dictionaries have no etymology, but I consider it very likely that here, in the vulgar *testamentum porcelli*, the root is present. It should be noted that, as Haupt points out, *cocina* for kitchen (see footnote 1 on this page), also unique, is a precursor of Spanish *cocina*, Italian *cucina*, French *cuisine*, German *Küche*, English *kitchen*. The strongest support for my interpretation, of course, comes from the following clause, *ubi abundant cymae*, 'when herbs (or vegetables, cabbage) abound' (*ubi* in temporal application).

[4] Even in the case of a military will somehow the intent to make a will had to be demonstrated. It was not enough, for instance, to tell a beneficiary privately: 'You can have such-and-such a thing of mine.' The calling together of witnesses was an almost necessary step: *convocatis ad hoc hominibus*, D.29.1.24, Florentinus *X institutionum*, I.2.11.1, quoting a rescript of Trajan.

[5] *Dimittere* in the sense of 'to leave something' is met in G.1.195 and G. *Ep.* 2.7.8.

[6] Laconian wheat is bearded, hairy; cf. Pliny, *Hist. Nat.* 18.20.93, and (for *arista* used of human hair) Persius, 3.115.

80   Lecture 2. SOCIAL ASPECTS

Gruntress, whose wedding I shall be unable to attend,[1] I give
and bequeath to be given 30 pecks of barley. And of my organs
I shall give and donate to the cobblers my bristles, to the
brawlers my head-armament,[2] to the deaf my cars, to the
pleaders and prattlers my tongue [it is exactly the kind of will
our transplanting surgeons wish everyone of us to leave
behind] to the sausagemakers my entrails, to the stuffing-
experts my thighs, to the women my loins, to the boys my
bladder, to the girls my tail, to the sodomites my bum, to the
runners and hunters my heels, to the robbers my claws.[3] And
to the unmentionable cook,[4] I apportion as bequest the soup-
ladle and pestle which I brought with me[5] from Trevest right
to Triest; he may wear them on a cord tied round his neck,

[1] *Potui* again in the sense of I cannot: see above, p. 78 n. 4.

[2] *Capitina*; the translation is my guess.

[3] Haupt aptly quotes Plautus, *Pseudolus*, 852, where thievish cooks have *ungulae*. *Vom Schwein wurde alles verwendet*, says Orth, 'no part of a pig went unused'; Pauly-Wissowa, 2nd series, vol.2, 1923, 810, art. *Schwein*.

[4] *Nec nominando coco*. In D.28.2.3 pr., Ulpian *I ad Sabinum*, a father disinherits his son, calling him *non nominandus*. We also, however, find testators insulting beneficiaries. D.28.5.49.1, Marcian *IV institutionum*, *filius meus impiissimus male de me meritus heres esto*; D.32.37.2, Scaevola *XVIII digestorum*, *Maevio liberto meo de me nihil merito dari volo lagynos vini vetusti centum quinquaginta*. In D.28.5.9.8, Ulpian *V ad Sabinum*, *non tamen eo quod contumeliae causa solet addi* shows that Ulpian gave a ruling about these cases; but it was the opposite of that before us, and the reviser betrays himself by the most inelegant way the clause is squeezed into its present position. (D.30.54.pr., Pomponius *VIII ad Sabinum*, traditionally adduced as concurring with 28.5.9.8 – e.g. Biondi, *Successione Testamentaria e Donazioni*, 2nd ed., 1955, 210 – deals with an entirely different situation.) It is just conceivable that the piglet omits the proper name of the cook, *Magirus* (Butcher, see above, p. 78), in order not to do him too much honour. Even in an ordinary will the beneficiary's name is not essential, it is enough to designate him in unmistakable fashion: D.28.5.9.8.

[5] *Quae mecum attuleram*. Surely these were gifts of military objects made to him when he enlisted. If the pluperfect may be pressed, it is: which I had brought with me. Cf. D.49.17.4 pr., Tertullian *singulari de castrensi peculio*: *Miles praecipue habere debet quae tulit secum in castra concedente patre*. In the edition by Buecheler and Heraeus, incidentally, *attuleram* is followed by a colon; that is to say, *de Tebeste* and so on is connected with *liget* and so on, 'from Tebest to Triest he may wear them'. This is not impossible, but I prefer to take *de Tebeste usque ad Tergeste* with *attuleram* and start a fresh clause with *liget*.

Economic Realities: the Filiusfamilias

that's best.¹ And I want a monument inscribed with golden letters – M. Grunter Hyena the piglet lived 999½ years; had he lived another half year, he would have completed 1000 years. My very good friends and consuls of my life, I ask you that you deal well with my body, season it well with good condiments of nut, pepper and honey, in order that my name be honourably mentioned for all time. My masters and relations, you who are attending this making of my will, let it be signed'. Bacony signed. Morselly signed. Spicy signed. Sausagelump signed. Porkrind signed. Charles Lamb signed.² Weddingpig signed.³"

This *peculium castrense* meant nothing to the mass of *filiifamilias*. How was it possible, then, for the position to remain virtually unchanged till Constantine? An essential part of the answer is that, for the bulk of the population, these rules did not operate at all. In the urban areas at least, the vast majority of residents were have-nots, with not much to litigate about and certainly lacking the means to litigate with. In theory, if a beggar's son hired out his services, the wages paid him belonged to his father; so did the cigarette stubs he picked up from the gutter. The reality was totally different, he would never be

¹ Trying to reproduce the jingle in the Latin: *Tebeste – Tergeste – de reste*. An alternative: from Reeds to Leeds, he may wear them from his neck, as beads. The piglet has come from Tebessa in North Africa: Numidian auxiliaries were esteemed in the Roman army. He ended up at Triest, which city may conceivably have been chosen by someone who shared the notion that it was Thracian (see above, p. 78, regarding Jerome's description of the *testamentum* as of Thracian origin). Istria (where Triest lies) is represented as Thracian by both Apollodorus and Skymnos; see Oberhummer, art. *Thrake*, Pauly-Wissowa, 2nd series, vol. 11, 1936, 395. But I am almost tracing the piglet's peregrinations as if he were Gaius.

² *Celsinus*. Haupt refers to Apicius, *De Re coquinaria*, 8.7.12, giving the recipe for *porcellus Celsinianus*, sucking-pig à la Celsinus. I think Charles Lamb's essay on the origin of roast pig has earned him the honour of being Celsinus's English counterpart.

³ Maybe the pig to be used for the wedding-cake *mustaceus*, into which an enormous amount of lard was put; see Orth l.c., 809, and art. *Kuchen*, in Pauly-Wissowa, vol.11, 1922, 2092. A soldier's will would have been valid even if not signed by seven witnesses; but who would want to miss out any of these funny names?

bothered. Among the have-nots, whatever your status in the family, the little you acquired was yours from the age you had sufficient wits to acquire anything. In the slums, there was no distinction between a citizen and a Greek or Jew. Poverty is a great equalizer.[1]

The texts bear out what commonsense suggests. It suffices to recall the money distributions made by the Emperors. 'To each member of the plebs of Rome I paid out 300 sesterces under my father's will; in the twelfth year of my tribunate I gave to each 400 sesterces for the third time. These distributions never reached less than 250,000 people' – so Augustus informs us in the account of his reign.[2] The younger Pliny, in his eulogy of Trajan, praises the Emperor for making provision for those among the poor whom illness or absence might prevent from collecting on the appointed date, 'so that none of the Roman plebs, when you bestowed largesse, should feel himself a mere man rather than a citizen'.[3] They did not sort out *patresfamilias* and *filiifamilias*; and the thought that the former might lay hands on what was doled out to the latter simply did not enter their minds. That whole system did not apply to this class.

It follows that our question is to be re-formulated far more narrowly: how to account for the long-lasting propertylessness of a *filiusfamilias* in the small, well-to-do stratum of Roman society? The prospect a *filiusfamilias* had of some day not only being rid of his seniors but also lording it over others was a help – more so than it would be today, since expectation of life was shorter. By the time you were thirty, statistically there was a good chance that your forebears were all gone. But in many cases, of course, they were not,[4] and it must have been

[1] So is wealth, but more on the level of choice than that of necessity.

[2] *Mon. Anc.* 3.7ff., ch. 15.

[3] *Paneg.* 25: *ne quis e plebe Romana, dante congiarium te, hominem se magis sentiret fuisse quam civem*. Nowadays, in such a context, to feel oneself a man would be considered more desirable than to feel oneself a citizen; except, I suppose, in France.

[4] When the figures for expectation of life are not broken down, they include infants, among whom mortality was highest. But infants had no children. A *filiusfamilias* was interested in the mortality of those above the age of fifteen.

Economic Realities : the Filiusfamilias 83

precisely in the better-off circles that people tended to live longer than average. Again, Roman law admitted emancipation, the dismissal of a son from paternal power, so that he achieved the status of a *paterfamilias*. But this remedy was in the discretion of the father; it was, moreover, no unmixed blessing for the son; and it remained rather uncommon.[1] I shall come back to it.

Another mitigating factor was the custom – manifestly confined to the haves – of letting a *filiusfamilias* administer and live on a special fund, *peculium*. Too much, however, should not be made of this. For one thing, the *paterfamilias* might reduce or completely recall it at any moment. For another, even while it operated, the *filiusfamilias* was not normally entitled to use it for any liberality. He might buy, sell, hire and so on, but not (unless specially authorized by the *paterfamilias*) make a gift, manumit a slave, leave anything by will. Even with respect to the *peculium*, that is, he lacked true independence. It is significant that, as I mentioned a moment ago, when Augustus courted the sympathies of the troops, it was a liberality, the bequeathing of stipend and booty, which he allowed them. Conversely, Tiberius, from the moment of his adoption by Augustus, conducted himself like a good *filiusfamilias*, which meant that 'he neither made gifts nor performed manumissions'.[2] No doubt the *peculium* he had[3]

[1] D.37.12.5, Papinian *XI quaestionum*, tells us of a father who behaved outrageously to his son and was forced by Trajan to emancipate him. When the son died, the father claimed his possessions as *parens manumissor*. I am happy to add that he ran into difficulties.

[2] Suetonius, *Tiberius*, 15.2: *Nec quicquam postea pro patrefamilias egit . . . nam neque donavit neque manumisit*. The notice implies that, had he overstepped the rights of a holder of a *peculium*, he might have got away with it: his was, of course, an exceptional case. Suetonius goes on to record that even inheritances and legacies left to him Tiberius accepted only as additions to the *peculium* (cf. D.15.1.7.5, Ulpian *XXIX ad edictum*, quoting Labeo). Again, he might have got away with treating them as independent property. As is well known, it was only Justinian who finally made such gifts the property of the *filiusfamilias* (and even then with a usufruct for his *paterfamilias*): C.6.61.6, AD 529. It is interesting how early, in very special circumstances like those of Tiberius, the idea could be entertained.

[3] Mentioned by Suetonius, *ibid*; see the preceding footnote, on the matter of inheritances and legacies.

enabled him to transact any business necessary to his comfort. But liberality was open only to a *paterfamilias*, which he no longer was and in fact wanted to demonstrate that he no longer was.

Liberality – connected with *liber*, free – is the ultimate test of power, whatever the rules of a system. The parable of the two sons in Luke is set in a non-Roman world, where a son is not legally debarred from having property of his own in his father's lifetime. The elder brother, however, stays at home on the farm, as a member of his father's household, working with him, being fed and clothed by him. No reason to doubt that he participates in all business of the farm – yet when it comes to liberality he has no standing. 'Lo', he complains to his father, 'these many years I serve thee, and yet thou never gavest me a kid that I might make merry with my friends.'[1] Aristotle defines things owned as things I have power to alienate, and he adds specifically that by alienation he understands gift as well as sale.[2]

I think that this concentration of liberality in the Roman *paterfamilias* has enormous implications. Jolowicz in his section on *patria potestas* writes[3]: 'One limitation there was . . . *Patria potestas* has no concern with public law, and a son under power could vote and hold a magistracy just as freely as a *paterfamilias*.' In a formal sense this is correct, like the proverbial saying that anybody may stay in the Ritz. Realistically, however, the private law restrictions on a *filiusfamilias* could not but carry over into the public, political domain. It is not only that, up to a point, a *paterfamilias* might give his *filiusfamilias* direct orders to embark on or refrain from a course of action. We must consider the overall effects of the legal set-up. Say, a *filiusfamilias*, in the late Republic, wished to campaign for a magistracy. An ordinary *peculium* was not enough. He needed money, a great deal of it, to give away as largesse: which

---

[1] *Luke*, 15.29; see Daube, *Zeitschrift*, 72, 1955, 329ff.

[2] *Rhetoric*, 1.5.7.

[3] *Historical Introduction to Roman Law*, 2nd ed., 1952, 118. He quotes D.1.6.9, Pomponius *XVI ad Quintum Mucium*: Filius familias in publicis causis loco patris familias habetur, veluti ut magistratum gerat, ut tutor detur.

means, he needed the specific support of his *paterfamilias*. Admittedly there were unlawful ways of enrichment. Verres was a *filiusfamilias* with a *peculium*[1] and no doubt, at the start of his career at least, his father had conceded him the privilege to make gifts; but he soon managed to mobilize independent – and necessarily illicit – resources. But not everybody was as unscrupulous. In general, even in public life, a *filiusfamilias* remained rigidly controlled by his *paterfamilias*, who held the purse strings. It is difficult to conceive of a more powerful brake on any deviation from traditional family politics or, indeed, on any tendency to detract in a thorough-going way from the old-established scope of *patria potestas*. The means for such a platform would not be forthcoming. In a sense it was precisely in the public sphere that even a *filiusfamilias* with *peculium* was most fettered. Present-day demands for student power arise out of the increased economic independence of the youthful bourgeois; they would be impossible without it.

Here it may be worth while to remind ourselves that the – from the political point of view – most important fruits of liberality were withheld from foreigners; above all, the Roman *cursus honorum*, open to a *filiusfamilias* – if supported by his *paterfamilias*. In his own state, of course, a foreigner could attain office, and do so whether or not his father was alive. Another example of containment in regard to liberality: a foreigner, by releasing a slave, made him free but could not make him a Roman citizen.[2] A *filiusfamilias*, indeed, owned no slave; he was propertyless. It is highly doubtful whether, in classical law, he could manumit a slave in his *peculium* even with his *paterfamilias*'s authority.[3]

The principal explanation of the tenacity with which the Roman upper classes – for it is only a question of that minority – stuck to these incredible rules is that they saw them as expressing, and safeguarding, their innate superiority over the foreign rabble and probably, in course of time, also over the

---

[1] Cicero, *in Verrem*, 2.1.23.61, assigns importance to the *tabulae patris*
[2] Buckland, *The Roman Law of Slavery*, 1908, 534, 594.
[3] Buckland inclines to consider it possible: *op. cit.* 458f., 718ff.

rabble at home. There is no limit to the hardship people will bear for the sake of status, national or sectional. Here lies the clue, and if only we look, the sources contain a good many corroborative hints. Gaius, for example, repeatedly stresses that *patria potestas* is more exclusively Roman than other institutions which, under Roman law, apply to citizens only: it is found, he declares, among practically no other men.[1] Hadrian himself attached great weight to the exclusiveness of the institution.[2] In this feeling a *filiusfamilias*, however inconvenient his condition, was united with his Head. The rarity of emancipation, adverted to above, certainly has something to do with this. The better citizens were proud of this grotesque family structure.

The old English Public Schools, Eton, Charterhouse, Winchester, furnish a close analogy. Future historians will be hard put to it to understand how it was that, in the first half of the twentieth century, the boys attending these establishments would put up with strict hours, corporal punishment, fagging for seniors, no girls, no pictures, when all the time they could watch their contemporaries at the High School next door leading a jolly life. We have to do with the self-imposed discipline of an elite; rules, the original function of which is gone, but which are retained religiously for the sake of their present, almost more important function – to symbolize and strengthen the select and noble over against the common. If you think that I am over-emphasizing this aspect of the Public Schools, you are right. But there are amazing parallels. For instance, the Roman system of *patria potestas* evoked the admiration of certain foreigners, as do the Public Schools today. Dionysius of Halicarnassus, who was more Roman than most Romans, who sympathized with the senatorial party and who advocated statutory limitations on the manumission of slaves because he considered them an undesirable addition to the citizenry,[3] characterizes *patria potestas* as one of the points in which Rome is vastly superior

[1] G.1.55, 189; cf. 1.9.2, D.1.6.3, Gaius *I institutionum*.
[2] G.1.55, 93f.
[3] 4.24; cf. below, p. 94 n. 3, p. 120.

Economic Realities : the Filiusfamilias 87

to Greece; and he especially singles out the life-long power of the Head, his power over sons who are adults, married men, high magistrates.[1] The only major Public School founded in Britain in the past thirty years was founded by Kurt Hahn, a refugee from the Nazis on account of his race, who had previously directed a school on the English model in Germany.

There are other areas in Roman law which may be compared or contrasted. The laws imposing restraint on feminine luxury were often defended as protectors of native high-mindedness against alien vulgarity. On the other hand, it is clear that the Roman women, many of them, longed for that vulgarity. Livy represents a speaker against such a statute as pointing out that, while it might prevent jealousy between Roman women, they were all resentful at seeing their foreign rivals attractively decked out. A grievance of this nature, he adds, must weigh more heavily on women than it would on men who have offices, priesthoods and so on to make up for amenities foregone.[2] Once again, of course, we move in affluent company. The wives of the poor were affected neither by the enactment of a luxury-limiting measure nor by its abrogation, nor did their husbands hold offices and priesthoods. In the end, the women – the rich women – did get the restraints removed. The *filiifamilias* remained under the old-fashioned regime for many more centuries. But then, in the circles where it was of realistic significance, they as well as the *patresfamilias* might aspire to those honorific posts which rewarded hardship and which, remember, were closed to foreigners; and the old-fashioned rules, as I have explained, underlined the distinctiveness of the higher breed.

I would now, however, add a further point. From as early as

[1] 2.26.1ff.

[2] Livy, 34.7.5f. The speaker is the tribune Lucius Valerius, advocating the abolition of the Oppian statute in 195 B C. Cf. below, p. 125. By the way, Sage, in Loeb Classical Library, *Livy*, vol.9, 1953, 439, mistranslates 34.7.11. The *scilicet* introduces two rhetorical questions: 'If you repeal the Oppian law, will it not still be in your discretion to forbid (if you so wish) what now the law forbids? Will your daughters, wives, even sisters be less *in manu* (subject to your control)?' The thought in 13 connects up with this: 'They prefer their luxury to be in your discretion rather than in the statute's.'

the second century BC, the system of absolute propertylessness of a *filiusfamilias* developed the most unpleasant creaks. Sons wished their fathers dead, and more and more frequently the wish was father to the deed. No use shutting one's eyes to it. The references in literature must be taken seriously. In the comedies, naturally, the grimness of the situation is apt to be given a humorous coating. In Terence, a father is furious that his son, in his absence, allowed a court to sentence him to take to wife a poor pretty girl though he could have got out of it by providing her with a dowry and marrying her off to somebody else. The young man admittedly had not enough cash for the transaction but he could have raised it, the father exclaims, from the usurers. This argument, however, is countered by a slave who is in league with the son: 'Who would lend him while you are alive?'[1] The audience would laugh, but the nasty implication is obvious. Another play of Terence's contains a rather tragic monologue of a father in the course of which he says in so many words that his sons are just waiting for his death.[2] The laughter quite ceases when we turn to serious literature. Cicero's earliest speech in a criminal trial was in defence of a man accused of murdering his father.[3] Suetonius comments on how different early Emperors viewed the terrible penalty prescribed for parricide: one would approve, another would be put off. There were enough cases of the crime for a ruler to develop his own style of dealing with it.[4] Seneca praises a father who did not cut the allowance of a son who had plotted his death.[5]

A *filiusfamilias* resorted to manifold devices to improve his lot. Prior to a senatusconsult of the first century AD, one of them was to go to the usurers who would lend him money, repayable when *patria potestas* came to an end, i.e. when great-grandfather, grandfather, father had passed on. It was an ex-

[1] Terence, *Phormio*, 302f.
[2] *Adelphoi*, 874: *meam mortem expectant*.
[3] *pro Roscio Amerino*.
[4] *Augustus* 33, *Claudius* 34; cf. Seneca, *de Clementia*, 1.23.
[5] *de Clementia*, 1.15.2.

Economic Realities : the Filiusfamilias

tremely risky business for a usurer: if the *filiusfamilias* died before becoming *sui iuris*, the money was lost.[1] Obviously, a usurer would try to get as much security as he could, by methods necessarily questionable. He could hardly enquire into the provenance of an article of value which the *filiusfamilas* handed him as pledge. Indeed, he might not mind it if the *filiusfamilias* thought of means of hastening the departure of a long-lived father. A senatusconsult about the middle of the first century AD had the definite, avowed aim of protecting a *paterfamilias* from the peril to his life if his son got into the hands of moneylenders. It was called, the sources tell us, *senatusconsultum Macedonianum*, after a *filiusfamilias* Macedo who, in this situation, had killed his father; and it laid down that henceforth a person who lent money to a *filiusfamilias* could not sue for repayment even when the debtor became *sui iuris*.

In the eighteenth century the traditional account was declared apocryphal: the dastardly crime must have been perpetrated by the moneylender in the case, not the *filiusfamilias*. This theory, which so well chimes in with the romantic picture of ancient Rome, has become fairly fashionable; so much so that in the leading Latin dictionaries – Lewis and Short, Georges – Macedo is entered as the name of a Roman usurer. Another theory is that no murder took place at all. Most scholars, rejecting the account given in the sources, identify *filiusfamilias* with young man – a fallacy which, on the subconscious level, underlies a good deal of thinking about the *filiusfamilias*, 'child' in English, *Haussohn* in German. The senatusconsult, they believe, was designed to safeguard a young man from his improvidence: he should not waste his prospective wealth. But a *filiusfamilias* might be a mature statesman. As late as around AD 200 Ulpian writes that the regulation covers a *filiusfamilias* who is a consul.[2] Or take a citizen *sui iuris* who promises repayment of a loan to be made to him, then he is adopted by another citizen who thereby

---

[1] Cf. the remark quoted above, from Terence's *Phormio*: 'Who would lend him while you are alive?'

[2] D.14.6.1.3, *XXIX ad edictum*.

becomes his *paterfamilias*, and now he receives the loan. The senatusconsult, the jurists decide, does apply: the loan will never become actionable.[1] Conversely, if a *filiusfamilias* promises repayment of a loan to be made, then becomes *sui iuris* and now receives the loan, the senatusconsult does not apply, he can be sued.[2] It is not youthful extravagance which is the criterion, but solely the debtor's status as *filiusfamilias* and the resultant danger to him who stands between him and independence. It has been argued that a *filiusfamilias* heavily in debt would never commit parricide; on the contrary, as the usurers could proceed against him only when he was *sui iuris*, he would wish his *paterfamilias* many years of good health. But this is to look at the rules in a vacuum, totally disregarding what actually happens in these circumstances. I wonder whether the holders of this view have ever read the plays of Plautus. Once a *filiusfamilias* was involved with moneylenders, the latter, if he did not satisfy them, were in a position to blackmail him mercilessly. They could withhold further support of the grand life he was by now used to. Worse, they could threaten exposure of his loans, of the manner in which he had spent them, of the embezzlements and other offences he was guilty of in connection with them. At any rate, this is how the Romans saw it: from the speech of Cicero I just mentioned it may be gathered that heavy debts and a zest for high living ranked as standard motives for parricide in the trials.[3] I am afraid (as I have demonstrated in greater detail elsewhere[4]) the repulsive information transmitted concerning the occasion for the *senatusconsultum Macedonianum* is true.

[1] D.14.6.6, Scaevola *II quaestionum*.

[2] D.14.6.3.4, Ulpian *XXIX ad edictum*.

[3] *pro Roscio Amerino* 14.39: *Luxuries igitur hominem nimirum et aeris alieni magnitudo et indomitae animi cupiditates ad hoc scelus impulerunt*, 'Doubtless, then, it was riotous living, the enormity of his debts and unbridled passions which drove the accused to this crime?' Cicero finds it easy to deal with these hypothetical imputations since his client lived quietly in the country.

[4] *Zeitschrift*, 65, 1947, 261ff. On pp. 308ff. I argued that a date under Claudius is likelier than one under Vespasian. I should have mentioned two of the texts quoted above, Suetonius, *Claudius* 34, and Seneca, *de Clementia* 1.23, as lending support to my suggestion.

Economic Realities : the Filiusfamilias 91

There were indeed other awkward complications caused by the *filiusfamilias*'s disabilities. Say, a *filiusfamilias* studying at a place distant from home lends his allowance to a friend or has it stolen from him. Repayment or restitution is owing to his *paterfamilias*: the allowance remains the latter's property. So, in strictness, if the friend or the thief does not settle, the *filiusfamilias* has no action. Difficulties of this kind are discussed by several jurists.[1] The point to bear in mind always is that the parties involved belong to the comfortable fraction of the population; those on the right side of the case at least – not, necessarily, the thief.

[1] E.g. D.5.1.18.1, Ulpian *XXIII ad edictum*, 12.1.17, 44.7.13, Ulpian *I disputationum*. On how Cicero financed his son's studies at Athens, see Kroll, *Die Kulter der Ciceronischen Zeit*, vol.1, 1933, 118f. A father's dishonest management of an estate left to him with a *fideicommissum* in favour of his son could be ended only by the Emperor's intervention: D.36.1.52, Papinian *XI quaestionum*, see Daube, *Studi in memoria di Emilio Albertario*, 1950, 445ff.

II. ROMAN SOCIETY

A. Altruistic Dodges

I come to the second part of this Lecture, devoted to some hitherto neglected results of the compact nature of upper Roman society. It is well known that the mutual duties among the group went far beyond what would be expected nowadays. Recently, I did some work on evasions of law, dodges, at Rome and particularly on their social and economic setting.[1] One conclusion which emerged, and which I think is valid far beyond Roman law, was that dodges were the preserve of the well-to-do: the poor break the law, the rich get around it (or at least try to).

However, this is not what I want to enlarge on here. What I want to talk about is a specifically Roman phenomenon, anything but universal: an inordinately high proportion of dodges reported in the sources are operated from altruistic motives, in order to assist a friend or a relation in need, or even an inferior provided he is attached to you, a loyal slave, for instance, or a freedman.[2] For Cicero, when he inquires at length whether one may or ought to do wrong for the sake of a friend, this is more than academic speculation; it is an acute problem.[3]

---

[1] A summary is printed in *Proceedings of the Classical Association*, 61, 1964, 28ff.

[2] When I speak of altruistic motives, I am aware how vulnerable a notion this is. Psychoanalysts tell us that I may help you because I hate you; even orthodox psychology knows of the association of charity and self-satisfaction; and the instances of benevolence I am going to discuss are confined to those inside the group – my very point. Nevertheless I am undeterred, using the term altruistic in its naive signification, of that action which the ordinary person affected would describe as a good turn done to him.

[3] *de Officiis*, 3.10.43f., *de Amicitia*, 10.35ff. The problem has a long history before Cicero.

His answer is in the negative, but as the experts remind us,[1] as far as his own conduct is concerned, we often find him sailing near the wind. He would, for example, write to a judge before whom a friend is to be tried, saying that of course right must triumph, but the judge might wish to know that in Cicero's opinion the man is a splendid, upright citizen. I feel sure that Cicero knows what he is doing. He must not directly infringe the moral or legal code; but anything short of that, in the interest of a friend in trouble, is permissible or, indeed, obligatory. In a letter to his brother he expresses the view that the latter – who was then governor of Asia – had gone too far in interfering with the course of law on behalf of a friend. 'In some matters', he writes, 'there is no room for favours': 'in some matters', so in general there is room.[2]

1. *The Insolvent Debtor.* The Digest tells us of a strange dispute among Republican lawyers.[3] I owe you 50 pounds and pay you 5. You return the five-pound note to me, by way of gift, and I immediately hand it to you again; and so on, till I have given you the same note ten times. Question: Have I paid you 5 pounds or 50?

At first sight it looks like one of those legendary riddles: Achilles and the tortoise; or Epaminondas, the Lacedaemonian, says, all Lacedaemonians always lie – can this, then, be true? But there, the old jurists are serious about this five-pound note, and it is finally the great Servius whose decision is accepted: I have paid you 50. The explanation is that in ancient Rome infamy befell an insolvent debtor not only if it came to an auctioning off of his goods, but also if he got his creditors to be satisfied with less than the full amount, if

---

[1] Kroll, 60ff., Kelly, 56ff.

[2] *ad Quintum Fratrem*, 1.2.10: *Via iuris eiusmodi est quibusdam in rebus ut nihil sit loci gratiae.* The point is noticed by Kroll, 65. I shall not conceal the fact that Cicero's censure followed a visit paid him by the man hurt by the governor's action, and that this man was then praetor-designate.

[3] D.46.3.67, Marcellus *XIII digestorum*; see Daube l.c., 30, Watson, *The Law of Obligations in the Later Roman Republic*, 1965, 208ff.

cum eis pactus est se soldum solvere non posse.[1] In the case of the same note or coins being shoved to and fro, what happens in reality is that the creditor consents to an arrangement: he takes a portion of the debt and calls it quits. It is only in a formalistic sense, by way of fake, that he receives all. Why this jugglery? Because if the poor debtor is to be saved from infamy, the reality has to be covered up, and – here I come to my point – the creditor is prepared to help in this. From the fact that the question is taken up by a number of writers it looks as if this circumvention of the rigorous treatment of insolvency had been resorted to more than once; maybe in certain circumstances it became the thing to do. Legal opinion prior to Servius seems to have been prevalently against condoning it: the truth being that the debtor *pactus est se soldum solvere non posse*, he must suffer accordingly. From Servius on, the dodge is admitted and a creditor can avert infamy from the debtor who pays only part of what he owes.[2]

2. *Slaves and Freedmen*. Slaves and freedmen, too, 'belong', and a generous master or patron will go to great lengths to nullify obstacles the law puts in the way of rewarding them. When, in 2 BC, Augustus restricted the number of slaves a man could free in his last will,[3] with such certainty were attempts at evasion anticipated that the statute itself contained a clause invalidating transactions designed to get around it.[4] It did not stop people from trying; of course not, since one could always

---

[1] *Tab. Heracl.* 114f., Bruns, 108. That the provision, or the gist of it, figured in the *Edict* is shown by Lenel, *Edictum*, 79. He does not, however, refer to the text under notice. By the way, infamy on account of theft, assault or *dolus* befell a man not only if he was condemned in an action but also if he had compromised: Greenidge, *Infamia*, 1894, 25, 130f. The equation, as far as infamy is concerned, of a debtor's arrangement with a total seizure of his goods reveals a suggestive affinity of insolvency with those contemptible delicts.

[2] For a dodge to help a man who needs a surety, D.12.6.18 (Ulpian *XLVII ad Sabinum*), see below, pp. 122f n. 4.

[3] Legislation of this nature had been recommended by Dionysius of Halicarnassus some five years before: see above, p. 86, and below, pp. 119ff.

[4] G.1.46: *lex Fufia Caninia quae in fraudem eius facta sint rescindit*.

Roman Society : Slaves and Freedmen

contend that the transaction in question was no fraud on the law but within it.

For instance, an owner of four slaves, who was allowed only to release two, would bequeath the other two to an acquaintance, with a direction to free them. It seems that this stratagem was tolerated by the classics.[1] They did not tolerate another one. The statute provided that if a testator manumitted more than the permissible number, the gift would be valid for those named first, up to the limit. One master who wished to give freedom to more than he was entitled to wrote all their names in a circle, so that each could claim to be the first. Alas, the decision was that none would be free.[2]

Again, a freedman's patron was entitled to services, and furthermore he had a limited right of succession. It was permissible, however, for a freedman to buy off these burdens. There is evidence of a friendly dodge in this connection: the parties went through a fictitious redemption, that is to say, a

[1] D.35.1.37, Paul *singulari ad legem Fufiam Caniniam*. The legatee's role was not entirely shadowy: he did obtain the advantage of patronage. *E contrario*, I suppose that if a man appointed his son heir, directing him to manumit the supernumerary slaves, this would not have been approved since the son-heir would obtain nothing by manumitting them that he would not have obtained had the testator conferred freedom directly.

[2] G.1.46; see my article in *Law Quarterly Review*, 80, 1964, 225ff. The device was thought up by one who knew of the Delphic oracle which, to the question how the Seven Sages were to be ranked, had replied that their names should be arranged in a circle – each of them was first. The same legend inspired the idea of the Round Table by means of which King Arthur settled the quarrels about precedence among his knights: it is one more instance of the transplanting of a classical motif into medieval material. Significantly, the Round Table appears relatively late in the tales of King Arthur: it was in Ausonius's *Ludus Septem Sapientium*, popular in the France of the Middle Ages, that the romancers found the oracle. From King Arthur's Round Table derive not only all round table conferences and similar uses of this kind of seating but also the round robin of the fleet, the demands of mutineers signed in a circle in order to make it impossible to single out (and string up) the ringleaders. Occasionally nature might seem to write in a circle. D.1.5.15, Tryphoninus *X disputationum*, discusses the case of a slave-woman manumitted if and when she had borne three children. Evidently a fourth child would be born free. But there was a complication: this woman gave birth first to one child and then to triplets. Cf. 1.5.16, 34.5.10.1, Ulpian *VI disputationum*.

figure was named but the understanding was that the patron would never exact it. In this case, while the classical lawyers refused to cooperate, under Justinian's law it was no longer necessary to have recourse to a dodge since he allowed the gratuitous remission of the freedman's obligations.[1]

3. *Fideicommissa.* The whole institution of *fideicommissa*[2] came into existence as a device to leave your estate or some of it to a person the law said you could not leave it to. Under the law of the late Republic, you could not name as heir or legatee an alien, anyone who was proscribed, outlawed, or, if you belonged to the wealthiest class of the census, a woman. So a testator who wished his possessions to go to his Greek teacher would institute a Roman friend his heir, adjuring him to pass them on to the Greek. The nominal heir was under no legal compulsion to carry out the testator's desire; what force the latter had was founded entirely on religion and trust. Augustus legalized (and in the process, I shall argue, tamed) the procedure. Before that, however, it was manifestly a dodge of the type I am here concentrating on, for somebody else's benefit.[3]

Cicero reports the case of a rich citizen with a daughter.[4] He appointed a friend his heir and, in the will, mentioned that he had requested the heir to hand over the estate to his daughter. For Cicero, a father taking this course was asking what he was morally obliged in his daughter's interests to ask, *quod rogare debuisset*. The heir, however, not only denied that the request had ever in fact been put to him, but also expressed doubt as to whether, even had it been put, he could have complied. Why? It was contrary to the statutes (the *lex Voconia* in particular)

---

[1] D.18.1.36, Ulpian *XLIII ad edictum*, C.6.4.3, AD 529. See Daube, *Studi Arangio-Ruiz*, vol.1, 1952, 192ff., *Zeitschrift*, 76, 1959, 177ff.

[2] Buckland, *Text-Book*, 353ff.

[3] The machinery is interesting. Moral pressure is substituted for legal, and also use is made of an *interposita persona*: the heir stands in front. See Daube, *Proceedings of the Classical Association*, 61, 1964, 29.

[4] *de Fin.* 2.17.55.

Roman Society : Fideicommissa 97

which, as a magistrate, he had sworn to uphold[1]; and he retained a large part of the estate.[2] Cicero clearly does not believe in the honesty of the man's scruples. But whether honest or not, they do illustrate the tension I referred to above between your duty within your circle and the more general dictates of rectitude.

The same tension dominates an affair brought up by Cicero against Verres; in fact the moral issue was here rather more complicated.[3] One Publius Trebonius wanted to provide for a proscribed brother. The method he chose was, if not exactly *fideicommissum*, something quite similar.[4] He appointed a number of friends and a freedman joint heirs, directing that each of them should bind himself by an oath to see that at least half of what he got would reach the proscribed Aulus Trebonius. On Publius's death, the freedman did take the oath. The others went to Verres, then *praetor urbanus*, who did two things for them. First he let them off the oath, so they could keep their portions without sharing with Aulus. Of this part of Verres's handling of the case Cicero more or less approves: after all, a *lex Cornelia* expressly prohibited any aid to an outlaw. But, secondly, Verres punished the freedman by depriving him of his portion, thus making it accrue to the portions of the others. This, according to Cicero, was motivated solely by Verres's

---

[1] Cf. Cicero, *de Off*. 3.10.43: *neque contra rem publicam neque contra ius iurandum ac fidem amici causa vir bonus faciet*, 'neither contrary to the public good nor contrary to an oath and faith will a good man act for his friend's sake'.

[2] Not, it seems, all of it. He seems to have followed the advice of a number of persons he consulted, to the effect that he should let the woman have 'no more than would have gone to her under the *lex Voconia*'. I take this to mean one of two things: either that he should hand over only as much as would fall into a lower class of the census, or (see G.2.226) that he should hand over only half. Surely it does not mean – a possibility suggested by Rackham in the Loeb Classical Library (*Cicero, de Finibus*, 1921, 142) – that he hand over nothing.

[3] *in Verrem*, 2.1.47.123f.

[4] As *fideicommissum* was not yet at the time incorporated in the legal system, a higher degree of variability is only natural; and it is perhaps somewhat unhistorical to confine the term to such arrangements as were recognized by the jurisprudence from Augustus onwards.

contempt for the lower orders: he could not stand seeing a freedman come into a large fortune. There was no genuine good reason, Cicero holds, for this measure. The freedman could be blamed neither for obeying an instruction of his dead patron Publius Trebonius nor for standing by his present patron Aulus Trebonius, despite his proscription.[1] If, in fulfilment of this oath, he was going to infringe the *lex Cornelia*, by actually giving something to Aulus, there would then be the time for a charge under that statute.

I shall not probe Cicero's argumentation, having said enough, I think, to demonstrate the role of those pre-Augustan *fideicommissa* as altruistic dodges – altruistic, that is, within the group. But I will add a word about subsequent developments. Augustus's recognition of *fideicommissa* was designed not only to support these arrangements (though I am not doubting for one moment that the official motivation is part of the truth) but also to control and indeed restrain them; at least it did have this effect. It is well to note that he left the heir free to destroy a *fideicommissum* by refusing the inheritance and thus creating intestacy.[2] As far as *fideicommissa* of single objects are concerned, this is not perhaps remarkable: it merely put them on the same level as ordinary legacies, which were equally gone if the heir of the will declined. But it was, of course, precisely in the case of a *fideicommissum hereditatis*, where the fideicommissary is to receive the estate in toto, that an heir was most likely to abstain. It was not till AD 73 that a senatus-consult (*Pegasianum*) ensured the operation of such a *fideicommissum*. By that time, *fideicommissa* had been thoroughly domesticated, generosity undesirable from the government's point of view suppressed.

Let us look at women, aliens and persons out of step with

[1] It would seem that the freedman was originally released by the father of Publius and Aulus. When the father died, the two sons became joint patrons.

[2] True, if he himself was the person that would inherit on intestacy, he might get into difficulty with the praetor when claiming under the latter head; see Lenel, *Edictum*, 363f. What happened if he was a *suus* is controversial.

Roman Society : Fideicommissa

the family legislation of the Principate. Women, it is true, had their position bettered: they could obtain even a large fortune by way of *fideicommissum*. But this was part of a general change of attitude in the question. They were rapidly becoming capable of being made heirs without restriction. We have the testimony of Gellius that by the middle of the second century at the latest the *lex Voconia* was quite obsolete.[1]

As for aliens, I would distinguish four stages. Augustus shrewdly entrusted jurisdiction in this matter to the consuls. No citizen in his senses would provide for an alien unacceptable to them, and if he did it would be useless or worse.[2]

---

[1] In 20.1.23 he represents Africanus as listing it together with other archaic statutes which, sound in their day, were totally obliterated. When Gellius wrote this work, Africanus was already dead (Kunkel, *Herkunft und soziale Stellung der römischen Juristen*, 1952, 172). Gaius was still alive, yet in G.2.274 he speaks of the *lex Voconia* as in force: one of the numerous instances of mechanical copying from an older work – see Daube, *Natural Law Forum*, 12, 1967, 31f.

[2] As is well known, under Augustus there was a proposal to suppress the free expression of opinion about the Emperor in a will. I suppose the sanction would have been forfeiture of the estate. Anyhow Augustus set his face against the measure: Suetonius, *Augustus*, 56.1. This does not mean, however, that people did in practice feel free. Suetonius also tells us, 66.4, how anxious Augustus was to receive generous bequests from his friends, and they had to be flatteringly worded too (though he was not greedy – confirmed by Tacitus, *Annals*, 2.48). From Tacitus, *Annals*, 6.38, and Dio Cassius, 58.26, we learn that Fulcinius Trio abused Tiberius in his will; Trio's sons concealing the will, Tiberius, who had got to know of it, ordered it to be divulged to the senate. But Emperors did not as a rule act this way, else the incident would not have been carefully recorded. What was generally expected is shown by the fact that Trio's sons were frightened. Tacitus, *Annals*, 3.76, mentions Tiberius's civil reaction when a prominent wealthy lady made bequests to anybody who was somebody, omitting him. Under Nero, if you left him too little, you ran the risk of forfeiture to the fisc because of ingratitude: Suetonius, *Nero*, 32.2. If you perished in disgrace, institution of the Emperor as chief heir and eulogies might save something for your family: Tacitus, *Annals*, 14.31.11, 16.11.2, 16.19.5. Domitian, after a more promising beginning (Suetonius, *Domitian* 9) ended up by being not much better than Nero: Tacitus, *Agricola*, 43. Lucian, *Nigrinus*, 30, represents the philosopher as remarking that Romans while alive flatter their superiors and reveal the truth only in their wills when they need no longer dread the consequences. This seems to me a general criticism, with no special reference to the Emperor.

Though in special cases, say, that of an important foreigner who befriended Romans abroad, a *fideicommissum* would be upheld.[1] Then, second stage, came a period of more laxity – small *fideicommissa* were supervised by praetors – and for a while a *fideicommissum* in favour of an alien was generally actionable.[2] Third stage: actionability was removed.[3] Which, as one might expect, led to testators once again going outside the law and asking an heir, though the request was not enforceable even as a *fideicommissum*, to show his loyalty by voluntarily giving so-and-so much to such-and-such an alien friend. That this happened is apparent from the fourth and final move: Hadrian ordained that a *fideicommissum* for an alien was forfeited to the fisc – ruthlessly stamping out all evasion, all extra-legal benefaction.[4]

Fideicommissa for unmarried persons or persons married but childless went through a similar evolution, only, as the Emperors had here far more at stake, the end of the road was reached sooner. Augustus himself was the spiritual father of the legislation which, in order to promote marriage and improve the birthrate, placed enormous obstacles in the way of these recalcitrant groups getting inheritances or legacies. At

---

[1] G.2.285: *et fere haec fuit origo fideicommissorum*, I.2.25 pr., primarily about codicils, with stress on Romans finding themselves abroad.

[2] This stage is represented by the opening part of G.2.285: *ut ecce peregrini poterant fideicommissa capere.*

[3] G.2.285: *sed postea id prohibitum est.*

[4] G.2.285: *sed nunc . . . senatusconsultum factum est ut ea fideicommissa fisco vindicarentur.* Hadrian had wide sympathies. At the same time, as we saw above, he was jealous of the old Roman institution of *patria potestas*, and there are indications that he had his reservations about things foreign. For example, 'he diligently cultivated Roman religious observances, but despised foreign ones': Aelius Spartianus (*Scriptores Historiae Augustae*), *Hadrian*, 22.10. His eradication of *fideicommissa* for aliens belongs to this side of his thinking. I have received no assistance from historical works. Henderson (*The Life and Principate of Hadrian*, 1923, 206) cursorily refers to legislation about 'technical questions such as inheritance and bequest', but he finds it of no interest: 'Hadrian's rescripts concerning these must be left to the appreciative enthusiasm of the professional student'.

Roman Society : Fideicommissa

first sight it looks as if *fideicommissa* for them had been valid, enforceable. This, of course, would have made hay of his laws, which might just as well – or almost as well – not have been enacted at all. The problem is so perplexing that most authorities look the other way.[1] To solve it, we must again realize that, to begin with, no express ban on *fideicommissa* was needed. In Augustus's reign, a testator would hardly try to achieve by means of *fideicommissum* what he could not achieve otherwise; he knew that a *fideicommissum* fell in the competence of the consuls, who would react strongly against anything the Emperor disapproved. But here, too, there followed a laxer period when a *fideicommissum* was actionable, or more probably, the jurists argued that it might be.[2] This phase, however, did not last long. The senatusconsult of AD 73, which I have already mentioned, once for all put a stop to any attempt at circumvention: a *fideicommissum* for a person against whom these laws were directed was to be no more actionable than if he had been named heir or legatee,[3] and indeed, like an ordinary inheritance or legacy it would go either to other, worthy beneficiaries under the will or, if none existed, to the treasury.[4]

---

[1] de Zulueta is one of the very few to draw attention to it: *The Institutes of Gaius*, vol.2, 1953, 115. Kniep, *Gai Institutionum Commentarius Secundus*, 1913, 430, indeed draws the conclusion that the admission of *fideicommissa* for *caelibes* and *orbi* was the price Augustus had to pay for getting passed their exclusion from inheritance and legacy; so his victory, Kniep urges, was of a formal nature, these groups could in reality obtain most testamentary benefits. At least this theory is a genuine, courageous attempt to come to grips with the problem. But it is utterly incredible.

[2] G.2.286, 286a. Note that whereas in 2.285, concerning aliens, we are told that *poterant capere*, in both 2.286 and 286a, concerning *caelibes* and *orbi*, we are told that *videbantur capere posse*.

[3] G.2.286a: *capere posse prohibiti sunt*, with the same meaning as in 2.285 quoted above.

[4] G.2.286a: *eaque translata sunt ad eos . . . aut ad populum*. This clause corresponds to *sed nunc* etc. in 2.285; except that in the case dealt with in 2.285 there was an interval between the establishment of non-actionability of a *fideicommissum* and its penal re-direction, while in that dealt with in 2.286a the one senatusconsult declared a *fideicommissum* non-actionable and a *caducum*.

So here, already Vespasian closed the loophole which, with regard to aliens, was closed only by Hadrian. What is relevant for us is that such extreme measures were required to prevent testators favouring people contrary to the spirit of the laws.

4. *The Undowered Bride.* My last illustration will be dodges to make a dowry appear larger than it is or indeed to simulate the existence of a dowry where none has been given. I shall delineate the background somewhat more fully than is strictly necessary, first because the figure of the *indotata*, the undowered bride, is rather touching, and maybe I can induce somebody to write her history, in life and in literature; and secondly, because the case is instructive as to the very special complications which are apt to affect our legal evidence as distinguished from all the rest. One difference which strikes one right away is that whereas historians, playwrights, orators and so on from early times pay considerable attention to the *indotata*, prior to the Byzantine period she plays a negligible part in the writings of the lawyers.

The ideas voiced about her in general literature are strongly influenced by Greek models. The word itself is doubtless a translation of *aproikos*, maybe also of *anekdotos*. We find it in the comedies of Plautus and Terence, in comments on the advantages of an *indotata* and equally – regardless of the inconsistency – on the magnanimity of him who takes one. It should be realized, however, that the very concept *indotata* presupposes a well-to-do society where a dowry is the rule: you speak of a girl as *indotata* only because *au fond* her situation is not what one would expect. Among the proletariat the fact would not be worth noting.[1] The truly prevailing attitude

---

[1] Cf. above, p. 72 n. 2, on the formation of negatives: *confiteri, confessus, inconfessus. Dotare* is coined in an era when it signifies a striking act, and the *dotata* is an exception. Indeed, when we look at the Roman population as a whole, she never ceases being that. But, in the upper stratum where a giving of dowry becomes the thing to do, it is the omission which may receive notice – hence the appearance of the term *indotata*.

Roman Society: the Undowered Bride

peeps out even in the comedies in the – Greek – sanction that the ravisher of a girl must marry her without a dowry; so this is, after all, unpleasant. The daughters of Fabricius Luscinus and Cn. Scipio, as their fathers were too devoted to public service to provide for them, were dowered by the state.[1] Appius Claudius (who dedicated a book to Cicero) never forgot that his father left him in such straitened circumstances that he had to give away a sister without dowry.[2] Horace advises Scaeva not to beg from his benefactor too flagrantly, by saying 'my sister is *indotata*, my mother destitute'[3]; and Martial mocks a father embarrassed to scrape together a dowry for an overaged daughter.[4] Evidently, a dowry is highly desirable.

The word *indotata* is not met in good classical prose; presumably it is not yet quite incorporated in Latin.[5] In the rhetoricians, the Greek rule just mentioned, with some modification, grows into a favourite theme: the girl at her father's bidding may choose whether her ravisher is to suffer death or to marry her.[6] Not surprisingly, the alternative death – marriage is so stark and dramatic that in course of time the quality of the marriage as undowered recedes into the background: in the elder Seneca we still find the attribute *indotata*

---

[1] Val. Max. 4.4.10, Appuleius, *Apol.* 18.

[2] Varro, *R.R.* 3.16.2.

[3] *Ep.* 1.17.46.

[4] 7.10.14: *poscit iam dotem filia grandis*.

[5] Cicero once uses it in a tropical sense: the civilian Scaevola's art was *indotata et incompta*, 'undowered and unadorned', whereas Crassus enriched her with *dote verborum*, 'a verbal dowry' (*de Or.* 1.55.234). This looks a deliberately decorated, 'dowered' way of putting it.

[6] *Pace* Bonner, *Roman Declamation*, 1949, 89ff., this is Greek. C.9.13.1. 2, which he adduces in support of a Roman setting, is very late, from Justinian, AD 533, and directed against Hellenistic-Oriental practices. Jewish law, for instance, knows of circumstances where the man guilty of rape or seduction must marry the woman who, however, may refuse him: *Babylonian Ketuboth*, 39b, Philo, *Leg. Spec.* 3.71.

in the law, in Quintilian it has dropped out.¹

The classical jurists rarely, if ever, use the verb *dotare*²; and they never describe a woman as *indotata*.³ In fact, the adjective is confined to Justinianian statements. It does not occur in the *Codex Theodosianus*. Of the four constitutions in the *Codex Justinianus* which contain it, three are from Justinian and the fourth, though ascribed to Alexander, some three hundred years before, is falsified.⁴ Similarly, though it is found over a dozen times in the Digest, all the passages are spurious and probably all due to the compilers.⁵

---

¹ The cases under the law are amusing. 1. The father delays producing his daughter for the purpose of choosing, thus keeping the ravisher on tenterhooks. 2. The ravisher flees, the father gives his daughter to somebody else, the ravisher returns, and now the father claims that his daughter may still opt – it being virtually certain in the circumstances which way. 3. The girl chooses marriage but the ravisher denies the deed, he is convicted in a trial, and now the girl claims to have a free option again. 4. A twin is ravished and hangs herself. The father produces the other twin who demands that the ravisher be executed: as nobody notices the substitution this is done. The substitution is discovered and the father charged with causing the young man's death. 5. A man ravishes his absent brother's fiancée. At their father's intercession she chooses marriage. Later the ravisher-husband catches the returned brother in adultery and, though their father again intercedes, kills him. He is disowned by the father. 6. A rich man asks a poor girl's father for her hand and is refused. Father and daughter are shipwrecked and find themselves on the suitor's land. He again entreats the father, who silently weeps. He marries her. Returned, the father wishes his daughter to exercise the option – in which direction is obvious. 7. A married man ravishes a girl. She chooses marriage. He divorces his wife, who charges him with unjust, groundless divorce. 8. A young man in one night ravishes two girls. He is condemned to death by one, to marriage by the other. Here are the sociable aspects of Roman law for you, if you have done with the social ones.

² Beseler, *Zeitschrift*, 57, 1937, 35f., says never, and he may well be right.

³ Levy, *Der Hergang der römischen Ehescheidung*, 1925, 12.

⁴ C.5.17.1, Alexander, AD 229. It is a pity that the *Thesaurus* takes no note of this fact, which was already seen by Mitteis, *Römisches Privatrecht*, 1908, 70, and naively gives 229 as the date.

⁵ Take 21.2.24, Africanus *VI quaestionum*. This connects up with fragment 22.1, Pomponius *I ex Plautio*: a woman buys land and hands it over as dowry, a third party claims to be owner and is successful in his action, the woman may proceed on the ground of eviction at once (without

Roman Society: the Undowered Bride

Why no *indotata* in the classics, and why does she crop up in later dicta? Under the classical regime, technically, she raises no problem: there is no enforceable duty to provide a dowry,[1] and moral or humanitarian considerations are accorded little room in the discussions. Things change as time goes on. The concern not to have a decent girl undowered finds more expression, sentiment is allowed to intrude, and besides, the father's discretion is gradually curtailed: by Justinian, dowry has become a legal or at least semi-legal obligation (for the well-to-do, it goes without saying: in this matter, too, the traditional expositions of Roman law tend to generalize what in reality applied to a tiny fraction of the population). It is as a result of this development that quite a few old decisions are revised and the word appears. Some of these interpolations were spotted as early as by Faber in the seventeenth century.

---

waiting for the marriage to end) *quasi minorem dotem habere coepisset, vel etiam nullam si tantum maritus optulisset quanti fundus esset*, 'since she has a reduced dowry from this moment, or also none if the husband paid as much as the land was worth'. The portion from *vel etiam nullam,* 'or also none', is interpolated. Besides being (or trying to be) over-meticulous, it gets a great deal wrong. It assumes that the land is all the dowry there is, whereas that may or may not be so; and it distinguishes between the case where, as a result of the third party's action, the dowry is merely reduced because somehow or other the husband managed to pay less than the full value of the land and the case where the dowry is wiped out because he had to pay up. None of this, of course, is envisaged by the classical author: his argument was simply that the eviction had an immediate adverse effect on the dowry, justifying immediate regress by the woman-buyer of the land (an eminently practical decision). It should also be observed that the interpolation reckons with simple damages whereas the classic was no doubt thinking in terms of double the price. If we now go on to 21.2.24, we are told that if the husband himself proves to be the owner, then, as there has been no eviction by means of an action (but a sort of automatic self-eviction), the legal situation is different *quamvis aeque indotata mulier futura sit*, 'though the woman will equally be going to be without dowry'. Whether or not other bits of this fragment are spurious, the words quoted, it is clear (*aeque*, 'equally'), refer back to that interpolated clause in 22.1 which remarks on the possibility of elimination of the dowry. They must have been inserted when this section of the Digest title was put together – by the compilers.

[1] Except, it would seem, in special cases from Severus and Caracalla, about AD 200: D.23.2.19, Marcian *XVI institutionum*.

Ulpian, for example, puts this case[1]: I hand over an object to someone contemplating marriage, on the terms that ownership is to pass for the purpose of dowry if and when the event takes place. I die before it takes place. As at this moment my heir becomes owner and – this is important – as there is no binding contract to which he would succeed, the arrangement falls to the ground. So far the text makes sense. Now follows an appendix: 'But it is more benign to impose on the heir the necessity to consent in order that the woman should not be *indotata*.'

One fragment, though it does not contain the word, very much reflects the new trend. It is attributed to Paul and constitutes something of a proclamation in the Digest title on dowry: 'It is in the public interest that women should have their dowries safe, on account of which they can marry.'[2] No classic could have written that they can marry because of their dowries. In its original context the fragment had to do with privileged creditors, who, when an insolvent debtor's goods are auctioned, need not share with the rest but, as far as possible, are satisfied in full. Dowry was privileged (as was, for example, a ward's claim against his tutor): if a husband's goods were auctioned, his wife got her dowry entire, before other creditors took their dividends.[3] Already we have arrived at a far more circumscribed and sober range of the dictum.

We can, however, establish exactly what Paul wrote. He dealt with the case of a girl taken to wife before she had attained marriageable age. The man went bankrupt. Was she a privileged creditor? On the one hand, there was no legal marriage, hence no valid dowry; on the other, if the two stayed together, a legal marriage would ensue and the dowry would come into operation.[4] Paul held that she was privileged,

[1] D.23.3.9.1, *XXXI ad Sabinum*; see Buckland, *Text-Book*, 230, n.7. The *Thesaurus* is unaware of the position.

[2] D.23.3.2, Paul *LX ad edictum*: *Rei publicae interest mulieres dotes salvas habere, propter quas nubere possunt.*

[3] Lenel, *Palingenesia*, vol.1, 1078, *Edictum*, 429.

[4] D.12.4.8, Neratius *II membranarum*, is relevant. If a dowry was given where a couple were under marriageable age, Servius had allowed *condictio* at once. Neratius was prepared to leave the matter in suspense: *condictio* would lie only if and when they separated before reaching

Roman Society: the Undowered Bride 107

and it was in arguing this decision that he said: 'For it is in the public interest that this girl, too, should obtain her full claim, in order that on reaching marriageable age she can be married to the man.' We actually have this explanation preserved in another part of the Digest.[1] The compilers, by a method they employed in many other cases,[2] generalized the statement[3] and accorded it a prominent place in a basic title, where it now says something quite different, in accordance with the new philosophy.[4]

The *indotata*, then, is absent from the classical evidence. Yet

---

marriageable age, but for the moment there was no *condictio* since, if they stayed together, the relationship would become marriage, with the dowry valid, and the interval was no more intolerable than where a dowry was given by a fiancée prior to her wedding.

[1] 42.5.18, Paul *LX ad edictum*: *Interest enim rei publicae et hanc solidum consequi, ut aetate permittente nubere possit.*

[2] Daube, *Zeitschrift*, 76, 1959, 176ff.

[3] They cut out *enim* and the reference to age, they replaced *solidus* by *salvus*, and they turned the singular *haec* into the plural *mulieres*.

[4] As usual, the revision has been somewhat clumsy, not thorough enough. Strictly D.23.3.2 advocates the safe restitution of a dowry with a view to re-marriage. It is true that the unambiguously final *ut possit* of 42.5.18 is replaced by the vaguer *propter quas possunt*. But at first sight the text still appears to contemplate what restitution of the dowry will enable a woman to do in the future. That is of course not what the compilers mean: they mean generally that dowries make possible marriages, first marriages. In the original version, there was indeed restitution with a view to a future marriage, namely, that which would come about once the girl reached the requisite age. – D.24.3.1, Pomponius *XV ad Sabinum*, opening the Digest title on restitution of dowry, has undergone a similar fate. 'The cause of dowries always and everywhere takes precedence; for it is also in the public interest that dowries should be preserved for the women since it is extremely necessary that females should be dowered for the procreation of offspring and the populating of the state with children', *Dotium causa semper et ubique praecipua est; nam et publice interest dotes mulieribus conservari, cum dotatas esse feminas ad subolem procreandam replendamque liberis civitatem maxime sit necessarium.* The generalization is betrayed right away by 'always and everywhere'. These words and the portion from 'for it is also in the public interest' are spurious. (Beseler, *Zeitschrift*, 57, 1937, 36, rejects the entire fragment, which seems too radical.) Exactly what case Pomponius discussed, it is impossible to say. It could have been that surviving in D.23.3.24, from the same book (it follows 24.3.1 in Lenel, *Palingenesia*, vol.2, 120); but one could think of any number of others – like 42.5.18, quoted above, or 24.3.66.2, Javolenus *VI ex posterioribus Labeonis*.

this is just the consequence of the technical preoccupation of the jurists. Socially and economically she played her role in that period no less than later, and, at times, even in reading the legal discussions we can sense her standing in the background. In this connection the stratagems adverted to in introducing this topic are significant: a woman with no dowry will be represented as bringing one, or a woman with a small dowry as bringing a large one. Already the Republican jurists examined such legacies by husbands as 'On account of the money given me by way of dowry, let my heir pay out fifty' when, in reality, less or nothing had been given as dowry; and they held that the figure named was payable – a doctrine carried on by the classics, confirmed by Severus and Caracalla and adopted by Justinian.[1] Modern authorities mostly take it for granted that the testators must have slipped up.[2] It is far more likely, however, that at least some were conscious of the discrepancy; and that they acted as they did because they cared not only for the woman's financial prosperity but also for her and her family's reputation. If so, that would have greatly facilitated the decision to recognize these bequests.[3]

[1] D.33.4.6, Labeo *II posteriorum a Javoleno epitomatorum*, quoting Servius, Cascellius, Alfenus Varus and Ofilius; 33.4.1.8, Ulpian *XIX ad Sabinum*; I.2.20.15.

[2] E.g. Riccobono, *Zeitschrift*, 43, 1922, 280, Beseler, *Zeitschrift*, 53, 1933, 17. By contrast, Voci, *Diritto Ereditario Romano*, vol.2, 2nd ed., 1963, 326, does not confine the doctrine to error. Riccobono adduces stipulations taking place after divorce, but these are not necessarily perfect parallels. E.g. D.45.1.21, Pomponius *XV ad Sabinum*, considers a promise, made after divorce, to return so-and-so much that was given as dowry when, in reality, nothing or less had been given. Admittedly the promiser seems to be in error. But, then, the setting of a promise *divortio facto* is utterly different from that of a legacy left *constante matrimonio*. In the former, we shall hardly look for a dodge resorted to by the ex-husband in order to procure his ex-wife a special advantage material or in respect of reputation. In the case of a legacy during marriage, such devices make sense. Actually, I wonder whether, if a legacy of the kind under review could be definitely proved to be the result of error, it would not be ineffective.

[3] It would have facilitated it whatever its technical basis. The latter, incidentally, varies in different periods and with different jurists. It was certainly not just *falsa demonstratio non nocet*.

Roman Society: the Undowered Bride

In an allied case, from Celsus,[1] we are expressly told that the testator knew. Here a dowry had been given but the husband had returned it to his wife during marriage. In full awareness he left her a legacy of forty by way of repayment of dowry. The legacy was upheld. In general, in Celsus's time, the return of a dowry during marriage was an invalid gift of *vir* to *uxor*. It was valid, however, in exceptional situations, say, the wife had pressing debts.[2] We may assume that in the present case such a situation had occurred, but the husband gallantly covered it up by his misleading phrasing of the legacy. That some greedy heir, unwilling to pay it out, exposed the scheme was not his fault.

We can unearth a dodge which the jurists did not allow. The Digest contains an extract from Julian,[3] in its present form quite incongruous. The main part is a long rigmarole, that if I make you a gift of money on the understanding that you should lend it to me, it is neither gift to you nor loan to me. Then comes an appendix reminiscent of one cited above: 'It is more benign that it should be gift and loan.' Indeed, why ever not? Why ever should I not be able to make you a gift of money even though for the moment I need the cash and take it back as a loan from you? In another part of the Digest a decision admitting such an arrangement is actually preserved,[4] and it is obvious from the details that the decision was needed not because of any difficulty of principle but because of a complication of the particular case, having to do with the *lex*

---

[1] D.31.21, *XX digestorum*. I agree with Levy, *Zeitschrift*, 46, 1926, 419 (against others, e.g. Schulz, *Einführung in das Studium der Digesten*, 1916, 49), that while *hoc tamen praetextu usus esset* is spurious, the clause *quasi dotis reddendae nomine eam summam legaret* is an essential element in the presentation of the case. As for *hoc tamen . . .*, the testator needs no pretext in order to make a bequest. As for *quasi dotis reddendae . . .*, this is the point: he leaves the money as if it were owing as dowry.

[2] D.23.3.85, Scaevola *VIII digestorum*, 24.3.20, Paul *VII ad Sabinum*; see Wolff, *Zeitschrift*, 53, 1933, 324ff., without reference, however (unless I have overlooked it) to 31.21.

[3] D.12.1.20, *XVIII digestorum*.

[4] D.39.5.33.1, Hermogenian *VI iuris epitomarum*.

Cincia.[1]

The puzzle is solved if we take note first of the provenance of the fragment – it goes back to Julian's discussion of restoration of dowry[2] – and secondly of a rescript by Severus and Caracalla dealing with a related case.[3] It emerges that Julian was concerned with a prospective husband giving his fiancée

---

[1] That statute rendered a gift above a certain amount unenforceable; that is to say, once the gift was fully carried out it could not be attacked, but so long as the donee had to go to court for it, the donor had an *exceptio*. (The statute was directed against bribery. The idea – a not unreasonable one – was that the moment the man from whom you wanted favours had definitely cashed in, he was free again and in a position to act for or against you as he thought fit. In connection with the purchase of votes we know that candidates often deposited the monies with a *sequester*, who was to pay voters if and only if they had done what was expected of them: this method gave security to both parties, the candidates and the voters; see Mommsen, *Römisches Strafrecht*, 1899, 869.) In the case in question a money gift exceeding the statutory limit was made, on the terms that it should be lent to the donor. This produced a neat problem: when the loan was reclaimed, could the borrower-donor say that he was being sued contrary to the *lex Cincia*, i.e. that plaintiff was going to law for the gift? Or if the borrower-donor had promised repayment of the loan (a frequent type of promise), could he avail himself of the *exceptio in factum* (Lenel, *Edictum*, 513) '*si non donationis causa promisi me daturum*', i.e. could he maintain that he had made the promise with a view to gift? The verdict, however, went against him: his original transfer of the sum to the donee had fully completed the gift, and when he received the money back by way of loan that was a new, different affair no longer falling under the statute. Some critics have taken exception to the fragment, the diction of which is below classical standards. But Schulz is right (*Roman Legal Science*, 1946, 223): Hermogenian is so late as to be practically post-classical, hence there is no point in purifying the text, he just did not write like a classic. As for the substance of the ruling, I see no reason to assume that it differs from the classical position. Even if it did differ, my argument would remain valid: the transaction would have been rejected only for the sake of a scrupulous (over-scrupulous) adherence to the *lex Cincia*, not because of anything inherently wrong with transfer of money as gift followed by re-transfer as loan.

[2] *Soluto matrimonio*; see Lenel, *Palingenesia*, vol.1, 369.

[3] C.5.3.1, about AD 200, quoted by Lenel *loc. cit.* The Emperors reject a Greek mode of creating a dowry, namely, by means of a fictitious acknowledgment of receipt of a dowry on the part of the husband (without even the formality of transfer and re-transfer). Much literature on *donatio in dotem redacta* and allied topics; see, e.g. Mitteis, *Reichsrecht und Volksrecht*, 1891, 270ff., 297f., 476ff., Meyer, *Klio*, 6, 1906, 437f., Rabel, *Zeitschrift*, 28, 1907, 329f., Jones, *Law and Legal Theory of the Greeks*,

money on the understanding that he would receive it back as dowry: evidently in order that she should not be without a dowry or with too small a one.¹ This transaction was not recognized, neither his transfer to her nor hers to him; which meant that on termination of the marriage, she could not claim this sum as her dowry. The text doubtless suffered some interference before it reached the compilers. But it is most probably they who resolved to generalize it, lift it from its specific application to dowry, suppress all mention of this institution and thus fit it for inclusion in *De rebus creditis*, their basic title about loan, where it would figure as a rule about that contract.² To suit the new scope, however, the original decision had to be turned into its very opposite, rejection of the transfer and re-transfer had to become recognition – hence the 'benign' ending (in conformity with the decision concerning the *lex Cincia*) by which gift and loan are both validated.

Here, then, we come upon a case from the classical epoch where the husband himself attempted, unsuccessfully, to dower his bride: an altruistic machination, whether his primary object was to secure her materially or to save her from disgrace or to do both. There could hardly be a better illustration of the extraordinary intricacies presented by our legal sources. Let me remind you that while the classics display incomparably

---

1956, 176. Betti's discussion of 12.1.20, incidentally, in *Bullettino*, 42, 1934, 322ff., by disregarding the palingenesia of the fragment, completely misses the point (as does Kaser in following him, in *Das Römische Privatrecht*, vol.2, 1959, 57). As a result, he also misconstrues the relation between this decision and C.5.3.1. He overlooks, too, the special reference of D.39.5.33.1 to the *lex Cincia*.

¹ Very likely, once again the purpose was not purely practical, to provide for her – or it could have been attained by an appropriate stipulation – it was also to make her look a better match.

² It is noteworthy that even now the text does not use the unambiguous technical term for 'to make a loan', *mutuo dare*, but throughout operates with the wider notion *pecuniam credere* or *in creditum dare* which one could imagine to have figured in Julian's dowry case. That the compilers were adepts at generalizing classical utterances and diverting them to different topics I have repeatedly observed: see above, p. 20 n. 1, pp. 106f., p. 110 n. 1, and below, pp. 122f. n. 4.

less interest in the *indotata* than does Justinian, in the text before us it is the latter who has eliminated the dodge in favour of a poor girl. That problem is no longer directly exhibited in this passage, and it is only by a critical analysis that we can establish its occurrence in the older, classical work on which Justinian draws.

Many hundreds of years later, in the *Chartreuse de Parme*,[1] the Marquis Crescenzi is about to marry Clelia Conti. Her father, Fabio Conti, is shocked to hear her called *une fille sans dot*. He purchases an enormous estate, with the Marquis's money, to serve as dowry. Stendahl tells us that the Marquis, however, an *être eminemment logique*, regrets the expense of the transaction.

I cannot resist the temptation, before leaving the subject of marriage, to introduce an episode from early Roman history, the dispute about the maid of Ardea,[2] which enshrines a motif recurrent in countless variations in many literatures: the girl between two suitors, one of her own humble class, the other higher up. As far as I can see, the motif has not so far been isolated; it does not figure in Stith Thompson.[3] Yet we meet it constantly, in folksong and elaborate poetry, in fiction and plays; not to mention reality. Think of little Em'ly in *David Copperfield*, courted by Ham, her cousin, and Steerforth; of the film *Le jour se lève*[4]; of the feeling of the immigrant group in *West Side Story* that their young women should take 'one of their own kind'. The girl may be enticed by the glitter or be loyal to her pal; or the latter may represent an inferior life unworthy of her, while the prince is to raise her to the status she deserves. One of the two may take her against her will. Again, she may find her choice opposed by her family, or indeed some of them may urge her one way and some the other. Often it is the mother who favours the ambitious match. Not always, however: in the memorable quarrel between Sancho Panza and his wife concerning their daughter's future, it is the wife who

[1] Ch. 23.   [2] Livy 4.9.
[3] *Motif-Index of Folk-Literature*, rev. ed., 6 vols., 1955-8.
[4] I believe the superb, original version can no longer be seen.

Roman Society: the Undowered Bride

represents sturdy, vulgar commonsense while he insists that only a grandee will be good enough. Of course, they need not have become so excited since no grandee has as yet asked for Mary Sancha's hand.[1] There are all sorts of combinations. The two rivals may be one, or virtually one: the lowly one, for example, may test the lady by disguising himself as a person of consequence, or by commissioning such a person to propose to her. *Così fan tutte* comes to mind.

About the middle of the fifth century BC there lived at Ardea, a Latin community not far from Rome, a fatherless girl of the plebeian order, whose beauty was the cause of a public disaster. She was wooed by a plebeian and an aristocrat. Her mother, wishing her a splendid alliance, directed her to accept the nobleman. Her guardians, on the other hand, were biased in favour of their fellow-plebeian and bade her marry him. She herself was not asked, it seems, and we do not know what her preference was. The controversy was submitted to the magistrates, who decided for the mother. Thereupon the plebeians abducted the girl by force. The nobles counterattacked. The plebeians, driven out of the city, besieged the latter and sacked the farms belonging to their enemies. These now invoked the aid of Rome, with which Ardea had a treaty. As the plebeians turned for help to the Volsci, a veritable war ensued. (It sounds very modern.) In the end, the Romans defeated the Volsci and subdued the plebeians.

It has recently been claimed[2] that the anecdote was invented (or, insofar as historical, preserved) in order to inculcate the gist of the *lex Canuleia*, the Roman statute of around 445 BC which rendered plebeians eligible to marry patricians. But whatever lesson may be aimed at, it cannot be this. Quite apart from the fact that the events are laid at Ardea, not at Rome[3] – if they

[1] *Don Quixote*, pt. 2, bk. 3, ch. 5.
[2] Ogilvie, *Latomus*, 21, 1962, 477ff. The main conclusions of this interesting article are summarized by the author in *Livy, Books 1–5*, 1966, 547f.
[3] Volterra in *Studi in onore di Antonio Segni*, 1966, 3ff., gives strong reasons for rejecting Ogilvie's assumption that Ardean marriage law is here thought of as identical with Roman.

were intended to exemplify this pro-plebeian reform, the girl would have to be a patrician and her tutors against her stooping to a union with a plebeian; or alternatively, she could be a plebeian, but in that case the resistance to the union ought to come from her patrician suitor's people; or yet again, she could be a plebeian on whom a haughty member of the upper order had illicit designs – one remembers Virginia (or even Lucretia) – so her guardians would object to misuse and demand honourable wedlock. Any of these versions would do, but not that before us. If you want a story to celebrate academic integration, you will not put the case of a negro's advisers forbidding him to register as a student at a wide-open, welcoming university; your case must be that of the university authorities forbidding the secretary to enrol him. It is most unlikely that the anecdote purposes to convey anything at all concerning the *lex Canuleia*. But if it does, it refers to a kind of Black Power movement, an ultra-radical section among the plebeians who deplored the statute and advocated abolition of the *conubium* between the orders introduced by it. I cannot believe this.[1]

Really, the existence of *conubium* between the plebeians and aristocrats of Ardea is taken for granted by the narrative; there is not the faintest indication of a problem in this respect. The narrative is in fact antiplebeian, or at least against the plebeians of Ardea, declared to be inferior to the Roman ones who, when they seceded from their city, deliberately refrained from

[1] Besides the innovation of the *lex Canuleia*, there are two more provisions, according to Ogilvie, which the anecdote is designed to bring out: namely, that marriage might be without *manus*, and that marriage without *manus* might be entered into by a woman *sui iuris* against the will of her guardians. However, again quite apart from the precarious identification of Ardean law with Roman, first, it is incredible that either of these provisions of the internal law would be illustrated by means of an incident leading to a war. Secondly, the possibility of marriage without *manus* surely did not need to be illustrated at all. Thirdly, it is extremely doubtful whether, in the fifth century BC, a woman *sui iuris* could generally marry without *manus* against the will of her guardians; if she could, this narrative which pitches the mother (and a court), not the girl herself, against the guardians would fail to illustrate the point. Fourthly and most conclusively, there is in the anecdote not the vestige of an allusion to the distinction between marriage with *manus* and marriage without *manus*.

Roman Society : the Undowered Bride 115

ravaging the farms.¹ The noble suitor of the maid is praised for being attracted by her beauty alone, without looking for the usual advantages of a match. Whereas the mother has the girl's welfare at heart and is happy about her chance, the plebeian guardians are depicted as motivated by sheer party interest. We must not forget that Livy is professedly recounting the episode as a warning of what a terrible thing the jealousy between factions can be. It is the plebeians who, instead of abiding by the verdict of the court, resort to violence. (That the magistrates themselves, who are presumably most if not all of them aristocrats, may not be quite free from prejudice is not noted by Livy, though the plebeians would no doubt be alive to it.) It is the plebeians who call in an outside power (the Romans, appealed to by the nobles, are at least allies of some sort); and it is they with whose discomfiture the affair terminates.

I shall attempt no deductions from the narrative as to the law of Ardea respecting the conclusion of marriage, and especially as to whose consent was required. *A fortiori* I shall not inquire whether the result would illumine ancient Roman law – it might do so either if the two systems were in fact close, or if, though they were not, the tale assimilates the Ardean to the Roman. The episode, however special and arresting, furnishes a nuance of the popular theme of the two suitors. This does not mean that it cannot have happened or at least contain a nucleus of historicity. A motif may be ubiquitous precisely because it is true to life. As far as the dissension within the girl's circle is concerned at any rate, we find a very similar one assigned for decision to a provincial governor at the end of the second century AD.²

¹ Livy, 4.9, *nihil Romanae plebi similis*. For the restrained conduct of the Roman *plebs* during the first and second secessions, cf. Livy, 2.32.4, 3.52.3.

² C.5.4.1, Severus et Antoninus, AD 199: 'When it is a question of the marriage of a girl and there is no agreement between her guardian and her mother and her relations as to the choice of her future husband, the verdict of the governor of the province is needed.' The affinity of this situation and its handling with Livy's story has long been seen. Ogilvie (*Latomus*,

481f.) tries to brush it aside: 'the dispute here (C.5.4.1) was not concerned with the giving of consent to a marriage but with the choice of a husband where the girl did not have or had not voiced any preference'. As for the girl's attitude, however, neither are we told in C.5.4.1 that the ruling contemplates a girl who is indifferent; nor, in Livy, that the maid of Ardea did reveal her feelings. And as for the former half of his statement, I do not see what else than consent to the marriage might be in issue. Ogilvie urges that if C.5.4.1 were thinking of the guardians' consent, 'by the same argument it could be maintained that the consent of the mother and the relations was required – which is palpably untrue'. But it is not palpably untrue by any means: see Buckland, *Text-Book*, 113f. From just about that period (probably in connection with tendencies to impose a duty to provide a girl with a dowry – see above, pp. 105f.) such controls came to be recognized here and there; cf. C.5.4.20, Honorius et Theodosius, AD 408–9. Ogilvie wants C.5.4.1 out of the way for two reasons. First, it should not be mixed up with the serious constitutional trial at Ardea, where he thinks *conubium* was at stake. Secondly, he is contending, it may be recalled, that at Ardea – standing for Rome – a girl *sui iuris* needed no consents for marriage without *manus*, yet unless C.5.4.1 is somehow explained away, it does require consents. As a matter of fact, though his thesis is untenable, he need not have been inconvenienced by this text: there might have been ever so many changes in the rules in the course of six-and-a-half centuries. It would indeed be surprising if the system presupposed in C.5.4.1 fully or even to a high degree coincided with that presupposed in the ancient anecdote.

B. The Protection of the Non-Tipper

The rest of this Lecture I shall dedicate to legislation and jurisdiction for the protection of the non-tipper. In the typical case, the law in appearance restrains a man from harming himself by an excess of generosity, while in reality it is designed to come to the aid of him who has no wish to be overgenerous.

We might start from a situation familiar to all of us. Many clubs have a rule against tipping. (I mean here tipping at discretion, not regulated things like 15 per cent on the bill or the Christmas box.) Admittedly concern for the dignity of the personnel may be one of the reasons, but another is that the system is easy on the member who is unwilling to tip (whether from lack of funds or from meanness) and would otherwise feel pushed. (Don't try to dispute this, for I have sat on committees charged with this matter and moved by just this consideration.) Again, when a Fellow of my College marries, the Bursar sends round a note asking for money to buy a corporate wedding present and he adds that contributions are not to exceed so-and-so much, say, two guineas. At Rome, in the late Republic and Principate, with the then prevailing strict notions of *officium*, of what was owing to one's friends and retainers, the problem of pressure was far more serious, so serious that it could not be left to convention. There is in fact a whole, so far unisolated, corner of jurisdiction and legislation dealing with it. It is this branch 'for the protection of the non-tipper', which I am going to characterize by a few examples.

I have already mentioned that a freedman could buy off the rights his former master retained over him and his estate, but that when a liberal patron went through a *proforma* sale, undertaking not to claim the price, the lawyers would not have it. There is more evidence of resistance against gratuitous renunciation of a patron's rights,[1] which was indeed not admitted till Justinian.[2] Why? It is not enough to reply that the *Edict* spoke of a buying off. That could have been interpreted less rigorously, or even changed. Surely, among the considerations in favour of an unbending attitude was this, that if gratuitous waiver was allowed, even a patron not so inclined might feel constrained to proceed that way. Decency is dangerous, a sort of plague. If one patron is kindly to his freedman, others will be, but what is worst, in the end the disease will belong to the *bon ton*, you cannot exclude yourself. So it is up to the law to prevent the infection.[3]

Gratuitous waiver – the very word 'gratuitous' may teach us something. In English, as in French, 'gratuitous' means either 'free of charge', 'liberal', or 'groundless' in a bad sense: *acte gratuit*. Both meanings already exist in Latin. The pleasant one occurs as early as in Plautus, the unpleasant one is first met in the younger Seneca[4]: 'Hatred is the result of a hurt, *ex offensa*, or groundless, *gratuitum*'. One factor in the rise of the latter may well be the fact that more and more frequently what purported to be given free, as a liberality, was in truth enforced by the social code. The element of active good-will was absent; what remained was the feeling of giving something for nothing. People still described such acts as done by way of grace and gratitude, 'gratuitous',[5] but what they meant was that they were done *sine causa*. From here to the bad sense is no far cry. Gratuitousness and duty are associated in numerous texts. Cicero writes that generosity, *liberalitas*, is not mercenary; it is *gratuita*, exercised for the

[1] D.38.2.47.2, Paul *XI responsorum*.
[2] C.6.4.3, AD 529.
[3] Regard for the patron's children certainly did play a part, but it alone would hardly account for the obstinate insistence on a price: after all, there was nothing to stop him from wasting the money received from his freedman or from bequeathing it to third persons not his children. Moreover, from D.38.2.47.1 just cited, it looks as if a patron's son also could not in classical law let off the freedman without charge.
[4] *Ep.* 105.4. Disregarding adumbrations in Livy.
[5] *Gratuitus* derives from *grates* and is related to *gratia*.

Roman Society : the Non-Tipper

sake not of reward, *fructus*, but of duty, *officium*.¹ Similarly, in his opinion, the dying Epicurus shewed his *probitas gratuita* by such fine acts as remembering the children of a disciple: *tanta officia*.²

What is (to me) fascinating is that the Hebrew adverb *ḥinnam*, derived from *ḥen*, 'grace', 'graciousness', has exactly the same two meanings, 'without recompense', 'freely', on the one hand, 'without cause' in the bad sense on the other.³ To be sure, the Old Testament world is not that of the Roman *officia*. Nevertheless the development is very comparable. Among the earliest extant Biblical laws are directions as to when a slave obtains his freedom 'gratuitously' whether the master likes it or not.⁴ Again, there are traces of an ancient legal custom according to which a junior member of a family was to serve the Head 'gratuitously'.⁵ So here, too, the compulsory graces may have contributed to a degradation of the notion.⁶

Once we are awake to the importance of this aspect of Roman legal life, other illustrations come readily to mind and, indeed, a number of puzzling features become explicable. Take Augustus's law of 2 BC, quoted above, which limited the

¹ *de Leg.* 1.18.48.

² *de Fin.* 2.31.99.

³ Indeed, the oldest instance of the latter meaning is 'people that hate without cause', strikingly reminiscent of Seneca's *odium gratuitum*. The noun phrase, 'hatred without cause', however, is post-Biblical: see above, First Lecture, p. 54.

⁴ *Exodus*, 21.2, 11.

⁵ *Genesis*, 29.15; see Daube and Yaron, *Journal of Semitic Studies*, 1, 1956, 60ff., Daube, *The Exodus Pattern in the Bible*, 1963, 62f.

⁶ The semantic history of 'gratuity' is in full flow. The word signifies (1) favour, attested from 1523; (2) money-gift, from 1540, often in return for services; (3) more particularly a money-gift by a superior to an inferior, a servant, from the nineteenth century – (3a) a bounty on discharge or retirement, from the beginning of that century, (3b) a tip, from the middle. Up to this point, it can all be found in the NED, vol.4, 1901. Recently, however, the term (or one conspicuous application at least) is moving away from gift altogether. It more and more comes to signify a payment firmly expected on a certain occasion, maybe even enforceable at law; and even the amount is less and less in the discretion of the payer.

number of slaves a man might release by testament. A few years before, Dionysius of Halicarnassus, favouring the senatorial party – what would nowadays be called the Right – had recommended legislation of this nature.[1] One of his arguments was that more often than not a master who released his slaves in his last will was actuated by the unworthy desire for posthumous reputation: people would notice the new freedmen among his cortège and acclaim his benevolence. Now for one thing, it can be proved that this unworthy motive was far from general. As we have seen, a method (one of many) resorted to to evade the statutory restriction was to bequeath a supernumerary slave to a third party, on the terms to manumit him.[2] Evidently, that slave could not grace the testator's cortège as a freedman: it was the third party who, on carrying out the terms of his legacy, would become his patron. In any case, the very fact that a testator who manumitted his household *en bloc* could look forward to leaving behind a name for magnanimity shows how the bulk of citizens viewed such conduct.

Dionysius's strictures, however, are revealing. It is a commonplace in moralistic instruction – we come across it in Cicero[3] – that munificence should not be overdone and that where it is, frequently the purpose is ostentation. This sounds simple, until we ask what, in any relationship, is overdoing and what is ostentation. To this, different traditions, classes, value systems will manifestly give different answers. But there are some constant determinants, among them a powerful resentment against those who threaten to establish standards beyond what we could happily comply with: we want to see them restrained, and in the society with which Dionysius was concerned it might be necessary to restrain them by law. The statute here discussed, needless to say, had several objects. The sources, in addition to repression of the lust for posthumous popularity, mention the stemming of the influx of

---

[1] 4.24.
[2] D.35.1.37, Paul *singulari ad legem Fufiam Caniniam.*
[3] *de Off.* 1,14.44.

Roman Society : the Non-Tipper

inferior elements into the citizen body.[1] That the *colluvio servilis sanguinis*, however, cannot have been a supreme consideration comes out in the fact that the Augustan marriage legislation, while encouraging a freeborn woman to have three children, encouraged a freedwoman to have four.[2] (Then, as today, more child-bearing might be expected from, *zugemutet* to, the females from the lower mass.) One object we must not overlook is the protection of the non-tipper, i.e. prevention of a state of affairs when an owner of slaves, not to be despised as mean and forgetful of what a good guy ought to do, had no choice but to ordain wholesale release in his will.

If we look at the legislation from this angle, clearly if involuntarily indicated by Dionysius, as a curb on intolerable liberality, we become aware of a distinct affinity with the sumptuary laws, directed against the intolerable display of wealth. I shall say something about them in a moment. Before, however, let me refer to a *lex Cornelia*, probably of Sulla, which provided that no one might be surety for one man to one man in the same year for more than 20,000 sesterces.[3] There is a longstanding puzzle attached to this statute. It is generally thought that it was combating the irresponsible assumption of risk: why, then, did it forbid only to go beyond 20,000 for one man? Which left you perfectly free to ruin yourself by standing surety for fifty. But the statute was not combating recklessness. Its purpose was not to prevent you from risking as much as you liked, it was to shield him who was averse to getting involved in other people's debts – he was provided with a means of keeping such items down without ceasing to count

---

[1] Dionysius, *loc. cit.*, Suetonius, *Augustus* 40.3, Dio Cassius, 56.33, G.1. 13ff. They mention also the safeguarding of legacies: G.2.228. If an estate was too depleted by manumissions, the debts might equal if not exceed the assets, the heir might refuse it and this would kill the testament including legacies and, indeed, manumissions – except, perhaps, if he was a *suus*; what happened in that case is controversial, the texts are far from telling a clear story.

[2] *Ius quattuor liberorum*: G.3.44, *Ulp. Reg.* 29.3; Buckland, *Text-Book*, 167.   [3] G.3.124.

as a gentleman.¹ But for the intervention of the legislator, in the late Republic and early Empire it was next to impossible to refuse a friend's or dependant's request to guarantee an obligation. How routine a service this was may be gathered from a series of letters of Cicero's where he cannot remember whether or not he made himself liable for a certain acquaintance²; while the way Horace declaims on the hatefulness of these demands³ is direct proof that they were widely resented – which is not inconsistent with the fact that a well-meaning friend of a person in need of a guarantor might do his best, by means of one of those altruistic dodges discussed above, to defeat the statute.⁴

---

¹ The statute also forbade only to go beyond 20,000 to one man; so you could exceed the sum for the same man if he had several creditors. According to Appleton (*Zeitschrift* 26, 1905, 42) this laxity was inevitable since one of several creditors might not know that another had already taken a guarantee from you; hence it would have been wrong to deprive him of the security your promise gave him. There is much to be said for this explanation. But even this part of the statute might reflect the main purpose as I see it (which does not force us to drop the factor pointed out by Appleton). There was no reason to discourage an enthusiastic benefactor from going around with his protégé and helping him with dozens of sellers of goods, estate agents and moneylenders. But except in very special circumstances, a request for such multiple support was hardly *comme il faut*; a non-tipper could normally avoid it, he was sufficiently protected by the statutory limit on an undertaking to one creditor. Appleton, incidentally, quotes Cuq for the view (drawing support from Cicero, *pro Murena* 34.7) that the *lex Cornelia* primarily contemplated the intercession of a mighty person for his client. If this is correct (or to the extent to which it is), the measure belongs to the same kind of climate as the opposition to gratuitous renunciation of a patron's privilege.

² *ad Atticum*, 12.14.2, 12.17, 12.19.2. True, the transaction would have taken place over twenty-five years before.

³ *Sat.* 2.6.23ff., esp. 27.

⁴ D.12.6.18, Ulpian *XLVII ad Sabinum*, says that if premature payment is made by one who owes under a condition which must materialize, there is no *condictio*, whereas if it is made by one who owes under another condition of which it is doubtful whether it will come to pass, there is *condictio*. A strange formulation. A condition which must materialize is *dies*: I promise you on a Sunday to pay so-and-so much if to-morrow will be Monday, *dies certus*, I promise you if X will die, *dies incertus*. Yet the text calls it *condicio* and goes on to speak of a real condition as *alia condicio*. The fragment comes from Ulpian's discussion of *adpromissores*

It all flowed from the tight togetherness of the club. In the second century BC a law (*lex Apuleia*) provided that if one of several sureties paid more than his portion, he could recover from the others.[1] This shows the spirit in which such arrangements were treated. The several sureties may have made no agreement between them; for the lawgiver, the mere fact that they guaranteed the same debt unites them into a body where none ought to have an advantage over the other. What is as

---

(Lenel, *Palingenesia*, vol.2, 1184), from where indeed we have a further dictum with the curious formulation, D.46.2.9.1: 'he who takes a promise under a condition which must materialize is held to take an unconditional promise.' Lenel connects the two statements with the rule (D.46.1.8.7, Ulpian in the same book, G.3.126) that a surety's position may be less but not more stringent than the principal debtor's; in particular if the principal debt is conditional, the surety's may not be simple, though the converse is allowed. This is possible, but I am not satisfied because it leaves totally unexplained the surprising concept of 'a condition which must materialize'; it looks as if it had surprised Ulpian himself who, in 46.2.9.1, denies it any force. I believe the statements are connected with the *lex Cornelia* which, Gaius tells us, 3.124, covers 'any money certain to become due, i.e. contracted for without any condition; therefore even such money of which we are promised that it will be paid at a certain date – *in diem certum* – falls in this category, because it is certain to become due'. A conditional debt, then, was clearly not covered. To get around the statute, an unconditional debt had to be dressed up as conditional, had to be provided with 'a condition which must materialize', as when I promise if a boat will be seen in Ostia harbour within the next three months. The jurists, however, did not pass this dodge. 46.2.9.1 lays down that such a 'condition' is not a condition. 12.6.18 explains that it does not count as a condition in the matter of *condictio*: premature payment by a debtor under such a 'condition' gives him no *condictio* though he has one under a real condition. In the original Ulpian, together with these passages, there must have been the verdict rejecting this 'condition' as a means of circumventing the *lex Cornelia*. It is not preserved: Justinian was no longer interested in this *lex*. Incidentally, I have shown elsewhere (*Zeitschrift*, 76, 1959, 167ff., though I had not yet gained clarity on 12.6.18) that Celsus was the first jurist, in the case of premature payment of a debt, to restrict *condictio* to condition and refuse it not only for *dies certus* (where it had been refused before him) but also for *dies incertus* (where it had been admitted). Gaius in 3.124 still treats *dies incertus* as on a level with condition: the *lex Cornelia* does not apply, he represents *dies certus* as illustrating its remarkable range. Whether this reflects a widely shared view or whether, as often, he takes over an out-of-date detail from his source I leave open.

[1] G.3.122.

illuminating as the regulation itself is its subsequent interpretation: Gaius conceives of the law as establishing between the sureties a sort of partnership, *quaedam societas*. A *societas* between persons whose bond is neither kinship nor *consensus*, but participation in the same *officium*.[1]

The *lex Cornelia* seems to have formed part of Sulla's sumptuary laws.[2] This would suit my thesis very well, for the protection of the non-tipper is an aim of most anti-luxury measures; it definitely played an enormous part in the Roman ones which got under way towards the end of the third century BC.[3]

One form of extravagance, namely, at burials, had been legislated against far earlier, in the XII Tables, and indeed, Roman tradition has it, by King Numa. Those early provisions may have been inspired by religious beliefs, and in particular by hostility to Etruscan ritual. By 200 BC, though an anti-foreign slant persisted, the enemies of high living appealed chiefly to the simplicity of the past, to the virtue of moderation or even frugality and to egalitarianism (of a sort – as far as appearances were concerned). It would be a mistake to dismiss these sentiments as altogether spurious. But surely, behind them or side by side with them there was at work the wish to put down the prodigals whose style set the tone and forced their parsimonious brethren to emulate them or be out of the swim. Many people's lives (among the upper crust) were overshadowed by the fear of being thought a miser, to judge by the frequent mention of it in literature.[4] Lavish spending would be a way out; but a cheaper one was to have laws which, by prohibiting lavishness, made the miser undetectable.

---

[1] We must not press the comparison, but I am not convinced that, say, in the classical period, in an action under this law, defendant may not have enjoyed *beneficium competentiae*.

[2] Westrik, *Adnotationes ad loca Gai Institutionum de sponsoribus, fidepromissoribus et fideiussoribus*, 1826, 37, 49f., quoted by Voigt, *Das Ius Naturale*, vol.4, 1875, 425.

[3] For a general account see Kübler, art. *Sumptus*, in Pauly-Wissowa, 2nd ser., half-vol. 7, 4A:1, 1931, 901ff.

[4] E.g. Horace, *Sat.* 1.2.1ff., depicting the dilemma when you want to be called neither a miser nor a spendthrift.

Roman Society: the Non-Tipper

Sometimes the cat is let out of the bag. When a statute limiting female luxury was to be repealed,[1] old Cato spoke for its retention – of course – and one of his arguments addressed to the women (the rich women) who clamoured for its abolition was this: 'For while it is perhaps natural to feel shame or anger when what is denied to one of you is granted to another, with the dress of all made alike what is there which any of you need fear will render her less conspicuous? What one is most ashamed of is stinginess and poverty: the statute relieves you of either since you do not have what you are not permitted to have.'[2]

A *lex Licinia* passed some time before 100 BC is traditionally entitled *de sumptu minuendo*,[3] which would indicate that it was intended to curb expenditure. From Macrobius we hear[4] that it was the aristocratic party who had pressed for it. From which Kübler infers[5] that it must have relaxed the provisions of a prior *lex Fannia* and that we should replace *de sumptu minuendo*, 'concerning expenditure to be reduced', by *de severitate legis Fanniae minuenda*, 'concerning the austerity of the *lex Fannia* to be mitigated'. This, however, is to forget about the non-tippers who, at times, may form an influential lobby precisely among the highest circles where a few *bon viveurs* can make things dreadfully uncomfortable for everyone else. Gellius transmits a speech[6] apparently delivered in support of the *lex Licinia* and vehemently attacking extravagant entertainments: this can scarcely be squared with anything but 'expenditure to be reduced'.

There were, let me observe, certain types of munificence openly fought on behalf of such as were unwilling or unable to

---

[1] The Oppian statute, repealed in 195 BC: cf. above, p. 87.

[2] Livy, 34.4.12f. It is immaterial for my purpose whether or how far the speech is genuine. All that matters is that here is a source preserving an express reference to the interests of the stingy.

[3] Chapter heading of Gellius, 15.8.   [4] *Sat.* 3.17.7.

[5] *Loc. cit.* 907. The discrepancy between Macrobius and Gellius in respect of details of the statute is open to several explanations; at present none of them can be more than guesswork.   [6] 15.8.

compete. The most interesting is *ambitus*,[1] the effort of a candidate for high office to win votes by the display of costly array, the distribution of gifts, the arrangement of public games, the banqueting of friends. Throughout the Republic one law after another tried to keep *ambitus* in check. Sulla probably sponsored one.

The main reason the object of protecting the non-tipper was here freely admitted is that the tipper in this case did not act, barely pretended to act, from generosity. Everybody knew what he was after, he was 'ambitious' (related to *ambitus*)[2]; in fact he was doing business, he was buying,[3] and buying, moreover, a commodity which ought not to be for sale. Hence, in this case, the non-tipper was beset by no feeling of inferiority. There were other elements in the situation to boost his confidence. *Ambitus* often involved an unworthy degree of self-ingratiation with the public. Columella in the first century AD prefers to look after his land rather than 'to purchase the honour and power of the insignia at the price of dishonour, by abject servility, let alone the dissipation of his property'.[4] Again, recourse to *ambitus* showed that the man could not succeed by virtue of his and his family's reputation and real qualities (I mean what orthodoxy deemed the real qualities). According to Livy, the first law against *ambitus* in the fourth century BC was made because of the mode of canvassing of *novi homines*, upstarts.[5] No doubt the old set felt not only that this was wrong but also that it would be unpleasant to have to compete. Note the emphasis on expense at the end of Columella's observation.

[1] See Mommsen, *Römisches Strafrecht*, 865ff.

[2] *Ambire*, 'to go around in villages and hamlets among the electorate', conduct prohibited by a law of 358 BC: Livy, 7.15.13. (A candidate for election to the Académie Française has to call on every member.) Of the two nouns *ambitus* and *ambitio*, the former came to be confined to an unlawful mode of canvassing, the latter was less technical and acquired the sense of 'ambition', whence the adjective *ambitiosus*, 'ambitious'; see Mommsen, *loc. cit.* 866, and cf. above, First Lecture, p. 48 n. 3.

[3] Columella, 1 praef. 10 speaks of *mercari*; I shall quote the passage in full presently.

[4] 1 praef. 10; see the preceding footnote.   [5] 7.15.13, cited above, n. 2.

Mutatis mutandis the old considerations still apply to our modern treatment of electioneering expenses; nor am I sure that our control is significantly more effective than was the Roman. As for the latter, Mommsen remarks on the irony of the fact[1] that the term *candidatus*, 'candidate', taken literally, designates a person guilty of ostentation prohibited by an early law: it means 'dressed in shiny white'.

Dress, male and female, is indeed a means of social differentiation in all ages, whether major, between high and low, or subtle, between high and a little higher. It must have been irksome for a respectable citizen who would not or could not waste money to watch another becoming the talk of the town by his splendid attire. No wonder quite a few sumptuary regulations give relief to the former by obstructing the latter. Down to this day the feelings of the non-dresser can be a factor in the adoption of a fixed group apparel, say, by a religious order or a school. I am not saying that it is present in all instances, nor that, even where it is, other considerations may not be of weight: identity of outfit may give expression to genuine egalitarianism; it may enhance separateness from the outside world, solidarity and allegiance on the inside; it may serve such mundane purposes as easy mutual recognition, smooth administration, reduced cost, rapid equipment. It is these other considerations which predominate in the most notable case of all, the armed forces – though as soon as we enter the officers' mess, for example, we are again likely to come across conventions taking account of the member who cannot afford a silver cigarette étui.

Incidentally, in the matter of dress, the rather abstract concept 'uniform' was introduced, it seems, by Louvois, under Louis XIV, in the course of his reorganization of the French army: very fitting it should come from that powerful, centralizing, rationalizing reign. *Au fond*, the term still has its main base in the military domain. It entered English towards the

---

[1] *Loc. cit.* 866. An interesting monograph on a problem concerning American elections comes my way while I am proof-reading: Epstein, *Corporations, Contributions, and Political Campaigns: Federal Regulations in Perspective*, 1968.

middle of the eighteenth century. About the first, if not the first, English writer to transport it to outside its original sphere was Dickens, when he designed the uniform of the Pickwick Club.[1] For the readers of the time, the joke must have been far more amusing than for us who are accustomed to hearing of the uniform of nurses, of a gang, of the City.

I conclude with the history of the Jewish funeral.[2] An orthodox Jewish funeral is very simple: everybody gets a plain, white linen shroud. No doubt the idea that at that ultimate stage all are equal plays a part, as it did in Roman thought: Cicero, commenting on the disapproval of funeral pomp in the XII Tables and in Solon's legislation, declares it 'assuredly in accordance with nature that differences in wealth are ended in death'.[3]

Ah, if only the Talmud did not preserve the account of how the austere practice came to be established! By the beginning of the era, social convention required funerals so gorgeous that the non-tippers, people who had not the necessary means, or thought they had not, would leave relatives unburied and stealthily move to some other place. So the great and rich Gamaliel II, about AD 90, in order to remedy the situation, had himself buried in the most modest way. I can tell you from what I have seen in California that there is need there for a Gamaliel, in fact not only among men but also among beasts. When the dog I keep at San Francisco dies, I shall certainly take the next plane to Europe. Gamaliel's good deed had a little *Nachspiel*.[4] It was usual for the mourners, after committing the corpse, to forgather for some wine. The reform initiated by him was so popular that a toast in his honour was added, and in the end the drinking became so excessive that once again the Rabbis stepped in and abolished it altogether.[5]

[1] In 1837: 'the proposed uniform, sir, of the Pickwick Club.' See NED, vol.10, pt. 1, *U*, 1926, 223.

[2] See Kohler, art. Burial, in *Jewish Encyclopedia*, vol. 3, 1902, 432 ff.

[3] *de Leg.* 2.59: *tolli fortunae discrimen in morte.* French undertakers advertise *pompes funèbres.*   [4] *Babylonian Ketuboth* 8b.

[5] Cf. the ban on *circumpotatio*, round drinking at a funeral, promulgated by the XII Tables – Cicero, *de Leg.* 2.60.

3. PHILOSOPHICAL ASPECTS

I. Standards of Liability. A. *Dolus*, *Culpa* and *Casus*;
B. Differentiation in Life and Differentiation in Law
(1) Negligence (2) Intent. II. Reductio ad Absurdum

Whenever one considers the philosophy of Roman law, the relation to Greece is bound to come up. Roughly, while Greece furnished the great ideas, it was the Romans who transmuted them into something of practical applicability. Of this process there are many familiar examples, to which many more could be added. The apostle Paul affirms that among those who have become Christians, there is neither Jew nor Greek, neither bond nor free, neither male nor female.[1] With this may be compared a series of three Jewish thanskgivings of the period: a man expresses his gratitude for not being created a heathen, an ignoramus, a woman. (I always think this is very chivalresque, for how could one adore women if one were not created a man?). A triad attested from the fourth century AD, and even closer to Paul, still forms part of the orthodox daily morning prayer: thanks for not being a heathen, a slave, a woman.[2] Again, the dying Plato praised his guardian angel for being created a man, not an irrational animal, a brute; a Greek, not a barbarian, a foreigner; in the time of Socrates instead of in any other.[3] The third part, 'in the time of Socrates', we may assume, elegantly takes the place of something more usual.

[1] *Galatians*, 3.28; see Daube, *The New Testament and Rabbinic Judaism*, 1956, 80, 442.
[2] *Authorised Daily Prayer Book*, ed. Singer, 5f.; see Daube, *Theology* 69, 1966, 517.
[3] Plutarch, *Marius*, 46.1.

Clearly, there was floating in the Mediterranean world in those centuries a threefold division of the basic human condition, with all sorts of variations adapted to different circumstances; and one of these variations, I suppose, was the Roman trichotomy of *capitis deminutio*, change or loss of status, according as it affected a Roman's liberty (*capitis deminutio maxima*), citizenship (*minor* or *media*) or membership of a family (*minima*).[1] Very reminiscent of the other triple groups, but the practical twist is unmistakable.

Here we really know so little that such a suggestion is easily made: it is vague and harmless. Often we know just slightly more, and then we run into troublesome problems. I shall present two cases: first, certain grounds of liability or freedom from liability, and second, a mode of reasoning met in the legal sources.

[1] G.1.159ff. Schulz, *Classical Roman Law*, 1951, 72, is probably right in attributing the classification to Q. Mucius. The rest of his discussion of the institution, however, is not wholly convincing.

I. STANDARDS OF LIABILITY

A. *Dolus*, *culpa* and *casus*

Roman law is much admired for its three standards of liability: *dolus*, evil intent, *culpa*, negligence, and *casus*, accident.[1] I deliberately ram your car with mine: *dolus*. I bump into your car from lack of care: *culpa*. A sudden tornado thrusts me into your car: *casus*. There was a time when this classification was looked upon as a characteristic achievement of the Roman legal genius.[2] Nowadays scholars seem inclined to follow Kübler,[3] for whom it is a direct borrowing from Greece. This thesis, however, is at least an exaggeration. The truth is far more complicated.

The three standards are not, of course, met anywhere in Plato. But Kübler detects them in the *Rhetoric to Alexander* and in Aristotle. He is wrong. But this is not his fault. It is largely due to a long-standing serious misinterpretation of Aristotle.

We must begin with the earliest relevant work, the *Rhetoric to Alexander*. It recommends[4] that the accused in a criminal trial adopt one of the following positions: I did not do it, did

---

[1] I am aware that my renderings are inadequate approximations.

[2] E.g. Binding, *Zeitschrift*, 39, 1918, 5ff. By the way, it is in this article, it seems, that Binding coined the word *Interpolationenjagd*, 'interpolations hunt' (p. 10: *wie ich mich scherzhaft ausgedrückt habe*, 'as I have jokingly expressed myself'); and the man whom he accused of it was none other than Lenel who, seven years later, in *Zeitschrift*, 45, 1925, 17ff., published an article under this title against Beseler. Kalb had paved the way by his essay *Die Jagd nach Interpolationen in den Digesten*, 'The hunt for interpolations in the Digest', 1897.

[3] 'Der Einfluss der griechischen Philosophie auf die Entwicklung der Lehre von den Verschuldensgraden im römischen Recht', in *Rechtsidee und Staatsgedanke, Festschrift für Binder*, 1900, 63ff., apparently approved by Kunkel, *Römisches Recht* (on the basis of Jörs), 3rd ed., 1949, 179.

[4] 4, 1427a, 23ff.

not kill the man; I did it but it was lawful – say, killed him in self-defence; I did it but there were mitigating circumstances. Kübler's thesis is based on what the ancient writer has to tell us about mitigating circumstances. Prominent among them are *hamartema* (or *hamartia*) and *atychema* (or *atychia*), and these are opposed to *adikia*, deliberate evildoing, unmitigated. *Hamartema* is defined as harm inflicted as a result of ignorance; *atychema* as harm you do not intend, your intention is all right and things go wrong not through yourself but through other people or misfortune, bad luck. Kübler, sharing a common misunderstanding which finds its main expression in commentaries on Aristotle, translates *hamartema* by 'negligence'. With *adikia* corresponding to *dolus*, and *atychema* to *casus* (I shall presently have to make a reservation to the latter identification), this gives him the three standards of liability: *dolus*, evil intent, *culpa*, negligence, *casus*, accident.

The flaw is that the *Rhetoric*, in explaining *hamartema*, makes no reference whatever to negligence, lack of care or the like. It emphasizes ignorance, lack of knowledge, lack of information; and what it contemplates is the traditional situations of this type – for example, the killing of a friend in battle, intentionally but from error, mistaking him for a foe. (The Draconian inscription exempted this case from punishment.[1]) In contradistinction to *atychema*, accident, where for instance the spear with which you practice hits a bystander or the catapult you are demonstrating goes off, in *hamartema*, these disasters from ignorance, you do have the harmful intention – you do aim at that soldier, Oedipus did go for the old man who barred the way – only it is owing to a misapprehension, you believe that soldier to belong to the enemy, Oedipus was unaware the old man was his father. This has nothing to do with negligence. Whether the ignorance was inevitable or whether more scrupulous examination could and should have prevented it is immaterial. Similarly, negligence as such plays no part in *atychema*, accident. This embraces all unintended mishap

---

[1] Demosthenes, *in Aristocratem*, 53.637.

Liability : dolus, culpa and casus

whether blameless in our (the Roman) sense – the bystander suddenly moves into the playing-field, there is a hidden fault in the catapult – or not – you are careless in throwing the spear, in handling the engine.

The classification is essentially incommensurate with the Roman one, it is the outcome of totally different historical and dogmatic antecedents. Negligence has no part in it. To equate the two tables is to distort at least one of them. Even *atychema*, which at first sight looks the same as *casus*, is not quite the same, precisely because it includes unintended harm even if caused negligently, a wide sector excluded from the Roman *casus* which is opposed to *culpa*. If I bump into your car from lack of care, from the point of view of the *Rhetoric to Alexander* it is *atychema*, but in the Roman system it is *culpa*, not *casus*.

Let us now look at Aristotle, and first at his *Rhetoric*,[1] very close indeed to the *Rhetoric to Alexander*. Once again we are advised that the accused, though he has done the deed, need not be guilty of *adikema*, an unmitigated crime. He has available two equitable pleas in extenuation, *atychema* and *hamartema*. Except that *adikema* replaces *adikia*, the terms are exactly those of the *Rhetoric to Alexander*; and though, in expounding them, Aristotle strikes out on his own, they are employed in exactly the sense which they have in the older treatise. Indeed, it is the very purpose of the fresh elements appearing in his definitions to bring out that sense more clearly. *Atychema*, he explains, happens unexpectedly, *paralogos*, and is not due to wickedness, *mochtheria*. *Hamartema* does not happen unexpectedly, *paralogos*, and yet it, too, does not originate in vice, *poneria*. By contrast, *adikema* does not happen unexpectedly and is indeed the product of viciousness.

As in the *Rhetoric to Alexander*, we find distinguished *atychema*, the unintended mishap, where the harm occurs unexpectedly; and *hamartema*, where it does not occur unexpectedly, where you do intend it – and none the less you

[1] 1.13.15f., 1374b 1ff.

act without viciousness, *poneria*, because your motives are all right: your action springs from ignorance. It is quite unjustifiable to turn the latter category into negligence. If you shoot a member of your platoon who looks like an enemy, this killing in error is not, on the basis of the work before us, to be assigned to different classes according to the degree of circumspection applied: it is *hamartema* even in the absence of negligence, even, that is, if you are as conscientious in ascertaining the facts as is feasible in the circumstances. On the other hand, what for us are typical cases of negligence – you are incautious in practising with a spear, in demonstrating a catapult, in driving your car – fall under *atychema* no less than the same situations where the accused is free of fault, say, an abnormal gust of wind diverts the spear, a safety catch of the catapult breaks, the steering-wheel of the car jams. Aristotle's use of *paralogos* is most helpful in stressing the element of the unplanned, or even contrariness to plan, in *atychema*: I aim my spear at a board, the next moment, as a result of some coincidence, I find myself the cause of a man's death. This element is equally there whether or not I exercise proper care; and it is it which distinguishes the class from both *hamartema* and *adikema*, where there is nothing *paralogos* about the man's death – only, in *hamartema*, my decision to do him in is excusable when note is taken of the fallacious assumption underlying it. And let me repeat: there is no thought of marking off the avoidable, careless fallacy from the unavoidable one.

When we proceed to the *Nicomachean Ethics*, we are, it is true, confronted by a novel development; but even here it is wildly anachronistic to import the Roman standards. I shall deal with three sections.

The first[1] is devoted to the distinction between voluntary and involuntary acts, for the purpose of adjudging moral responsibility. It is not surprising in this context to find deeds committed through ignorance labelled as involuntary.[2] What

---

[1] 3.1.13ff., 1110b 18ff.
[2] I omit the requirement of compunction after the deed.

Liability : dolus, culpa and casus

is new is the wide scope of ignorance, the subsumption under this heading of both the *hamartema* and the *atychema* of the earlier works; in other words, of both the case where you mistake a fellow soldier for an enemy or, like Oedipus, your father for a stranger, and that where your spear is diverted from your aim, where you give a lesson in catapulting and the missile goes off or where your car runs into another. All these latter mishaps are now under deeds from ignorance.

This is a terrific attempt at reduction; and though somewhat forced, it is by no means irrational. After all, it is quite correct that even in the case of accident you are lacking some vital information, possession of which would make you act differently. In a way, the disaster may be attributed to the fact that you do not know what diverts your spear or makes the missile go off or makes your car bump into another.

Curiously, notwithstanding an enormous dissimilarity in background, a comparable trend is discernible in the *Pentateuch*, in the Priestly Code.[1] Priestly legislation started making allowance for ignorance in the field of levitical commerce where countless actions, innocuous in themselves, became illicit if done by or to a person or object belonging to a special category. It was all right to eat an ox or enter the sanctuary, but an offence to eat an ox dedicated to the temple or enter the sanctuary in a state of uncleanness. An offender unaware of the dedication or his uncleannesss was provided with a routine mode of atonement; and the law had a technical designation for this kind of error, *sheghagha*,[2] evidently corresponding to *hamartema* as used in the classifications I have presented: you do intend the deed – to eat the ox, to enter the sanctuary – and nevertheless you are guilty of no ill-will, you act from a misapprehension. The remarkable thing is that, ultimately, the notion of *sheghagha* was transferred to the regulation of homi-

---

[1] Some preliminary remarks of mine may be found in *Revue Internationale des Droits de l'Antiquité*, 2, 1949, 208, 211f.; a fuller discussion is given in my as yet unpublished Edinburgh *Gifford Lectures*, 'The Deed and the Doer in the Bible'.

[2] E.g. *Leviticus*, 5.18.

cide[1] and there referred to *atychema*, accident, unintended killing, say, by an unfortunate throw of a weapon. So here, too, 'error' became the over-all heading for involuntary harm, to the confusion of posterity – from the Rabbis of the Talmud to the Old Testament specialists of the present day – seeking to make one whole of the various strata of evolution.

Before leaving this section of the *Ethics*, an important point must be noted – important not only for its own sake, but also because a proper appreciation of it will make us less prone to the current misunderstanding of the following sections. Aristotle, we have seen, conceives of both the old *hamartema* (you mistake a friend for a foe) and the old *atychema* (your spear takes the wrong course) as involuntary since they are the result of ignorance. By an express proviso, he excludes from this heading crimes perpetrated in drunkenness, in a rage or in passionate desire.[2] These deeds are voluntary, for, though you act 'not knowing' (*agnoon*) what you are doing, you do not act 'from ignorance' (*di' agnoian*). Your action, he contends, is not, as in the other cases, due to lack of information concerning a specific circumstance (that the soldier you aim at belongs to your side, that a movement you make or a gust of wind is going to deflect your spear). It is due to your very drunkenness, anger or lust, and when you say that 'you do not know' what you are doing, what we mean is that you are unaware, not of a specific circumstance, but, more generally, of the nature of your deed, you are forgetful of the restraints incumbent on a decent citizen. In fact, 'you do not know' in much the same sense as an offender in cold blood: even he is ignorant in this wider sense, even he acts insensitively to his true interests, to the right end of man. Unlike Socrates, Aristotle refuses to accept this moral error as abolishing responsibility.[3] If we apply the categories of the rhetorical works, what you perpetrate in drunkenness, in a rage or in passionate desire is *adikia* or *adikema*; we shall presently find

[1] *Numbers*, 35, *Joshua*, 20.
[2] 3.1.14f., 21ff., 1110 25ff., 111a 22ff.
[3] Cf. Daube, *Sin, Ignorance and Forgiveness in the Bible*, 1960, 21ff.

Liability : dolus, culpa and casus

this conclusion borne out by further statements in the *Ethics*. There is so far, of course, no trace of anything resembling *culpa*, negligence.

Next, a section[1] where Aristotle is concerned to prove that virtue and vice are voluntary, within our power. Society at any rate proceeds on this basis, he observes. It metes out punishment to those who cause harm – except if they act under compulsion or from ignorance – and honours those who do nobly, thus repressing the former type and encouraging the latter. It would never exhort us to do anything involuntary, for instance, not to feel heat or hunger. Again, the argument is largely directed against the Socratic doctrine that, all wrong flowing from ignorance, no one sins voluntarily. For Aristotle, it may be recalled, wrong flows from ignorance only where you are mistaken as to a particular fact; while if your error is of the general, moral kind, about your calling, about the good, you admittedly act 'not knowing', but not 'from, as a result of, ignorance' – you do will your deed.

That society is with him, he goes on, comes out impressively in two cases. First, you may be held to account precisely for 'not knowing'. Your very blindness to right and wrong, that is, may be punishable if you are clearly seen as answerable for it. Thus the great lawgiver Pittacus (tyrant of Mytilene at the beginning of the sixth century BC) increased the ordinary penalty where a crime was committed in drunkenness. We have already seen that, in Aristotle's view, a drunkard's action is voluntary, it is *adikia* or *adikema*, his 'not knowing' is essentially the same as that of a criminal who is sober. We now learn that what is notable about drunkenness is that our responsibility for 'not knowing' what we are doing is more evident than in sober crime; so evident that it may attract an extra penalty.

It is hardly necessary to point out – but I must, in view of Kübler's thesis – that this treatment of a deed in drunkenness is fundamentally different from that which would bring it

[1] 3.5.7ff., 1113b 21ff.

under *culpa*, negligence, as something midway between *dolus*, intended harm, and *casus*, harm caused by accident. If we are to correlate at all, in Aristotle's system the deed in drunkenness falls under *dolus*, and he quotes Pittacus's legislation as shewing that it is sometimes judged even worse than the ordinary dolose deed. Negligence as a standard of liability simply has no look in.

The second case Aristotle invokes in support is punishment of a man even though he does not know a legal prohibition which one ought to know and which creates no exceptional difficulty. Here at least I can see how commentators coming from the Roman scheme might arrive at the standard of negligence. Aristotle distinguishes between difficult laws and laws readily intelligible; not to bother about the latter is certainly negligence, carelessness, blameworthy lack of application. Only, in Aristotle's system, this attitude does not bring the deed down from *dolus* to a less serious class of *culpa*. On the contrary, it is precisely this lack of application which (like drunkenness) lies at the root of vice, of *dolus*. The deed to which it leads is voluntary, dolose.

Aristotle, remember, is here out to demonstrate that society's practice makes no allowance for the 'not knowing' in a general, moral, Socratic sense. So he adduces a striking parallel – no allowance is made for being unacquainted with a prohibition of the positive law which is not beyond ordinary understanding. The contravention is considered voluntary, subject to the full rigour of whatever sanction is threatened. While it is easy to see how commentators got misled, the fact is that this passage no more than any of the preceding ones has to do with negligence as a standard of liability.

The analogy between an offender not knowing about the positive law he ought to know and an offender not knowing right and wrong in general is fully spelled out. Society inflicts punishment on the former: just so, Aristotle climaxes his argument, it inflicts punishment – I quote – 'in the other instances where the not knowing is the consequence of

Liability: dolus, culpa and casus

unconcern, so that the person is himself responsible for his not knowing, since it would be in his power to be concerned'.

This little sentence has been fatally misunderstood. What it does is to draw the conclusion from the parallel of not knowing such positive law as is easy to know. Just as in this case the wrongdoer does not get off, since his mental state is at fault, so society does not let off the wrongdoer for not knowing what he is doing in a general, moral way – he also is master of his character, he could be a better man had he applied himself. It is a fierce anachronism to turn this into a proclamation of *culpa*, negligence, as a standard between *dolus* and *casus*. Aristotle devotes a good many subsequent paragraphs to explaining how you have to train diligently to acquire the habit of right-doing and how unconcern and neglect make you prone to wrongdoing. His negligence is not placed side by side with *adikia*, voluntary crime, as another, lesser degree of guilt. It is the great factor in the genesis of crime, the soil in which the latter grows. It is the sloth, the reprehensible lack of moral fibre, which results in, and grounds your responsibility for, evil actions, actions which, in the Roman grouping, are to be assigned to *dolus*. Only a man constantly striving for perfection will remain free from evil, while evil – the dolose deed – is the ultimate outcome of lack of discipline.[1] Contrary to Socrates's teaching, sin is voluntary, the sinner's 'not knowing' (which cannot be denied) his own fault, a reflection of his carelessness. We must not harmonize this with the Roman scheme.[2]

---

[1] Considering this aspect of Aristotle's theory, I am not sure whether Kunkel (*Zeitschrift*, 45, 1925, 344) does not assume too close a connection between the *aner spoudaios* and the *diligens paterfamilias*.

[2] It is just conceivable that the clause 'in the other instances...' refers not to ordinary crime, but to the states of mind previously paired off with drunkenness, namely, rage and passionate desire (see above, p. 136). If so, what Aristotle is saying is that he who acts in such a state quite obviously does not know what he is about, yet society punishes him: his not knowing what he is about is due to defective discipline, a man must from the outset strive to tame himself. My main argument remains unaffected: there is no trace of a separate standard of negligence, negligence – in the sense of leading an undirected life – is what lies behind the doing of evil and what deprives an evildoer of excuse.

In *Deuteronomy*,[1] the idolatrous Israel is reproached: 'Thou hast forgotten God that formed thee.' In Roman and Roman-inspired law, forgetfulness is among the commonest varieties of negligence, the lesser guilt. But it would be wrong to think that this passage from the Old Testament is introducing the standard of *culpa* as midway between *dolus* and *casus*. Forgetfulness here means defection, rebellion, criminal sloth, it is the height of wickedness: 'They are a very froward generation.'[2] Similarly, the unconcern of which Aristotle speaks characterizes the criminal, it is not as if it were split off from vice as a lighter matter, but the two go together, the former being the attitude which produces the latter. The Deuteronomic forgetting and this Aristotelian remissness in the self-formation of the evil character[3] could exist in systems which never thought of opposing the deed from *culpa* to *dolus* or *casus*.

Lastly, we may look at a third section in the *Nicomachean Ethics*[4] which, while harking back to the distinction proposed in the *Rhetoric* for use in a criminal trial, at the same time incorporates the wider notion of a deed from ignorance worked out (we have seen) in a preceding part of the *Ethics*. The result of the combination is the appearance of *hamartema* in two senses: the narrow old one, you mistake a friend for a foe, and an enlarged one which embraces *atychema*, your spear takes the wrong course. But again, there is nothing corresponding to *culpa*, negligence: that is a foreign body introduced by later students of the work.

Aristotle begins by arguing that voluntariness is of the essence of just or unjust conduct, hence only voluntary wrongdoing can be blamed. Voluntariness is excluded by ignorance or compulsion, and the former may have regard to the person you are attacking (you do not know he is your father), the

---

[1] 32.18.
[2] 32.20.
[3] The very way in which I put this indicates that *Deuteronomy* and Aristotle's *Ethics* are widely different.
[4] 5.8.1ff., 1135a 15ff.

Liability : dolus, culpa and casus

instrument you are wielding (you believe the spear has a button on it), the effect of what you are doing (you mean to prick but it comes out as a grievous injury) or indeed the whole action (*ten praxin holen*, the catapult you are demonstrating goes off).[1]

This is the doctrine we found him expounding in a previous chapter: mistake, in the traditional sense, and accident are both subsumed under the one heading of ignorance. I have already pointed out that, though perhaps a *tour de force*, this compression is not without some rational foundation: if you knew that by an unfortunate coincidence what you intend as a prick will be a serious wound, or that the catapult's spring will break, you would proceed differently no less than if you knew the person you are about to strike to be your father. Viewed from this angle, harm caused by accident is construable as harm inflicted as a result of ignorance.

A few paragraphs further on,[2] Aristotle draws the consequence by affixing the label *hamartema* to the entire complex of mistake and accident. A deed springing from ignorance, he says, is a *hamartema*, and this includes the case where you do not mean to hit a man at all (say, you demonstrate a catapult) as well as that where you do mean to hit him but only because you are in error as to his identity. Within this broad area of *hamartema*, however, he goes on to distinguish – exactly as in the *Rhetoric* – between *atychema*, accident, where the harm occurs *paralogos*, unexpectedly, and *hamartema* in its narrower sense, where the harm does not occur *paralogos*, you do intend it, and none the less there is no *kakia*, badness, on your part – evidently the case where you mix up friend and enemy, father and stranger. It is interesting that, in his further elucidation of the difference between *atychema* and *hamartema*, he employs an idea which is not represented in his *Rhetoric*, though it is in the *Rhetoric to Alexander*. The latter, it may be recalled, defines

---

[1] Of the examples in brackets, the first is found in 5.8.3, 1135a, 30, the third in 5.8.6, 1135b, 15, the second and fourth in 3.1.17, 1111a, 10ff.

[2] 5.8.6, 1135b, 11ff.

atychema, accident, as the case where things go wrong 'not through yourself (as they do in *hamartema*, mistake, where, under the influence of an erroneous assumption, the harm is intended) but through other people or a mishap'. Aristotle explains that in the case of *hamartema* the origin of the train of events (*arche tes aitias*[1]) lies in you, in the case of *atychema*, outside.[2]

In contrast with *hamartema* in the wider sense – mistake and accident – is the deed perpetrated knowingly: *adikema*. There is no need here to go into the division between an offence committed in a passion, especially in a rage (and, more especially, under provocation), and a premeditated offence. In the former event, though guilty of a wicked deed, the doer need not be wicked, whereas in the latter he is.[3]

Kübler quotes this chapter of the *Nicomachean Ethics* for his thesis – *adikema* equals *dolus*, intentional wrongdoing, *hamartema* equals *culpa*, negligence, and *atychema* equals *casus*, accident. He is anticipated by Maschke, for whom 'Aristotle is the creator of the Greco-Roman and modern doctrine of liability'.[4] Note the 'and modern'. Throughout his discussion, Maschke attributes to Aristotle not only the establishment of the standard of negligence[5] but even highly specialized

---

[1] The popular emendation of *aitias* into *agnoias* is, of course, quite unjustified.

[2] The sequence *hamartema – atychema*, too, is the same as in the *Rhetoric to Alexander*.

[3] 5.8.8ff., 1135b, 20ff. Incidentally, it is generally held that the three types of injury Aristotle declares to exist in 5.8.6, 1135b, 11, are *hamartema*, *atychema* and *adikema*. This is possible, but it would make his arrangement awfully clumsy. I regard it as far more probable that the three types are *hamartema* in the extensive meaning (subdivided into *atychema* and *hamartema* proper), wrong committed in a passion, and wrong premeditated.

[4] *Die Willenslehre im Griechischen Recht*, 1926, 123.

[5] Proceeding from the traditional misinterpretation of the sentence cited above, 'in the other instances where the not knowing is the consequence of unconcern', 3.5.9, 1114a 1, he remarks, p. 154, that *damit ist eine generelle Diligenzpflicht in gewissem Umfange statuiert*.

Liability: dolus, culpa and casus 143

teachings of the early twentieth century.[1]

However, neither Kübler nor Maschke could have fathered the Roman scheme on Aristotle had the latter not been considerably Romanized long before. His transformation began as early as some fourteen hundred years ago. Gauthier and Jolif, in their masterly commentary on the *Nicomachean Ethics*, like everybody, identify *hamartema* with negligence, and they offer the example of a man who, practising with a weapon on a road, hits a passer-by; the same disaster on land duly assigned to such practice would be *atychema*. As the example is found in a work on the *Ethics* possibly dating from the sixth century AD, they believe it to be about as good as if it were from Aristotle himself.[2] But a great deal had happened in the intervening eight hundred years in the law and legal thought of the Mediterranean world. The Roman jurists had indeed brought the category of *culpa* to bear on cases of this sort: if you prune your tree and kill somebody's slave passing by, in principle you are liable only if he was walking on a public road, yet given certain conditions you may be guilty of *culpa* even if it all takes place on your property.[3] Or again, if, playing at ball, you push over and injure the caddie, it is *casus* rather than *culpa*.[4] On the basis of the authentic Aristotle, if, while practising, you unwittingly hit a passer-by, it is *paralogos*, unexpected, *atychema*, accident, no matter whether you are

---

[1] The entire treatment of 5.8.6ff., 1135b 11ff., on pp. 156ff., is vitiated by radical Romanization cum modernization.

[2] Gauthier and Jolif, *Aristotle, L'Ethique à Nicomaque*, vol.2, pt. 1, 1959, 401, referring to Heylbut, *Eustratii et Michaelis et Anonyma in Ethica Nicomachea Commentaria* (= *Commentaria in Aristotelem Graeca*, ed. Prussian Academy, 20), 1892, 238.

[3] D.9.2.31, Paul *X ad Sabinum*, cf. I.4.3.5; I omit details. See Watson, *The Law of Obligations in the Later Roman Republic*, 1965, 238ff.

[4] D.9.2.52.4, cf. 10.3.26, Alfenus *II digestorum*. In Antiphon's *Second Tetralogy*, where a boy is killed picking up the javelins in the gymnasium (3.6), the problem is conceived chiefly as one of causation; the prosecution holding that the person who threw the weapon caused the death, the defence that it was caused by the boy himself since he ran into the path of the weapon. See Maschke, *op. cit.* 73ff.

in the gymnasium or on a highway. Interestingly, Clement of Alexandria, about AD 200, who heavily draws on Aristotle, is not yet Romanizing at all.[1]

By the way, there is a significant time lag in the Romanization of Aristotle between the commentaries, the translations and the indexes. The commentaries are the first to bring him up to date – I have just mentioned a (possibly) sixth-century one – and they have little difficulty in going as far as they like. Gauthier and Jolif affirm that *hamartema* is *l'homicide par imprudence de notre législation*.[2] Translations are naturally more resistant. For instance, in the sixteenth and seventeenth centuries, *paralogos*, the quality characteristically attaching to *atychema*, accident, and not attaching to *hamartema*, ignorance, is still correctly translated *inopinato* or *praeter rationem*. A reader not misled by commentaries could still reach the right understanding: whereas in *atychema* the harm is unintended, comes about contrary to all calculation, in *hamartema* it is intended, by no means unlooked for (it is *nec inopinato* or *nec praeter rationem*) – only the intention is formed in reliance on a false premise, friend is taken for foe. An unbiased reader, that is, would hardly import the criterion of care or carelessness. By contrast, Rackham, the translator of the *Nicomachean Ethics* for the Loeb Classical Library, renders *paralogos* not by 'contrary to expectation', but by 'contrary to reasonable expectation'; so if you are careless, unintended harm, though it is unexpected, is not reasonably unexpected and therefore falls under *hamartema*. The standard of negligence is here smuggled into the very text, though even here with a certain restraint, and a footnote is still needed to

---

[1] *Stromateis*, 14f., 60.1ff. There is, needless to say, much deviation from Aristotle. For example, according to 15, 62.2, it is *hamartema* to lead a dissolute life, *atychema* to strike a friend believing him an enemy, *adikema* to violate a tomb. But the standard of negligence does not yet intrude. In 15, 62.4, he says – quite in the spirit of Aristotle – that readiness for education and obedience to the laws are within our power.

[2] *Loc. cit.* 401.

Liability: dolus, culpa and casus 145

make the modern meaning quite explicit.[1] The translations by Ross and others are *au fond* equally faulty. I cannot possibly list even a fraction of the distortions due to the fundamental flaw in this matter common to all students of Aristotle. Yet in the indexes of editions, whether in Greek or in another language, invariably we look in vain for entries under a heading 'Negligence' or the like. To this day, there has been no thorough, comfortable amalgamation of the misconception with the system as a whole.

The texts invoked by Kübler, then, cannot have furnished the model for the Roman standards. Should we make such a fuss about them? Since Freud we know we must do with *dolus* alone; there is definitely no *casus*. If I accidentally break my toothglass, it is either because I dislike it, or because I like it and want to punish myself, or indeed because I neither dislike it nor like it but substitute it for something else which I either dislike or like....

Kübler, however, claims that he has direct evidence of the take-over he alleges, namely, a reference by Paul – preserved in the *Institutes* of Justinian[2] – to *culpa quam Graeci adikema dicunt*, '*culpa* which the Greeks call *adikema*'. But for one thing, Paul, writing at the beginning of the third century AD, is a poor witness of what would have taken place two-hundred-and-fifty years earlier. For another, he associates *culpa* with *adikema*, not *hamartema* at all. So Kübler considers emendation, the substitution of *hamartema*. To this, however, he realizes

[1] Rackham, *Aristotle, The Nicomachean Ethics*, 1956, 300f.: '*atychema*, accident or misadventure, an offence due to mistake and not reasonably to be expected, and *hamartema* in the narrow sense, a similar offence that ought to have been foreseen'. In 3.5.9, 1114a, 3, incidentally, Rackham, p. 147, misparaphrases: 'as he could have taken the trouble to ascertain the facts'. As demonstrated above, the passage (literally, 'as he had the power to be concerned') does not envisage harm inflicted negligently in the sense that the doer ought to know more about the particular situation. It envisages lack of application as the source of dolose wrongdoing: 'as he could have taken the trouble to discipline himself.'

[2] I.4.4 pr. Pauline provenance is more or less guaranteed by *Coll.* 2.5.1, *libro singulari de iniuriis*, though the clause is part of a bit which has dropped out of the *Collatio*.

one may object because the reading *adikema* is confirmed by Theophilus's *Paraphrase of the Institutes*. He says one should not be put off too much: maybe the authors of the *Institutes* themselves replaced *hamartema* by *adikema* since they were no longer familiar with Aristotle's classification.

Well, *hamartema* is not there. Worse, even if it had the meaning attributed to it by Kübler, it would be the wrong word and *adikema* the right one. Paul is thinking of the *culpa* which grounds liability under the *lex Aquilia*, concerning damage to property. He represents it as synonymous with *iniuria*, the term occurring in the *lex*. It comprises *dolus* as well as negligence – anything not accident.[1] *Hamartema* would be out of the question even if it signified negligence. I do not think I need go on with this text.[2]

Among the reasons for the difference between the Greek scheme and the Roman is this, that the former is primarily

---

[1] This is rightly stressed by Kunkel, *Zeitschrift*, 49, 1929, 163, 171. Whether, as he considers possible, the classic wrote *damnum culpa datum* where we now find *culpa* may be left open. Schulz, *Roman Legal Science*, 1946, 196, upholds the present version, *culpa*.

[2] Still, a note on a further argument of Kübler's. In the following part of the text, Paul mentions another application of *iniuria*, namely miscarriage of justice, *iniquitas et iniustitia*, for which the Greek, he says, is *adikia*. Kübler urges that as *adikia* is used in this very bad sense, *adikema* could not be used for the far milder *culpa*; here, he concludes, is support for his replacement of *adikema* by *hamartema*. However, first, as *culpa-adikema* in this passage embraces both negligence and *dolus* (which fact Kübler overlooks and has to overlook), the sense is not quite so mild. Secondly, in Greek writings *adikema* is often met as denoting or at least including an unintentional offence; Philo speaks of 'voluntary and involuntary *adikemata*' (*De Posteritate Caini* 13.48). Thirdly, *adikema* and *adikia* are, after all, two different nouns and a writer may well endow them with different nuances. Fourthly, *non constat* that Paul's two definitions of *iniuria* – as *culpa-adikema* in the area of the *lex Aquilia*, as *iniquitas et iniustitia-adikia* in that of miscarriage of justice – go back to a single source; so the postulate of absolute consistency is hardly justified. It would be dubious even if the definitions did come from the same source. *Hamartema* itself is a good illustration of the lack of rigour in such matters. In his *Rhetoric*, 2.22.7, 1396a, Aristotle understands by it an evil deed, without any mitigation. The verb *hamartanein* in *Nic. Eth.* 5.8.8, 1135b,23, refers to an offence committed in a passion.

Liability: dolus, culpa and casus

concerned with a criminal law trial, the latter with a claim for payment of damages.

The Greek scheme proceeds from the trial of a crime, indeed, from homicide. According to the Greek experts, the defence has three possibilities. (1) It can deny the deed: the accused did not kill at all. (2) It can admit the deed but maintain that it was lawful: for instance, the accused killed in self-defence. Or (3) it can admit the deed but raise special pleas – such as ignorance or accident, the accused did not know the man belonged to his own army, the accused was only demonstrating the catapult which went off. In this scheme, if negligence were to be given a place, its chief role would be that of a counter-plea to accident. The prosecution would be able to reply: Yes, the catapult went off unexpectedly, but you could and should have been more careful, so though you are less blameworthy than a real murderer, you are not free of blame. In antiquity, however, the need for this counter-plea is not too pressing. Were it not for rather novel features of our civilization such as whole-sale surgery and, above all, road traffic, negligence would not be very prominent in criminal law. 'In modern times', say Cross and Jones, 'most cases of manslaughter by criminal negligence ... arise in connection with the driving of a motorcar by the accused.'[1] In other words, in ancient criminal law, once allowance is made for the unwitting character of a deed, little urgency attaches to the splitting off of negligence as something between accident and *dolus*.

The deed from ignorance, let me remark – I mistake the man for an enemy soldier – has an enormous fascination for the ancients, an incomparably greater one than accident. If we survey homicide in Greek lay literature, accident is rare but error of all kinds abounds. Oedipus kills his father unaware of their relationship; the daughters of Pelias kill theirs expecting Medea to bring him back rejuvenated; Prokris is killed by her

---

[1] *An Introduction to Criminal Law*, 5th ed., 1964, 152. I like the 'by the accused.' As careful legal writers, they point out that the dead are not called to account before our tribunals.

husband who mistakes her for a doe; Pentheus is torn to pieces by his mother and other Bacchantes who think he is a lion; Aktaeon is hunted to death by his own dogs and friends who see a stag in him; Theseus fatally curses his son Hippolytos whom he believes to have seduced Phaedra; Kreon, misjudging his authority over against the higher laws of heaven, sentences Antigone to death. Similarly, in the Biblical narratives, Old Testament and New, there is only one case of accidental homicide, and it is so insignificant *qua* homicide, this aspect is so little made of, that you will never think of it: I offer a third of my Gray Lecturer's stipend – the whole fee for this Lecture – to whoever can name me the case at the end of the next quarter of an hour. By contrast, homicide from ignorance plays a considerable part, up to the putting to death of Jesus by them who know not what they do.

Of the three postures of the defence, (1) the accused did not kill at all, (2) he did kill but lawfully, (3) he did kill but he has an excuse such as ignorance or accident, posture (1) is least interesting from a philosophical point of view. It involves a simple question of fact, a matter for the police to clear up. The literary genre representing this posture is the detective story, opening with a number of suspects each of whom professes innocence, 'I did not do it', and going on to pick out the culprit. An author may excel in psychological finesse and style; nevertheless, considering the essentially flat theme, it is understandable that this branch of writing ranks relatively low.[1] It is postures (2) and (3) which furnish material for the magnificent, searching works of the Greeks and Hebrews. Antigone insists that her transgression of the king's command was lawful, dictated by a superior principle. Oedipus invokes his total ignorance of the relevant circumstances. The Amalekite who slew Saul mistakenly thought his deed would be agreeable to David.[2] In *Jonah*, the sinful people of Nineveh are pardoned because they cannot discern between their right

---

[1] I love it.
[2] II *Sam.* 4.10.

Liability: dolus, culpa and casus

hand and their left hand – a consideration foreshadowing Jesus's prayer for forgiveness for his enemies. Here lie the worth-while puzzles for those who ponder human ways: where it is a question of the justification of a prima facie wrongful deed, and, above all, where it is a question of an agent under the influence of error.

Accident, however, though it falls under the same heading of special pleas as ignorance, defence no. (3), is found far less deserving of deeper study. The deed in error is felt to be the real problem of man as man, as a thinking being; error – where things proceed not unexpectedly, not *paralogos*, not *praeter rationem*, but on the contrary as intended, everything goes according to plan, in the language of Aristotle you are the author of the train of events – and yet it is all flawed by ignorance, misapprehension, misjudgment, when the desired result is finally achieved, when you have killed the soldier you aimed at, it turns out to be a calamity. The accidental deed does not show up the defective nature of man at his highest level, the level of thought. Essentially it is just an expression of that subjection to fate which is common to all that exists: men, beasts, even inanimate objects. If the javelin with which I practise hits an onlooker, that is no different, *au fond*, from his being hit by lightning – except that heaven has used me as instrument instead of an electric current. It has nothing to do with my rational self.[1] It is highly relevant that, for Aristotle, tragedy is characterized by that peculiarly human plight, where the rational design is carried out and then proves to

[1] To be sure, to the religious mind even the accidental deed did pose a worrying problem: why is this particular man used as fate's instrument? Philo and the Rabbis answered, because of a previous sin he must have committed: see my article in *Vetus Testamentum*, 11, 1961, 267. In that article I left it undecided whether the idea reached Philo from the Rabbis or the Rabbis from Philo. (Independent development is ruled out by the strikingly similar way in which the idea finds expression in the two.) I would now accord priority to Philo, for the idea occurs (as I had not noticed) in Antiphon's *Second Tetralogy* 3.8 (see above, p. 143, n. 4, and below, pp. 168ff). The prosecution argues that if the stain of unwitting killing falls upon a man from heaven for his impiety, it would be wrong to impede this visitation and acquit him. So Philo is drawing on his Hellenistic education.

have been disastrous. A person accidentally smashing his toothglass is not tragic, in Aristotle's sense.[1]

Here I would note that the current misinterpretation of his *Rhetoric* and *Ethics*, which turns *hamartema* into negligence, quite overlooks the close link with the theory of tragedy set forth in his *Poetics*. The tragic hero, he explains, is overthrown not through badness and wickedness, *kakia* and *mochtheria*, but through some great error, *hamartia megale*; and it is his discovery of his error, his passing from ignorance, *agnoia*, to knowledge, which fully completes his tragedy.[2] The terminology is too similar to that in the *Nicomachean Ethics* to warrant the assumption of two utterly disparate lines of thought. But surely it is impossible to bring negligence into the *Poetics*. Aristotle instances Oedipus and Thyestes as typifying his tragic hero. Are we to impute negligence to Thyestes because he did not examine the meat set before him by his brother in order to make sure that it was not his own son he was eating? Was that the essence of his tragedy? Would the myth of Oedipus really be the same if Oedipus had taken a corner with more haste than caution would demand, and had bumped into his father – whom he knew – so that the latter succumbed? For that matter, would it make no difference to the story of the New Testament if Jesus had died being struck by a tile which fell from a roof as a result of the carelessness of some Jewish and Roman workers engaged on repair?

I am far from denying that, in certain areas of the law, the

---

[1] From the moment that, as in the *Nicomachean Ethics*, the accidental deed is subsumed under ignorance and consequently becomes *hamartema* in an extended application, it does partake of the nature of the tragic, it does represent a flaw in reasoning. But Aristotle's theory of tragedy is based on the narrower meaning of *hamartema*, be it that he worked it out before he arrived at the wider meaning, be it that only a theory based on the narrower meaning did justice to the actual tragic material before him.

[2] *Poetics*, 11, 1452a, 29f., 13, 1453a, 7ff., 14, 1453b, 30f., 1454a, 3f. Discovery as conceived by Aristotle has a wide range; it can, for example, take place in time so as to prevent the horrible deed. There is no need here to enlarge on this topic.

Liability : dolus, colpa and casus

Greeks did fairly early make (or come near to making) negligence into a standard of liability – for instance, in connection with the holding of offices, but in other contexts too. There are advances in this direction in Antiphon's *Tetralogies*; under Plato's regime a guardian of an orphan is subject to a penalty if guilty of negligence or knavery (*amelein* or *kakourgein*).[1] Aristotle was of course familiar with all such developments.[2] My point is that not only do they occupy a very subordinate place in myth, saga, drama, but, above all, they are simply not reflected in the passages which I have reviewed as relevant to Kübler's thesis, that is to say, in the threefold scheme of the *Rhetoric* and *Nicomachean Ethics* from which he affirms that the Romans took their division.

Whether or not Roman law was influenced by those cases where Greek philosophers, orators and jurists approached or achieved the standard of negligence, I shall not discuss; I think some influence is highly probable. What chiefly accounts for the Roman classification *dolus*, evil intent, *culpa*, negligence, *casus*, accident, as distinct from the Greek one, is that its root is in civil law, concerned with compensation, rather than in criminal law or, more narrowly, the law of homicide, concerned with retribution.

In the latter, as I have just argued, at a time when there are not large numbers of negligent killings, to protect from retribution, or excessive retribution, the unwitting doer, the man actuated by no *dolus*, is good enough; there is no urgent need to refine and exclude negligence from this protection. In disputes about compensation, however, such an arrangement would not do. Neither in delict (you damage my boat) nor in contract (you fail to deliver the merchandise promised) would

[1] *Laws*, 928B.
[2] The lawgiver, when regulating education, must start with procuring the most promising material, hence the most suitable parents: 'he must first bestow diligence (*epimelein*) on marriage', *Politics*, 7.14, 1134b, 31. Note, however, that this is one of those numerous recommendations of diligence which cannot be said to create a technical standard: there is no court to conduct an inquiry into diligence or negligence in any given case and render its verdict in accordance with the result.

it make sense generally to relieve of accountability everyone but the deliberate offender. In some relationships, no doubt it is all right to allow a claim only on the ground of *dolus*, for example, where you gratuitously execute a commission for me. As a rule justice, it is felt, requires that he who causes loss or disappointment, with or without intent, should make it good – unless indeed events were beyond his control: the book you borrowed from me perishes in a conflagration.

It is this latter limitation which is a vital factor in the Roman scheme. At a primitive stage, when the sifting of evidence as to the precise situation and conduct of a party presents huge difficulties, recourse may be had to fixed external criteria; say, a borrower is free if the object disappears as a result of fire, earthquake or armed robbery. This objectively based liability will work fairly, in the vast majority of cases, though admittedly a less dramatic occurrence may exceptionally be as overwhelming as one of the recognized acts of God, while some other time it may be possible to save a book even from a fire. In course of time the courts tend to dispense with these rigid criteria and go by the merits of any given case. (The development is neither uniform throughout the entire legal order nor irreversible. For a variety of reasons the past fifty years have seen a revival of strict liability in many branches of the law.) Once the subjective attitude of each individual defendant is gone into, the Roman classification is a plausible one to emerge: the defendant will assert that he could not help things, and that plea will collapse not only if he displayed *dolus* but also if he displayed negligence.

Even in Greece, let me repeat, in quite a few cases negligence is recognized as grounding liability. But it does not figure in a system of standards comparable to the Roman, most definitely not in the chapters from Aristotle we have considered.

The Roman rhetorical works show an intriguing mixture. The basic structure, borrowed from the Greek predecessors, is still largely dominated by the criminal trial; but the cases discussed have shifted to lesser crimes and even near to private

Liability : dolus, culpa and casus

law, and blameworthy behaviour other than sheer *dolus* plays a considerable part.[1] Thus we are told of a Rhodian decree under which a ship with a ram entering the harbour will be confiscated: what is to happen to a ship driven there by a storm? Prima facie, this is an instance of accident, act of God. But the decision, we learn, is not so easy. It will depend on whether the necessity could have been avoided, the storm foreseen, on whether there was *inertia, neglegentia, fatuitas*. What in Antiphon is adumbrated in speeches about a peculiar mishap and in Aristotle is confined to a few contexts mainly to do with public or semi-public office,[2] has become articulated and generalized, an established component of forensic theory. It is now possible to raise the question of negligence wherever accident is invoked to escape from a fine or the like. Maybe some of this advance already goes back to late Hellenistic writings lost to us; but I should be surprised if a good deal of it were not genuinely Roman.

When did the Roman jurists start speaking of *culpa* in connection with negligence – be it that the term meant fault in a wide sense, whether *dolus* or negligence (this usage seems to have come up first), be it that it meant negligence as such, specifically?[3] In the field of the *lex Aquilia*, concerning damage to property, the date is relatively early, about 100 BC. Quintus Mucius Scaevola employs *culpa* in a decision quoted above, about a man who prunes trees and kills a slave passing by, and Alfenus Varus, some sixty years later, is obviously familiar with the concept; one of the cases where he works with it I have also adverted to already – the ball-player pushing over and injuring a caddie.[4]

---

[1] *Ad Herennium*, 2.16.23ff., Cicero, *De Inventione*, 2.31.94ff.

[2] And, of course, in ethics, sloth is the root of all evil; but this, as I have tried to demonstrate, does not make it into a legal ground of liability.

[3] I am simplifying: even by the end of the classical period there were few cases in which *culpa* was fully synonymous with *neglegentia*. For the purpose of my argument, however, these finer points may be disregarded.

[4] D.9.2.31, Paul *X ad Sabinum*, 9.2.52.4, Alfenus *II digestorum*. The case of the pruner illustrates the precedence of negligence in private law.

[continued over

For other fields, the earliest evidence is found in Servius, who flourished about 50 BC, between Mucius and Alfenus. He declares that in respect of objects received by way of dowry, a husband is liable for both *dolus* and *culpa*. (He would be liable under the latter heading, for example, if he allowed a fine house to deteriorate.) It is generally believed that this was laid down already by Publius Mucius Scaevola, father of Quintus Mucius – so that *culpa* would have operated, or at least would be attested, in dowry one generation before it operated, or is attested, in damage to property, instead of one generation after.

However, Publius Mucius went less far than Servius. His niece was married to C. Gracchus. In 121 BC there was a riot, Gracchus was pronounced a public enemy, his house plundered by the mob, he himself killed and his property confiscated. The authorities resolved, however, to let the widow have back her dowry. It was then that her uncle contended that this ought to include everything she would have got had she reclaimed the dowry from her husband; hence it ought to include compensation for dotal objects destroyed in the riot, since the latter had been caused by her husband's *culpa*. Not surprisingly the authorities did not accept this advice.[1]

If we do not let ourselves be blinded by later developments, it emerges that, basically, Publius Mucius still adhered to a husband's liability for *dolus* alone. Certainly he did apply the term *culpa*; not, however, in the sense of negligence but in that of reprehensible activity leading to an unfortunate result.

Mucius is concerned with the monetary claim of the owner of the slave killed. A *lex Cornelia* of Sulla, imposing severe punishment on the killing of a man free or unfree, is applicable to the deliberate deed only. In D.48. 8.7, Paul *singulari de publicis iudiciis*, we are expressly told that a pruner who does not call out, thus causing the death of a passer, does not fall under the statute – though, admittedly, *P.S.*5.23.12 adds (no doubt on the assumption that the pruner would be of low status) that nevertheless he will be sentenced to work in the mines.

[1] D.24.3.66 pr., Javolenus *VI ex posterioribus Labeonis*, Plutarch, *C. Gracchus* 17.5, Appian, *Bella Civilia*, 1.3.26; see Daube, *Studi Biondo Biondi*, vol.1, 1963, 199ff.

Differentiation in Life and Law

(One might compare, also from the law of dowry, the notion of a divorce which, though effected by one spouse, yet is brought about by the *culpa* of the other.[1]) Again, he did unquestionably extend liability: the husband's wrongdoing had no specific relation to the dowry, it was not as if Gracchus had committed *dolus* in dealing with the goods brought in by his wife, his misconduct merely caused the incident, the sedition, in the course of which they perished. The jurist, then, was moving in the direction of inclusion of negligence. But it was Servius who took the decisive step in establishing the wide scope of a husband's liability: *dolus* and *culpa*, dolose behaviour and negligence. That is, after all, why this rule is associated with his name. Very probably he invoked the opinion of Publius Mucius Scaevola in support, and later jurists – Labeo, Javolenus – saw that opinion as anticipating his statement.[2] This should not make us overlook the gap between the two – a typical one: in those three-quarters of a century between Publius Mucius and Servius there was much evolution of this kind, from carefully-groping first steps in a particular case to fully formulated principle.

What is of special interest is that Servius was able to exploit an opinion using *culpa* in the sense of dolose, criminal activity for his rule that a husband is answerable not only for *dolus* but also for *culpa* – signifying negligence. The oscillating character of *culpa* remains important throughout Roman law. Earlier on in this discussion I cited Paul referring to *culpa* as a condition of liability in damage to property, *culpa quam Graeci adikema dicunt*: here *culpa* covers *dolus* as well as negligence,

---

[1] E.g. *Fr. Vat.* 121, Papinian *IV responsorum*; see Bonfante, *Corso di Diritto Romano*, vol.1, 1925, 256. From the field of the *lex Aquilia*, cf. D.9.2.52.1, Alfenus *II digestorum*. Somebody removes a lantern in front of a shop; the shopkeeper runs after him; the fugitive strikes him with a whip; in the ensuing scuffle the shopkeeper puts out one of the man's eyes. No damages, Alfenus holds: *culpam penes eum qui prior flagello percussit residere*, '*culpa* rests with him who first struck with a whip'.

[2] D.24.3.66 pr.: *Dolum malum et culpam eum praestare oportere Servius ait; ea sententia Publii Mucii est.*

anything not *casus*.¹ All this renders it even more unlikely that the triad *dolus-culpa-casus* represents a simple transfer into Roman law of a ready-made Greek classification.²

¹ I.4.4 pr., cf. *Coll.* 2.5.1, Paul *libro singulari de iniuriis*.
² By the way, I wonder whether the English 'guilt' may not be etymologically related to *culpa*. I am not saying that it is probable, but neither does it strike me as impossible.

B. Differentiation in Life
and Differentiation in Law

1. *Negligence.* I wish to make some remarks to dissociate myself from a widespread fallacy.[1] Historians often fail to distinguish between the idea that application is desirable and negligence to be avoided – an exceedingly old idea – and the operation of diligence or negligence as a legal standard in the sense that a court's decision will turn on whether defendant has acted as he ought to – a far later phenomenon. For that matter, as I shall elaborate below, they often fail to distinguish between the condemnation of *dolus* – very old – and *dolus* as a standard in the sense that the verdict in a trial will depend on whether or not the individual accused has behaved dolosely – not always so old.

In early Roman law the tutor of a person under age, or the curator of a lunatic, could be proceeded against only if his conduct was dishonest, dolose.[2] This does not mean that a tutor was not from the beginning expected to *tueri*, 'guard his charge', a curator to *curare*, 'look after him': a great deal more than abstention from embezzlement. It would be as wrong to infer from their exclusive liability for *dolus* that the duty to do a decent, diligent job was not seen, as it would be to infer from the designation 'tutor' or 'curator' that any remissness in *tueri* or *curare* would lead to judicial accountability. Again, there is an aedilician edict imposing a substantial fine on you if an animal you keep by the wayside escapes and kills somebody or

---

[1] Cf. Daube, *Vetus Testamentum*, 11, 1961, 246ff.
[2] E.g. *actio de rationibus distrahendis*, Buckland, *Text-Book*, 163.

does damage. You must pay up no matter how careful you may have been: strict liability.[1] Yet it would be foolish to deny that circus-owners were unaware of the need for and usefulness of scrupulous precautions. A General may be answerable for treachery only, or for treachery and carelessness, or for any defeat, even an inevitable one. Whichever system prevails, people know that a General had better exercise care and foresight. These reflections stand to reason, but they are apt to be forgotten. Let me be more specific.

Frequently it is thought that, because in a certain matter diligence is recommended or a warning against negligence given, that must be the technical standard applied by the courts. However, it need not be. I shall give one typical example of such a mistaken deduction, which then serves as basis for a major historical judgment: Goodenough's attribution of this standard to the Jewish practice at Alexandria around New Testament times.[2]

According to Biblical law, if a man kindles a fire on his land and it spreads to that of his neighbour, he is obliged to compensate the latter. His liability is absolute: there is no clause to restrict it to the case where there has been negligence on his part.[3] Tannaitic law, that is to say, the early Talmudic law of, say, 100 BC to AD 200, still adheres to this regulation.[4] Goodenough claims that Philo, however, writing at Alexandria in the first third of the first century AD, depicts a more progressive state, with the standard of negligence fully recognized: so Alexandrian Jewish practice is in advance of the Rabbinical one of the same period.

What is this claim founded on? On a series of admonitions by Philo which, while accompanying the precept in question, are anything but a part of it. Philo in his work on Biblical law, modelling himself on Plato who held that laws should be

---

[1] D.21.1.40, 42, Ulpian *II ad edictum aedilium curulium*, I.4.9.1.
[2] *The Jewish Courts in Egypt*, 1929, 163f.
[3] *Exodus*, 22.5.
[4] *Mekiltha* on *Exodus*, 22.5, *Mishnah Baba Qamma*, 1.1, 6.4ff.

supported by reasons, usually gives detailed comments on a provision, setting out its function and making us appreciate Moses's wisdom in promulgating it. With regard to fire,[1] he begins by enlarging on the danger of this element and the desirability of the utmost caution. Then he goes on to state the regulation, and he states it exactly as it appears in the Bible and early Talmud: if a fire you kindle on your land escapes, you must make restitution – no proviso that the judge should probe and let you off, for instance, if the wind turned in a way you could not foresee. Finally he returns to the theme of his introduction, adding that the offender, having to make amends, will learn to be more careful in future.

What Goodenough does is to mix Philo's socio-moral advice and the law into one – an unwarranted procedure. All that Philo says about the importance of being careful with fire must have been known to Prometheus, let alone Moses or the Tannaitic Rabbis. If they none the less ordain strict liability, exacting compensation even if the damage is the result of accident, it is chiefly because, in their age, it would be too difficult to get at the evidence for each individual case. In general if your fire spreads, it is due to negligence; so in general the precept is fair – the occasional exception just cannot be provided for. But neither does Philo provide for it. He takes it for granted that if your fire does harm you are at fault – the fine, he remarks, will make you more careful – which is by no means the same as saying that you need pay only if you are at fault in the actual case. As many of us know to our cost, quite a few modern traffic laws fine you for the act, making no allowance for the case where, exceptionally, you are free from negligence. A future historian will err if, from a newspaper article which says that traffic laws are needed because of young people speeding to their amorous engagements, he concludes that you are let off if you can

---

[1] *De Leg. Spec.* 4.6.26ff. *Exodus* 22.5 is also mentioned in *Leg. Alleg.* 3.89.248ff. where fire stands for the irrational impulse which, with the help of the passions, consumes virtue and so on.

prove you were on the way to a meeting of the College Council.[1]

Goodenough's erroneous conclusion unfortunately has major consequences, since it is among the vital props of the thesis to which the book in which it occurs is devoted. His argument runs as follows. Early Talmudic law does not use the standard of negligence. First century Roman law does. First century Alexandrian Jewish law does. Ergo – his main thesis – in weighty matters the Jewish courts in Egypt follow an independent line, looking not to the Rabbis but to Rome.

Only the first step of the argument is correct: Tannaitic law does not work with the standard of negligence. The second step is wrong. When Goodenough asserts that the first century Roman law regarding fire marks off negligence from accident, he is basing himself on utterances of second and third century

---

[1] I incline to regard Plato's law about fire as essentially identical with Philo's and, indeed, a probable source of inspiration for the latter's presentation. In *Laws*, 843Cff. neighbours are exhorted to take care (*eulabein, dieulabein*) not to commit unfriendly acts against one another and, above all, not to encroach on one another's land. There follow several laws which seem to envisage dolose trespass, and then one to the effect that if a man in burning down his waste does not take care and the fire spreads to the adjoining field, he shall pay a fine to be fixed by the officials. At first sight this looks like liability for negligence: negligence is mentioned, not as in Philo in the exposition, but in the law itself. I greatly doubt, however, whether even Plato intends to make negligence by the particular defendant a condition of the fine. The reference to lack of care, it seems to me, simply reflects his concentration on the normal situation, his assumption (shared by Philo) that the spreading of such a fire must be due to negligence: the exceptional case just does not enter into consideration. Even here, that is, liability is absolute and all the officials have to do is to adjust the fine to the nature and extent of the damage. *Exodus*, 21.36 is very similar. While ordinarily, if A's ox kills B's, the two owners share the loss, if an ox is known to be wild 'and his owner does not guard him', the law ordains full reparation. This does not mean an inquiry in the individual case whether A did in fact guard the beast. The lawgiver takes it for granted that he did not, else no damage would have been done – which is true of the generality of cases. 'And his owner does not guard him' for practical purposes equals 'and the ox kills another ox'. See Daube, *Zeitschrift für die Alttestamentliche Wissenschaft*, 50, 1932, 153. To be sure, in course of time, in the hands of subsequent exponents, such *obiter* phrases are apt to be re-interpreted and become part of the substantive rule.

Differentiation : Negligence

jurists, and even in this material the distinction is not genuine but interpolated by later hands.[1] On the third step, referring to Alexandrian practice, I have said enough.[2] Clearly, as Philo does not introduce the standard of negligence into the Biblical ruling, and as neither he nor anyone else in Egypt could get it from Roman law where by this time it does not yet operate, the thesis of the book collapses.

The converse fallacy is equally common: the belief that where a legal system does without negligence as a standard of liability, negligence cannot yet be thought of or at least its role not yet be appreciated. But it may be fully appreciated: there are plenty of reasons, apart from lack of understanding, for not making it into a standard.

I have already argued that a rule prescribing compensation if your fire spreads to another's field is based (partly at any rate) on the realization that, in most cases, some carelessness does come in. It would be impracticable to ask the courts to find out about the presence or absence of fault behind each incident. So the thing to do is to generalize, to resort to strict liability – which, in a sense, is liability for negligence, namely in the sense that it is negligence which the lawgiver is out to repress: only he objectivizes it, treats it as established by the very spreading of the fire. This is not mere speculation: Philo,

---

[1] See Kunkel, *Zeitschrift*, 45, 1925, 331ff. In passing, from texts like D.47.9.9, Gaius *VI ad legem duodecim tabularum*, 49.19.28.12, Callistratus *VI de cognitionibus*, *P.S.*5.20.1ff. (*Collatio*, 12.2.1, 2, 4.1, 5.1, 2), *Coll.* 12.5.1f., Ulpian *VIII de officio proconsulis*, 12.6.1, Paul *singulari de poenis paganorum*, it seems to me that the XII Tables distinguished between the ordinary case of making a fire on your land and its spreading to your neighbour's and the case of making a fire on your land just next to your neighbour's dwelling so that it burns down. In the former case you must make restitution, strict private law liability. The latter case falls under criminal law, like the direct setting fire to a house. The code threatens capital punishment, though only if you are guilty of evil intent, *dolus*; presumably in the absence of *dolus* the obligation to compensate will take over, but we cannot be certain. There may well have been a time when, if you made a fire near a dwelling, *dolus* was assumed.

[2] Or, if not, let me add that other passages from Philo adduced by Goodenough are even less in his favour than that about fire. See, e.g. below, pp. 162f. n. 6, regarding the liability of a depositee.

we just noticed, in expounding the strict rule makes it quite clear that what it is directed against (at least as he sees it) is irresponsible conduct.[1] He makes it so clear, in fact, that Goodenough is misled into ascribing to negligence the function of a standard, with each decision depending on whether the particular defendant was at fault or not.

The Biblical shepherd must replace an animal which he loses to an ordinary thief but need not replace one taken by an armed gang.[2] A similar distinction is made in many ancient laws. Surely one important consideration is that, in general, with sufficient diligence he can prevent ordinary theft. From this angle, once again we may speak of liability for negligence in that special sense, negligence objectivized.[3] A shepherd's moral duty to do his best and, say, take what measures he can to keep his flock away from the route of an armed gang will be recognized even though the courts go by rigid, external criteria.[4] The law had not basically changed by New Testament times; yet 'the good shepherd giveth his life for the sheep'.[5]

Or take a depositee, a person who gratuitously guards an object you entrust to him. In Biblical and Tannaitic law, as in a number of other ancient systems, he is liable only for *dolus*.[6]

---

[1] Plato mentions this aim in the rule itself; see above, p. 160 n. 1.

[2] *Exodus*, 22.9ff.

[3] There are other factors. For example, ordinary theft leaves little trace: one would largely have to accept the shepherd's word for it. By contrast, the presence of an armed gang in the region will normally receive wide notice.

[4] Cf. *I Samuel*, 17.34f.

[5] *John*, 10.11.

[6] *Exodus*, 22.6ff. and *Mekiltha* on this section. It is only later, in Amoraic law, that liability is extended to negligence; see Daube, *Festschrift Schulz*, vol.1, 1951, 124ff., and *Libro Jubilar de Belaunde* (*Mercurio Peruano*), 1963, 231ff., reprinted in *Juridical Review* 76, 1964, 212ff. Goodenough, 169, 227, contends that Philo thinks of negligence as the basis of action in deposit: the Alexandrian Jewish courts had imported that standard from Rome. But for one thing, by Philo's time this standard had not yet entered the Roman law in this domain (it never entered it apart from one text about *culpa in concreto*). For another, in Philo's exposition, a depositee who alleges that the object was stolen from him must take an oath that he has not misappropriated it (*nosphisasthai*), nor

Differentiation : Intent

But it can be shown that, in religion and ethic, he is expected to watch scrupulously over your property. Josephus, in introducing the relevant paragraphs, compares the custody of a deposit to that of a sacred object.[1] The Hebrew *shomer*, 'keeper', 'guardian', which is used of a shepherd and a depositee, is used of countless other varieties of keepers, some liable absolutely, some for *dolus* only, some not at all. Always a degree of care is envisaged: the very word implies it (as does Latin *tutor* or *curator*). 'Behold', says the Psalmist,[2] 'he neither slumbereth nor sleepeth, the guardian of Israel'.

2. *Intent*. It is bad enough to deny the ancients insight into the nature of negligence. But over large and important areas they are deemed incapable even of grasping *dolus*.

The commandment 'Thou shalt not covet'[3] again and again puts Biblicists off. Ancient courts deal with facts, theft, robbery and the like, not with thoughts. So the conclusion is drawn that either this commandment is late, or *ḥamadh* for once denotes not 'to covet' but 'to misappropriate'.[4] But the commandment is not meant to come before the courts; it is addressed to the conscience. Certainly courts get busy only when a theft has been committed and, indeed, it must be a provable theft.[5] This does not imply that they did not know, from the time of Adam and Eve in paradise, that theft – like many another sin – springs from coveting. In fact a man who,

---

colluded with the thief (*koinopragesai*), nor been telling an utter lie when pleading theft by a third party (*holos synepipseusasthai klopen*). This is manifestly a denial of *dolus*, a kind of oath which would be senseless if there were liability for negligence. Goodenough says Philo is not writing a Digest, there must have been further formulas. Well . . .

[1] *Jewish Antiquities*, 4.8.38.285.
[2] 121.4.
[3] *Exodus*, 20.17, *Deuteronomy*, 5.21.
[4] E.g. Noth, *Exodus*, transl. by Bowden, 1962, 166.
[5] How narrowly circumscribed provable theft was at some stage in Biblical legislation I have shown in *Studies in Biblical Law*, 1947, 89ff.: a man was found guilty of theft of an animal only if he had slaughtered or sold it.

say, could show that he had been loaned his neighbour's plough would never be sentenced for theft – from the outset *dolus* is an essential ingredient. There is absolutely no reason why a collection of warnings should not, even in the earliest period of the Old Testament, contain 'Thou shalt not covet', with no need to give the verb a more concrete sense than it has.

Let me go on to a more dramatic illustration. It is a dogma that, in dealing with homicide, not only does early law equate the unwitting doer with the witting, but this course is taken from blindness or indifference to what separates the two. In reality, full equation occurs much more rarely than the prevalent view has it, and where it does occur it is a *pis aller*, resorted to because of the insurmountable practical obstacles in the way of determining which side of the line a given case falls: by treating as a murderer, say, anyone who kills by a direct blow or anyone who kills with a piece of iron, justice is done in the vast majority of incidents though, now and then, an innocent person gets trapped. The alternative would be for the law to abdicate altogether.

In the *Pentateuch* both stages – death to whoever kills by a direct blow and death to whoever kills with a piece of iron – are preserved.[1] The latter statute is part of a legislation avowedly concerned with confining the rigour of the law to those who deserve it. But the former too is designed to get at *dolus* – the *dolus* being objectivized, established by the external situation.

Latte in his authoritative article in Pauly-Wissowa[2] affirms of early Greek law: 'Murder (*phonos*) is a unitary concept, determined by the result; he who kills a man is a murderer, intent or other circumstances being quite immaterial; *es herrscht reine Erfolgshaftung*, there prevails pure liability for the outcome'. He quotes two stories. One is from the *Iliad*[3]:

---

[1] *Exodus*, 21.12, *Numbers*, 35.16 – in their original setting, as yet unprovided with the reservations which in the text before us modify them.

[2] Art. *Mord*, in vol. 16:1, 1933, 280 f.   [3] 23.86ff.

Differentiation: Intent

Patroclus recounts how, as a young man, he killed a chap in wrath over the dice. He willed it not, he says, *ouk ethelon*, he was in a fury. He had to go into exile. The other is found in Hesiod and Pausanias.[1] Hyettus surprised his wife with a paramour, son of a mighty person. He slew the adulterer and he, too, was exiled. These two were lucky they lived when they did. Some *Erfolgshaftung* indeed. In England, the latter, since 1671 at least, would have his charge reduced to manslaughter. The former, prior to 1957, could have been hanged; and even between then and quite recently that might have happened to him if he shot his victim. Otherwise – for example, if he strangled or knived him – from 1957 he could get only life imprisonment. And that, I must warn any of you who may be thinking of imitating either of those bravoes, you could still get now: life imprisonment.

There is not a single case in the whole of Greek literature – myth, saga, history – or, for that matter, in the Bible, of a man who killed without intent being put to death, be it in the course of self-help, blood-vengeance, be it by public authority; and this although there are laws which (as I have just remarked) objectivize *dolus* and impose the death-penalty, say, on any killing by a direct blow. Not a single case: let that fact sink in.

It is true that exile – honourable exile as a rule – may be inflicted. Foremost among the factors accounting for this practice is the attitude of the victim's family and friends who, then as today, will be slow to accept explanations. Nor, in judging their reaction, must we forget that, even in the absence of intent, homicide is hardly ever purely accidental, nearly always negligent – to which feature the ancients are fully alive. It is also true that even the unwitting doer may feel guilty, unworthy, singled out as a source of disaster.[2] But such feelings are not unheard of in the 1960s. Adrastos, having unintentionally killed his brother, was exiled and hospitably

---

[1] Hesiod, fr. 144 (Rzach), Pausanias, 9, *Boeotia*, 36, (4).
[2] Cf. above, p. 150 n. 1, about a doctrine found in Antiphon, Philo and the Rabbis.

received by King Kroisos. It appears that he was accident-prone, for, at a hunt, he unintentionally killed the son of his host. The latter forgave him, but he could not forgive himself and committed suicide. Far from lumping together witting and unwitting homicide, this story reveals a perfect awareness of the difference. Had Adrastos acted with intent, on the one hand Kroisos would not have forgiven him and on the other, paradoxically, he would not have killed himself but have been quite happy to live on.

A word about the violent end of Antinoos in the Odyssey, the interpretation of which has suffered much from the prejudice I am combating.[1] Odysseus, returned but as yet disguised as a beggar, sits in his hall among the feasting suitors who resent his uncouth presence. He boasts that he can handle Odysseus' (his own) bow: none of them can. They tell him that he is drunk and should leave it alone, and that if he persists he will only do terrible things with it and draw dire punishment upon himself, much like that abominable centaur who, having imbibed too much wine at a wedding, raped his host's bride and had his nose and ears cut off. Of course, Odysseus takes the bow. He starts by some preliminary display of prowess, then announces that he is going to aim at a novel target and shoots an arrow into the throat of Antinoos, the most prominent member of the company. The suitors at this moment do not yet realize that he perpetrated the deed with full deliberation, but attribute it to his drunken raving. Yet murder it is. They run for their weapons, vowing that they will make him pay with his life.

It is widely held that the suitors at this stage believe Odysseus to have killed Antinoos without any intent, by a shot that went wrong. As they nevertheless threaten him with death, we have before us a mode of thought – it is inferred – to which the distinction between *dolus* and accident is alien. But an unbiased reading shows that they believe him to have acted not without intent but (as I have described it) without

[1] 22.1ff.; see, e.g. Maschke, *op. cit.* 6.

Differentiation: Intent

set purpose. That is to say, they do attribute intent to him; but intent the result, not of rational planning, but of a drunken fit. Just note these points: as Odysseus is about to seize hold of the bow, what he is likely to do is compared to the crime of a drunken monster who committed rape. Again, just before he slays his hated enemy, he proclaims in so many words his resolve to hit a target of an unusual kind. Further, as soon as Antinoos falls dead, the suitor, we are told, run for their shields and spears: why, if they are under the impression that the deed was unwitting? A mere accident is unlikely to be repeated, and these people are not given to nervous fears. Lastly, the phrase used to inform us that they as yet look on the killing as not fully deliberate is the same as characterizes Patroclus's killing of a friend in a gambling dispute. There is intent in both cases. What there is not is rational reflection: it is ruled out by uncontrolled anger in the case of Patroclus, by drunken wildness (the suitors believe) in that of Odysseus.

However, even if we conceded that the suitors at this moment deem the killing entirely unintentional, due to a shot which went wrong – it would be utterly mistaken to think of them as blind to the difference between *dolus* and accident. Unless we expect them to follow some doctrinaire academic line, how are they to behave in this situation? What kind of accident is this? A worthless tramp interferes where he has absolutely no business and, despite the most insistent warnings, recklessly causes a noble young man's death. It is only natural that they should be fiercely enraged at what later Roman law would call *culpa lata, lascivia* or the like.[1]

John O'Hara writes in the America of the mid-twentieth century. In his *Hope of Heaven*[2] a dubious character, long estranged from and despised by his family, returns and inflicts himself on his son and daughter. He always carries a revolver around with him and there is no love lost between him and his

---

[1] E.g. D.48.8.4.1 (*Coll.* 1.11.1), Ulpian *VII de officio proconsulis*.
[2] Panther, 1960, 87.

son. Still, it is by accident that the revolver goes off and the son killed, and his grief is genuine. None the less, as he departs for good, his daughter's fiancé refuses to shake hands with him.

A common failing of modern research into ancient law is the inclination to primitivize the sources, to press the naive side of any statement or custom and overlook the element of sophistication which is often quite strong. I cannot here pursue this vast subject and confine myself to a very few illustrations.

The Hittite laws define accidental homicide by the phrase: 'only his hand transgresses'.[1] From such a formulation modern authorities will take it that full responsibility for the result was seriously assigned to the organ. It is obvious, however, that the construction must not be taken too literally: the Hittite laws do not provide that if a man kills unwittingly, his hand – the transgressor – should be cut off. That would indeed be small comfort to its owner.

At Athens, proceedings might be instituted against a weapon which caused a death. Plato, Aristotle and Demosthenes agree in restricting them to two cases: where no person had handled the weapon, and where somebody did do the killing with it but escaped undetected, leaving it behind.[2] Instead of deducing from the narrow field of this trial that people were alive to its precarious, second-best character, Maschke argues that they must have regarded the weapon as the exclusive cause even where the person who had killed with it was available, provided his killing was accidental. So in this case, too, no matter what the sources say, there must have been proceedings against the instrument. I need hardly remind you that there are many early systems (such as the Biblical, the Hittite, the Babylonian) without a trace of such proceedings, a fact which should give pause to those who would see in them a crude, naive stage.

My third and last illustration is Antiphon's *Second Tetralogy*, like the other tetralogies a model debate, an exercise, not a

---

[1] I3f.
[2] Plato, *Laws*, 8.873Ef., Aristotle, *Ath. Pol.* 57.4, Demosthenes, *Against Aristocrates*, 76.

Differentiation: Intent

series of speeches meant for an actual trial. Listen to how Maidment, the editor-translator in the Loeb Classical Library characterizes it in his Introduction[1]: '*Tetralogy II* . . . is concerned with the case of a boy who was accidentally killed by a javelin-cast in the gymnasium. Now it might be expected that . . . the author would make the prosecution take the line that the victim met his death as the result of a deliberate intention . . . or else as the result of criminal negligence; while the defendant would reply . . . that death occurred by misadventure. But instead both sides admit from the start that the death was purely accidental, because for the writer it makes no difference. A life has been lost by violence . . . (the thrower) will have to make reparation with his life . . . . It is hardly necessary to point out how extraordinarily primitive are the beliefs which lie behind this conception of blood-guilt. They have their roots in the dim past. . . . Homicide, whatever the circumstances in which it is committed, is punishable with death.' Maidment fully realizes that already Dracon – and, indeed, pre-Draconian law – distinguishes between intentional and unintentional killing, and he admits that he cannot explain the discrepancy with this *Tetralogy*. But he sticks to his guns.

Well, after this, we are prepared for a quick, crass, gory exchange. What do we get? An argument so subtle and daring, especially on the side of the accused, that the latter himself is represented as apologizing for upsetting accepted commonsense notions and directing attention away from appearances to the deeper truth.[2]

The case put is simple: a man throws a javelin in the gymnasium, and the boy who picks up the thrown javelins runs into the path of the weapon and is killed. Under the Attic law of the time, such misadventure in the course of a contest or practice for a contest would have been *phonos dikaios*,[3] killing within the law, a justifiable deed – hence exempt from punish-

[1] Maidment, *Minor Attic Orators*, vol.1, 1953, 39f., 45.
[2] Speech 2, par. 2.
[3] It is immaterial whether this terminology was used in statutes or not, sufficient that it is found in the orators.

ment. The *Tetralogy*, for the purpose of its discussion, assumes a law which does not confer automatic exemption.[1] The defence pretends to be able to prove that, even in the absence of a special proviso, the javelin-thrower must be let off: he did not kill at all, it was the boy who, moving into the way, brought about his own death. The prosecution argues that the boy conducted himself correctly, so cannot be held responsible. Moreover, even if it were granted that his movement was a cause of the result, at least the javelin-thrower by his action became a joint killer: he should be sent into exile.

There is here a most searching, disturbing analysis of a certain variety of misadventure, yet the editor thinks that 'both sides admit that the death was accidental because it makes no difference'. So the *Tetralogy* would need no modification if the boy had been murdered by a jilted lover; accident is chosen simply, I suppose, because it makes a good story. But preconceived opinion has led to more distortion. 'A life has been lost', the editor says, 'the thrower will have to make reparation with his life'. The fact is that at no point in the *Tetralogy* is there a request for the death penalty: the deed (if a deed at all) is accidental, exile is all that may be demanded.[2]

---

[1] This is the sense of the law invoked in Speech 2, par. 9, and Speech 3, par. 7, and forbidding 'to kill unjustly or justly'. Its artificiality, its *ad hoc* nature, stares one in the face. Of many impossible comments that of Maschke, *op. cit.* 53, is perhaps the most impossible.

[2] Besides several references to exile (e.g. Speech 1, par. 2), for good measure a direct contrast to the death penalty is drawn in that part (Speech 3, par. 10) where the prosecution argues that, even if the boy's movement were deemed a cause of the disaster, the javelin-thrower furnished a joint cause. The boy, the prosecution continues, incurred harsher punishment than an unwitting killing warrants: he died. It would be unfair, therefore, to allow the joint killer to escape scot-free, scil. to be spared even the proper punishment, exile. Maidment (p. 45) quotes Speech 2, par. 9, as mentioning the death penalty for any kind of homicide. This must be a misprint. Probably he has in mind Speech, 3, par. 9. Here the prosecution urges that the defence ought not to invoke the javelin-thrower's honourable life as a consideration against rigorous punishment: the poor victim who lived just as honourably was punished with death! There is nothing in this clever rhetorical flourish to warrant the conclusion

Differentiation : Intent

To return to Maschke, this is what he says[1] about the early Greek epic: 'Intent (*Vorsatz*) has no legal relevance because it has no ethical relevance. The Homeric Greek feels a deed by which he is hurt to be the doer's fault, guilt (*Schuld*), without asking in the least about imputation or even causation: guilty, *aitios*, is anybody from whom harm comes.' In evidence he cites an altercation between Achilles and Agamemnon. The former says he joined the war because of the wrong done by Paris and his people to Agamemnon and Menelaus, not for anything they did to him personally – they did not drive away his cattle nor ravage his lands: 'the Trojans are in nothing at fault, *aitioi*, against me.'[2] I can detect here no vestige of liability without imputation or causation: the driving away of cattle and the ravaging of lands are dolose acts of banditry, and so, of course, are Paris's abduction of Helen and his fellow-countrymen's obstinacy in protecting and abetting him. Against Agamemnon and Menelaus, it is implied, they are indeed at fault, *aitioi*; but what they did does not strike me as exactly an act of God.

All this talk about *reine Erfolgshaftung*, intent without legal significance since without ethical significance, is nineteenth- and early twentieth-century mythology. It is really, come to think of it, just fantastic. Think of Greek and Hebrew insight into, and preaching against, hatred. Think of – outside homicide – Greek *hybris* and *klope*, Roman *iniuria* and *furtum*, old

---

that the accused, if condemned, would face anything worse than exile. Towards the end of the *Tetralogy* (Speech 4, par. 9) the defence warns the court of the bad conscience they will have if the accused *diaphtharei*, 'perishes', 'is demolished', 'is found guilty'. Maidment (p. 113) translates 'is put to death'. That would be the connotation if it were a trial for murder. On this occasion the meaning is 'sentenced to exile'. As the genuineness of the *Tetralogy* is controversial, I draw only subsidiary support from the *Choreutes*, a speech composed by Antiphon for an actual trial of unintentional homicide, where once again exile is the punishment envisaged in the event of condemnation (par. 4). On the sophisticated idea thrown up by the prosecution in the *Tetralogy* (3.8) that an unwitting homicide must be a sinner – that is why heaven makes him the cause of the disaster – see above, p. 149, n. 1.

[1] *Op. cit.* 6f. [2] *Iliad*, 1.153.

delicts with evil intent a primary element in them. Actually, the Homeric Greek does not ask only about causation and imputation and intent. He is sensitive to different kinds of *dolus* – of course. Had Hector killed Patroclus unintentionally, by a stone thrown into the air for fun, Achilles would not have maltreated his corpse. Had he been a vulgar robber who killed Patroclus in order to sell his armour, Achilles would not have honourably returned his corpse to his father. Yet that *reine Erfolgshaftung* is almost universally accepted – and this prompts a question. There must be something very special about a theory which, though so totally absurd, so totally without evidence, indeed contrary to it, could gain such wide credence. What is it?

The answer is that it satisfies two very deep divergent desires or needs, both of them exceptionally powerful in the last century and the first decades of the present (for it is in that period, not in the dim past, that those extraordinarily primitive beliefs have their roots): on the one hand the belief in steady progress – which enables us to look down on those childlike creatures of the beginning, who had no conception of the subjective data behind the visible ones, and to whom we are far superior and constantly more so in evaluating motivation and the like – and on the other hand the romantic notion of the heroes of antiquity as lapidary, classical figures whom we can only look up to, figures *aus einem Guss*, monolithic, dealing with facts and not, like the miserable bourgeois, with sentimentalities, hitting back without asking questions, true elemental forces of nature. (It does not need a psychoanalyst to guess why this latter half of the picture would have a special appeal to the scholar cooped up in his study.) I am not siding with those at the moment fashionable anthropologists who make the Papuan headhunters into avant-garde thinkers, preferably à la Teilhard de Chardin. But that dog of mine which I shall leave unburied at San Francisco[1] notices whether I kick him in anger or from inadvertence.

---

[1] *Second Lecture*, p. 128.

Differentiation: Intent

As for the havoc that the prejudice I am opposing causes outside classical and Biblical studies, I will submit just one minor example on which I hit recently. In *Beowulf*[1] King Hrethel's second son unintentionally kills his elder brother with an arrow, a deed – the romancer tells us – for which the father can impose neither a fine nor other, sterner punishment. Commentators agree that it is only because of the relationship that retribution is ruled out; had the king to do with a stranger, it would be exacted in full.[2] Indeed, the episode, thus interpreted, is constantly used to prove the premise of its interpretation – that accidental homicide in Germanic law ranked as a serious crime or even as murder.[3]

What a method! I very much doubt whether Hrethel would remain (or whether the story-teller thinks he would remain) equally passive had the shot been aimed with murderous intent. The narrator compares Hrethel to a man whose son has been hanged, i.e. executed, and may not be avenged. This comparison is particularly apt if meant to put justified killing by way of execution on a level with unwitting killing: in both cases the character of the deed demands that hostility to the doer be kept under control. (It would be somewhat reminiscent of the Greek scheme of defence, with the pleas of lawfulness and accident.) That the king considers his hands tied by the inadvertent nature of the killing rather than the relationship is corroborated by a detail conveniently overlooked in the literature: though resentful and, indeed, dying from grief, he

---

[1] 2435ff.

[2] Klaeber, *Beowulf and the Fight at Finnsburg*, 3rd ed., 1936, 213, Sedgefield, *Beowulf*, 3rd ed., 1935, 139, Wrenn, *Beowulf*, 2nd ed., 1958, 220f.

[3] Brunner, *Deutsche Rechtsgeschichte*, vol.2, 2nd ed. v. Schwerin, 1928, 820, Liebermann, *Die Gesetze der Angelsachsen*, vol.2, 1903–16, 265, 717. On p. 265 Liebermann dissociates himself from the extremists by suggesting that, whatever we may find in legal regulations, the ability to discriminate between intended harm and unintended harm is as old as mankind (*uralt-menschlich*) seeing that even the higher domestic animals acquire it.

leaves his second son his share in the kingdom.[1]

I repeat: the sources – Oriental, Greek, Roman – offer not one example of an unintentional killer being killed. I do not, of course, count the cases where the prevalent doctrine says, Ah yes, but he would have been killed were it not for such-and-such special circumstances. I want to be shown one instance where he is killed: surely a modest request. If the prevalent view is right, there ought to be hundreds. Even where an unwitting killer goes into exile, he is likely to find friendly hospitality – the case of Adrastos is typical – and the same goes for a slayer from intent, provided his motive is one people can sympathize with: remember Patroclus who murdered in a gambling quarrel and Hyettus who murdered an adulterer. There is displayed in these reactions enormous sensitivity to the subjective nuances of a deed.

I observed above that the ancients are less intrigued by the accidental deed than the deed committed in error. Even so they know or at least divine a good deal about the former. Nowadays if a lover inadvertently pushes his rival over a cliff, we pride ourselves on considering the possibility of unconscious volition. Perseus, by an unfortunate throw of the discus in the games, killed his grandfather, thus inheriting the kingdom. No version of this old myth mixes it up with murder. Nevertheless, while in some accounts he is represented as merely sorry – for he was fond of the old gentleman – others, perhaps

---

[1] Miss Whitelock, cited with approval by Wrenn *loc. cit.*, is the first to have noticed that the hanging contemplated is that of a criminal, which does not entitle the family to start a feud; and she is absolutely right in regarding this legal obstacle as the *tertium comparationis*—Hrethel too must not give rein to what resentment he may feel. As to why he must not, however, even she still thinks exclusively of his being the killer's father and pays no attention to the element of accident. I ought to add that the relationship may still be relevant as far as the exclusion of a fine is concerned: a stranger, that is, might well be forced to make some payment. But the poem seems to place special emphasis on the impropriety also of other, severer measures (they are in the foreground precisely in the verses which introduce the comparison), and it is here that the lack of *dolus* appears the decisive consideration. Of the explanations of the comparison prior to Miss Whitelock's, one was more far-fetched than the other; nor is Taylor, *Leeds Studies in English*, 7/8, 1952, 5ff., convincing.

Differentiation : Intent

earlier, make him seek a kind of exile and renunciation, by swapping countries with another king. Why does he do so? Because, we are told, 'he felt ashamed on account of the mutterings about his killing'.[1]

Now it is time to ask whether anyone got the only Biblical case of accidental homicide? Good, nobody. Remember the two whores who brought their dispute before King Solomon?[2] They shared a room and each had a baby. One of them overlaid hers in the night and, when she noticed it, crept across to her colleague's bed, put the dead baby there and took the live one back with her. Next morning the mother of the live one discovered the fraud and demanded that the exchange be undone, but the thief denied that anything wrong had occurred. Well, all the King is concerned about is that the true mother of the live baby should be established. Not the flicker of a thought is devoted to the overlaying, the unintentional killing. Today there would be a terrific fuss; there would be an inquest, and all sorts of disagreeable things might happen.

[1] Pausanias, 2.16.3, cf. Apollodorus, 2.4.4.
[2] I *Kings* 3.16ff.

II. REDUCTIO AD ABSURDUM

Reductio ad absurdum in the Roman jurists.[1] For a start let me present two cases from Labeo, who flourished under Augustus.

A husband in his will bequeathes to his wife the utensils for beautification, the toilet articles. Under this legacy, it is held, she gets only what objects had been set aside for her use, not, for example, a mirror in his study. Otherwise – here we come to the *reductio ad absurdum* – if he happened to be a manufacturer of such articles, she would practically dispossess the proper heir. Again, I sell you a major piece of land, say, for 50,000 pounds, reserving for myself the quarries, the beds of stone, on it. Some time later a quarry we had not known of when we concluded the contract comes to light.[2] Held, finally, that you may keep it since, otherwise, if the whole estate turned out to rest on beds of stone, you would just lose the full price of 50,000 pounds, and I remain with the land.[3]

Beseler regards all *reductio ad absurdum* as foreign to classical law; where it appears in classical writings, it is due to Byzantine revisers steeped in Greek ideas.[4] I dissent. His main evidence of Greek provenance is the use of the future tense

---

[1] On this subject I have given extensive documentation in two addresses, one in English (*The Use of* 'Reductio ad Absurdum' *by the Roman Jurists*), delivered at the joint meeting of the Societies for Roman Studies and for Hellenic Studies at Cambridge, 1958, and one in French (*Le raisonnement par l'absurde chez les jurisconsultes romains*), somewhat less full, delivered at the Institut de Droit Romain, Paris, 1958. The French address, with discussion, was cyclostyled and circularized by the Institut.

[2] That sort of thing happened: it is discussed for usufruct in D.7.1.9.3, Ulpian *XVII ad Sabinum*.

[3] D.34.2.39 pr., Javolenus *II ex posterioribus Labeonis*, 18.1.77, Javolenus *IV ex posterioribus Labeonis*; see Daube, *University of Ceylon Law Review*, 1, 1958, 1ff.

[4] *Beiträge zur Kritik der römischen Rechtsquellen*, vol.4, 1920, 16, *Tijdschrift voor Rechtsgeschiedenis*, 8, 1928, 293, and 10, 1930, 202ff., *Studi Bonfante*, 1930, vol.2, 72; cf. Schindler, *Zeitschrift*, 74, 1957, 226f., against wholesale rejection of all texts with *absurdum*.

Reductio ad Absurdum

for the objectionable consequence: otherwise it will come to pass, *fore*, that the proper heir is dispossessed, that the entire estate is reserved for the seller. But he must have been content to look at a very narrow selection of Greek texts. Having gone into the Greek *reductio ad absurdum* I find that its formulation is highly varied, definitely not such as would have suggested to a translator into Latin a peculiar association of this argument with the future tense. In fact, the latter is not employed in a large number even of Roman *reductiones*.[1]

Anyhow, the *reductio ad absurdum* is universal. Admittedly the Greeks made a fair analysis of it and the Romans learned a great deal from them. But the argument is so frequent in Cicero, Livy and precisely the classical jurists of the first century AD that what borrowing there was – and there was, indeed – must by and large have been early. Of course there are interpolated *reductiones*: there are interpolated *a fortioris*, analogies, anything. This does not alter the picture as a whole. In fact it would be a pity to subject the history of *reductio ad absurdum* in Roman law to simplifying distortion; for it furnishes yet another illustration of Greek thought being demonstrably influential, yet undergoing characteristic modification in the direction of pragmatism. It is interesting to watch the Roman jurists applying the *reductio* in just that manner and within just that range which are of maximum service to their specific purposes.

The usual philosophical definition of *reductio ad absurdum* is the establishing of a syllogism by showing the contradiction of its conclusion to be inconsistent with its premise. We must, however, distinguish between the logic of is (as opposed to ought) and mathematics on the one hand, and normative reasoning, the making of decisions, on the other. In the logic of is and mathematics, where premises and conclusions are unambiguously stated, the argument (the ideal one) is quite exact and reliable. It is really a *reductio*, not *ad absurdum*, but

[1] Beseler himself, in *Tijdschrift*, 10, divides the Roman material into two sections, with and without the future. The latter group, however, is condemned no less than the former.

ad impossibile, in Greek *adynaton*. If A is true of no B and B of some C, A is not true of some C since if it were true of all C, B would be true of no C – against the premise that B is true of some C. If laziness is never found in a law undergraduate, and some Cambridgemen are law undergraduates, some Cambridgemen at least are not lazy since, if all of them were, none of them would be a law undergraduate – contrary to the premise that some Cambridgemen are law undergraduates.

Even with regard to this strict *reductio*, Aristotle in his *Topics* enjoins caution. He urges that, in public dialectic disputation, where you put your conclusion as a question inviting your opponent's assent, you should – unless the impossibility you point out is absolutely obvious – refrain from this argument and give preference to others (*a fortiori*, analogy). For, thanks to the rather involved structure of a *reductio*, your opponent might deny your conclusion and get away with it, have the audience on his side.[1]

In his *Rhetoric* he explains in precisely what exceptional conditions dialectic *reductio* might avail a debater, and he illustrates it by a defeat that Pericles, who was a rationalist, inflicted on the soothsayer Lampon. Lampon refused to enlighten Pericles about the secrets of the Demeter cult: they were not for the ears of the uninitiated – and, of course, only women were initiated. So Pericles asked Lampon whether the secrets were known to him and Lampon replied that they were. 'How so', was Pericles's parting question, 'seeing that you are uninitiated?'[2] Another example quoted by Aristotle is Socrates's refutation of the charge of godlessness. His accuser Meletus himself had in his indictment mentioned Socrates's belief in entities inspirited (*daimonia*). Socrates shrewdly did not ask for confirmation of this: he did not need it, it was manifest, and a question about it might have given Meletus an

---

[1] *Topics*, 8.2, 157b 34ff.

[2] *Rhetoric*, 3.18.1, 1418b i.f., 1419a 1ff. Whereas in the passage from the *Topics* the adjective is *adynaton*, in the *Rhetoric* it is *atopon*. The latter is often used, as here, with reference to *reductio ad impossible*, though the former is not extended to *reductio ad absurdum* in the field of ought.

Reductio ad Absurdum

opportunity for wriggling out. What he did ask was whether spirits were not either the offspring of gods or something pertaining to gods.[1] Which Meletus admitted. There followed the concluding question: 'Is there, then, a man who believes in offspring of gods but not in gods?'[2]

When we come to normative logic, decisions (including legal ones), the argument mostly assumes a far less rigorous character, though it is not quite so lax and insubstantial as one might think at first sight. At first sight one might think of it as the propping up of a decision by showing the alternative to be inconsistent with what is desirable, reasonable, fair, lawful; in short, with the wider aim to which a person deciding feels called on to conform. We are in the realm of ought, and the *reductio* is not *ad impossibile* or *adynaton*, but merely – in accordance with the familiar phrase – *ad absurdum*, in Greek *atopon*. Take an umbrella with you when it rains since, otherwise, you will get wet. A buyer must pay since, if he does not, he goes counter to a binding contract.

If we proceed from this model, however, clearly almost

---

[1] Question of definition: *Rhetoric*, 2.23.8, 1398a.

[2] Cf. Plato, *Apology*, 15, 27b ff. There are differences, but according to the *Apology* as well as the *Rhetoric* Socrates, instead of asking Meletus whether entities inspirited did not form part of his, Socrates's, teaching, simply reminded him that the indictment acknowledged that much. It must be added, alas, that the text of the passage from the *Rhetoric* is doubtful. Especially if we compare *De Soph. El.* 15, 174b 8ff., 38f., it appears possible that Aristotle's point is that, at times, a way out of the precariousness of dialectic *reductio* is to relax the rules of disputation and put the final conclusion in the form, not of a question, but of a statement. On this basis, Socrates's conclusion should be translated: 'There is, then, a man – if we follow up your contentions – who believes in offspring of gods but not in gods – you must be joking.' That, grammatically, *estin hostis oietai* may denote an affirmative 'there is a man who believes' is certain: see, e.g. Sophocles, Fragm. 354 (*The Fragments of Sophocles*, ed. Pearson, vol.2, 1917, 26), *eisi d'hoitines ainousin anoson andra*, 'there are those who praise a healthy man'. It cannot be objected that in Plato and Aristotle the phrase generally implies a question: we have (on this alternative interpretation) to do with a deliberate deviation from normal practice. In the *Apology*, 15, 27D f., the final upshot of the debate is definitely summed up by Socrates without further attempt to make Meletus concur.

any reasoned decision is a *reductio ad absurdum*, at least by implication: any decision is chosen in preference to the opposite, less acceptable one. I never quarrel about nomenclature, and you are welcome to call it *reductio ad absurdum*. Only it is not what the Romans understand by it; and in general we, too, mean something more pregnant.

When do we, or the Romans, speak of conduct, a course a person has decided on, as absurd, with any precision? One application is where conduct is not just ill-considered but strikingly incongruous, in conflict with the conspicuous, professed purpose of the agent. Not if you simply go out without an umbrella, but if a valetudinarian who takes an umbrella in a drizzle goes out without one in a downpour. Not if a buyer does not pay, but if a man who charitably buys from an impoverished friend in order to assist him does not pay. A particularly clear instance is self-defeating conduct, where by going to extreme lengths in one direction you land at the other end, achieve precisely the reverse of your plan. Appeasement may be so viewed. Or *summum ius summa iniuria*: by over-meticulous, too anxious striving for justice you bring about the worst injustice, say, you give judgment for a general who, having concluded a truce for three days, attacked in the second night – a 'night' not falling under 'days'.[1] Evidently, there is affinity between the absurd and the ridiculous or downright foolish. In Greek, *geloion* is a frequent synonym of *atopon* and in Latin *ridiculum* of *absurdum* – it occurs even in juristic texts; and, incidentally, while I do not think the Romans needed the Greeks for hitting on *reductio ad absurdum*, the particular epithet *ridiculum* does look to me a rendering of *geloion*.

It is possible, then, to re-define *reductio* in the sphere of ought more closely, as the propping-up of a decision by shewing the alternative to be in striking contrast to the declared specific objective of the enterprise. Naturally, even within this narrower *reductio* there are degrees of absurdity (as

[1] Cf. Cicero, *de Off.* 1.10.33.

Reductio ad Absurdum

there are not of impossibility), so even after re-definition the range of the argument remains considerable. I shall in due course isolate a yet more circumscribed variety.

Before going on, however, I would draw attention to a little feature that relates to what I have propounded so far, i.e. to *reductio ad absurdum* (in the realm of ought) as the exposure of a specially notable incongruity. We shall see that the argument is apt to be put in a somewhat strident tone; above all, far more often than, say, in the case of an argument *a fortiori* or from analogy do we find the point made by means of a rhetorical question – 'What can be less charitable than to raise the hopes of an impoverished friend by buying from him and then not pay?', 'What will encourage an aggressor more than appeasement?'

The Digest[1] brings a longish section from Ulpian on legacies of wine, in the course of which he introduces a testator leaving his 'old wine'. At this point an extract from Hermogenian is interposed, with the decision that the legacy refers to such wine as the testator used to treat as old. If this cannot be established – and here the Digest returns us to Ulpian, whose verdict is that any wine not new counts as old, even last year's. Now comes a fragment from Paul, a *reductio*: 'On another ruling, what end or beginning of old wine could be assumed?'

Evidently, the compilers found no such *reductio* in Ulpian, otherwise they would not have switched to Paul. By the same token, it is clear that they did not make up this bit: if they had, they would have given it as part of Ulpian's discussion, not

---

[1] D.33.6.9.4, Ulpian *XXIII ad Sabinum*: *Item si vinum vetus sit legatum*; 33.6.10, Hermogenian *II* (should be *IV*, Lenel, *Palingenesia*, vol.I, 273) *iuris epitomarum: ex usu testatoris legatum aestimabitur, id est quot annorum vino pro vetere utebatur; quod si non appareat*; 33.6.11, Ulpian *XXIII ad Sabinum*: *vetus accipietur quod non est novum, id est et anni prioris vinum appellatione veteris continebitur*; 33.6.12, Paul *IV ad Sabinum*: *nam aliter observantibus quis finis aut quod initium veteris vini sumeretur?* See Daube, *Zeitschrift*, 76, 1959, 258f. The case doubtless comes from Sabinus: both Ulpian and Paul are commenting on him. The problem of 'old wine' arose in other connections, e.g. *mutuum*, D.12.1.3, Pomponius *XXVII ad Sabinum*, where the solution must have been quite different.

split it off as belonging to Paul, under a special, fictitious inscription.[1] Ulpian and Paul were contemporaries, beginning of the third century AD, Hermogenian is considerably later, practically post-classical.[2] Ulpian's decision – any wine not new is old – was rather drastic. Paul, however, seems to have concurred: he supported it by pointing out that, if one rejected it, the result – as the line could be drawn at no other point – would be worse than a less satisfactory decision: it would be no decision at all. That of course would mean destruction of the legacy, very deplorable: legacies were to be upheld at almost any cost. (In some modern systems the legacy might indeed be unenforceable for lack of determinability.) Hermogenian, later than Ulpian and Paul, did hit on a subtler answer: the testator's habits were to be the criterion, 'old wine' meant what he had treated as old.[3]

The *reductio* must be earlier than Hermogenian. Once his solution existed, it was no longer necessary to apologize by saying that the drastic course advocated was better than no course.[4] We may take it, therefore, that the *reductio* is not only not due to the compilers but stood in Paul's work.[5] Indeed I suspect that he took it over from Sabinus. In any case, it supplies a good example of a repulsive alternative – no decision

[1] And a correct one, too, for in Paul *IV ad Sabinum* there is a portion concerning legacy of wine or oil: Lenel, *Palingenesia*, vol.1, 1261. Such tiny fragments, broken off pieces, are rarely a fabrication of the compilers; see Daube, *Zeitschrift*, 76, 1959, 257ff.

[2] Cf. above, p. 110 n. 1.

[3] Ulpian and Paul got over the ambiguity by contending that a different verdict *multo minus commode fieri posse*, Hermogenian by deriving his interpretation of the testator's words *ex factis, dictis, animo atque vita eius*: Cicero, *de Inventione*, 2.40.117f.

[4] True, Justinian does incorporate the argument. But it is one thing to construct it and another to quote it once it is constructed. The final part of fragment 10, by the way, *quod si non appareat*, contemplating the possibility of Hermogenian's method proving impracticable, may well not come from him but be inserted by the compilers, with a view to combining this answer with the older one by Ulpian: see Lenel, *Palingenesia*, vol.1, 273.

[5] Incidentally, it uses not the future, but the imperfect subjunctive, *sumeretur*, a normal form in an 'irrealis'.

Reductio ad Absurdum

– presented in a high-pitched modulation.[1]

One thing is common to all *reductio* of the normative kind: a dependence on value judgments and, with it, uncertainties of many sorts. Admittedly the same goes for any reasoning as to ought, such as *a fortiori* and analogy; only the qualitative element as distinct from the quantitative is more obtrusive in a decision based on *reductio ad absurdum*. We all know how readily the conclusion is open to attack. The valetudinarian may retort that he catches cold more easily in a drizzle than when properly drenched. It is precisely justice at its highest, it might be contended, which rewards outstanding prowess and therefore upholds the sly general who attacked in the night. The hoary semi-utilitarian argument that you must not lie because, if everybody lied, belief would die out and you would be frustrated – well, the liar knows better: he will cross that bridge when he comes to it.[2] If the widow-legatee obtains virtually the whole estate, the testator being a manufacturer of cosmetic utensils, what harm is done? The heir still has the satisfaction of the compliment of being nominated in the will. In the case of a quarry being discovered after conclusion of the sale, the late Republican jurist Tubero did adhere to the strict wording of the reservation and adjudge the quarry to the vendor.[3]

[1] Here may be the place for a note on the opposition of the Proculians to assigning barter to sale. What they found fault with was the undecidability of all barter cases, which this classification, in their view, implied. Their argument runs more or less as follows: if the aim of classification of contracts is to determine the respective duties of the parties, and if sale involves delivery of an object for payment of a price, then barter must not be subsumed under sale since, if it is, each party's performance is to be treated as at once delivery and payment – absurd, it means a complete muddle with regard to their duties. The *reductio* sounds more cogent than it is; it can be attacked on various grounds. In fact Gaius, who records it (3.141), also records the rejoinder of a Sabinian that there are cases of barter where it is possible to distinguish between one party as seller, obliged to delivery, and the other as purchaser, obliged to payment – namely, if I clearly initiate the business by offering an object for sale and we then agree that you give me another object for it.

[2] Kant had good reason for preferring to condemn lying as an annihilation of the dignity of man: at least this stand is apodictic.

[3] A colleague of mine from English law prefers this unbending solution. By saying 'unbending' I am already expressing sympathy with the buyer: a highly subjective sentiment.

To Labeo's *reductio* that, on this basis, if all land turns out to be quarries, the vendor gets paid and yet keeps all, Tubero might have replied that this was no more than right: the buyer entered into precisely this contract. Failure to delimit 'old wine' would invalidate the legacy. Good: maybe the testator just wanted to tease the parties and their lawyers. We saw that Aristotle regards even the strict *reductio ad impossibile* as a *pis aller* in disputation because it might not convince. His reserve must surely embrace the *reductio ad absurdum* for the purpose of decisions.

The oldest mathematical *reductio* known to me is by Democritus.[1] This type *ad impossibile* alone is represented in Euclid and Archimedes, as also in Aristotle's *Prior Analytics* and *Topics*.[2] But already Plato is full of both the strict – is – type and the laxer – ought – type, several varieties of them, and so are other writers, early and late. It would be wrong to assume that the strict type, because first analysed and defined, is historically older in life and then softens into the laxer type. (Die-hards swearing by the logic of is would presumably speak of deterioration rather than softening.) The laxer, popular type is just as old as the strict, maybe older. Abraham, told by God that the city of Sodom will be wiped out, insists that God must not destroy the righteous with the wicked: 'Shall not the judge of all the earth do justice?'[3] If an ordinary chap leaves his umbrella at home in a downpour, it may be unwise; it becomes laughable if the person so acting is a valetudinarian. A man in his frailty will often do injustice: he will be simply

---

[1] Reported by Plutarch, *De Comm. Not.* 39. It is a twofold *reductio*, a neat puzzle: if a cone is divided into segments – if each segment is of the same extent as the next, the cone will not (as it does by definition) taper to a point, yet if each segment differs from the next, the cone will have distinct steps. The emerging position is described by the superlative *atopotaton*, 'most absurd', perhaps in order to call attention to the impasse where both the conceivable alternatives can be refuted.

[2] Russell is wrong in affirming (*The Listener*, 59, 1506, 6 February 1958, 255, also *Encounter*, 64, January 1959, 6) that Euclid would say 'which is absurd' of the denial that you know you have visible eyes.

[3] *Genesis*, 18.25.

Reductio ad Absurdum

wrong. But if the judge of all the earth does injustice, it is absurd. Note the rhetorical question, typical of *reductio ad absurdum* even in *Genesis*: should the judge of all the earth not do justice? A character in Cicero, defending a seller's right to keep quiet about defects of the object, argues: what would be so absurd as for an auctioneer at the owner's behest to cry, Here's an unsanitary house for sale?[1] Again, the conduct described as absurd involves a flagrant, more than ordinary incongruity: the owner pays an auctioneer in order to achieve the most effective advertisement possible, at the same time asking him to run down the object. And again, the rhetorical question – what would be so absurd?

Frequently, as the *reductio ad absurdum* must bring out a striking, foolish contradiction, it concentrates on the secondary results of the decision combated: the latter itself may not be so glaringly inconsistent with the premises, hence it is its consequences which are dragged in as revealing the absurdity. According to Livy, the decemvirs were advised not to restrict speech within the senate-house, otherwise more dangerous speech would ensue outside.[2] Appius Claudius warned the populace that if he were summarily arrested, what humble plebeian would be safe? Rhetorical question.[3] If a master was assassinated by one of his slaves, the law required all slaves in the house to be put to death. Under Nero a prefect, owner of four hundred slaves, was murdered. There was a suggestion to relax the law, but Gaius Cassius Longinus, head of the Sabinian school, squashed it[4]: 'Whom may his rank defend if it did not help the prefect of the city? Whom may the number of his slaves keep safe if four hundred did not protect Pedanius Secundus?' Rhetorical questions again. The *edictum Carbonianum* provided that if, on the death of a *paterfamilias*, a person below age, below puberty, set up as heir, was attacked as not being among the children, the suit might be postponed till he

[1] Cicero, *de Off.* 3.13.55.   [2] Livy, 3.39.6.
[3] And *fore*, the future I discussed above. Livy, 3.56.13.
[4] Tacitus, *Annals*, 14.43. His stern character, however, also impelled him to actions which must command admiration: see Daube, *Festschrift Leibholz*, 1966, vol.1, 311ff.

came of age. This protection was extended to the case where the young person was attacked as being a slave since, otherwise, scoundrels would be induced to make the graver allegation.[1]

In this form, the argument is often related to 'this would open the door to ...'. By the way, the outrageous secondary result need not be anything in the material world, it may be an unbearable thought. In his speech for Caecina Cicero argues that, if the interdict in question were to be understood in the way adverse to him, the forefathers who drew it up would emerge as a most inferior lot. Once again, the conclusion is put forward as a rhetorical question: if the interdict is inapplicable, what could be said to be more negligent or stupid than the work of our forefathers?[2]

A sub-species of this *reductio*, looking to secondary results of the course to be avoided, is common in the Roman jurists: what is claimed to be outrageous is not just any results of that alternative, but that alternative pursued to its utmost intrinsic consequence.[3] The two opinions with which I started are examples. If a widow to whom the toilet articles are bequeathed were to receive more than those which had been assigned to her use, say, a mirror in her husband's study, then, if her husband had been a manufacturer of toilet articles she would be entitled to the bulk of the estate. If a vendor of land who reserves for himself the quarries were to succeed in a claim to a quarry discovered after the contract, then, if the entire land turned out to be quarry-land he would pocket the price without giving anything in return. The objectionable decision is objectionable because it would commit you to an absurdity in a

---

[1] D.37.10.1.5, Ulpian *XLI ad edictum*.   [2] *Pro Caecina*, 14.40.

[3] Strangely, in the *Concise Oxford Dictionary*, under 'reduction to absurdity', apart from the loose application 'pushing of a principle to unpractical lengths', this is all that is listed: 'proof of the falsity of a principle etc. given by producing a logical consequence of it that is absurd'. According to the large *New English Dictionary*, too, this is the one meaning of reduction to absurdity – entered under 'Reduction 9, conversion into a state, b'. However, the strict *reductio* (above, p. 177) does appear, under 'Reduction 7, logic'.

hypothetical extreme case. In itself it is perhaps just tolerable, but it is spun out to what might follow on an unbending, 'logical' application, and it is the end-stage which damns it. The term *reductio ad absurdum* here often refers less to the exposure of the course to be rejected as incongruous than to this thorough spelling out of what it 'logically' involves; and, significantly, writers are apt to substitute *deductio ad absurdum* – the wrong decision is pursued, brought down, 'deduced', to its ultimate, unhappy implications. In a way, Labeo's interpretation of *morbus*, 'ailment', belongs here.[1] Under the aedilician edict, if a slave you bought in the slave-market proved to have a *morbus*, you had the right to return him. According to Servius (consul in 51 BC, friend of Cicero's), you could return him even if he lacked a tooth. Labeo (under Augustus) said no. If *morbus*, he explained, which denoted an abnormal state, *contra naturam*,[2] were extended to so normal a disability, babies would be born ailing because born without teeth.[3]

[1] Gellius, 4.2.12. His argument is taken over, with modifications I shall touch on below, p. 190 n. 1, in D.21.1.11, Paul *XI ad Sabinum*.

[2] To be exact, such a state *contra naturam* as diminished usefulness: Gellius, 4.2.3. Labeo's definition is largely adopted by Sabinus and subsequent jurists: D.21.1.1.7, Ulpian *I ad edictum aedilium curulium*.

[3] The argument is vulnerable, like most of these *reductiones*, but no more than the rest (see below, p. 190 n. 1). It has, however, been grossly misunderstood. Labeo is usually represented as maintaining that if a quality – like lack of a tooth – is a defect in an adult it must also be one in a baby; hence if a baby is not defective for lack of teeth, neither can an adult be. This is of course stupid reasoning: it would apply to walking and talking, a paralytic or dumb adult would be sound. But it is definitely not the reasoning of Labeo. He proceeds from *morbus* as an abnormal state; and he contends that if you treat as ailing an adult with a perfectly normal disability, then indeed you ought so to treat babies who have no teeth – nor walk or talk; while if you do not so treat them, you must not so treat an adult with no more than a normal disability. Manifestly, with this position, the attribution of *morbus* to a paralytic or dumb adult is quite consistent: it is a question of states *contra naturam*. From the point of view of *Wissenschaftsgeschichte*, it is interesting to note the attitude of different scholars to the – as they see it – silly argument. Most of them keep mum. Buckland sturdily concludes that even a great classic is capable of nonsense (*Yale Law Journal* 33, 1924, 347). Riccobono thinks

There is affinity not only with 'this would open the door to . . .' but above all with the warning of the thin end of the wedge. We do, of course, meet this variety outside the law, for instance, when it is said that the hydrogen bomb is the *reductio ad absurdum* of warfare. Warfare is designed to settle a conflict to one's advantage; it cannot, however, but lead to nuclear fighting; in which extreme case it will be found self-defeating, the quickest route to self-extinction. I need hardly remark on the vulnerability this *reductio* shares with most in the area of ought.[1] At Cornford's University everybody knows everything about the wedge in academic government:[2] 'The *Principle of the Wedge* is that you should not act justly now for fear of raising expectations that you may act still more justly in the future.' He even saw the character of the argument as a last resort, a *Notbehelf*: 'A little reflection will make it evident that the wedge argument implies the admission that the persons who use it cannot prove that the action is not just. If they could, this argument would be superfluous.'

Why are the jurists keen on the thin-end-of-the-wedge *reductio*? *Reductio ad absurdum* counted as a second-best argument. Hence it tended to be employed in rather nearly balanced questions, where you would show up as unacceptable not so much the alternative course itself as its secondary

---

Footnote 3 contd.

(*Bullettino* 6, 1893, 146) that Labeo joked, and he refers to Gellius, 13.10.3; but that passage is far from saying that Labeo made jokes. Beseler (*Tijdschrift* 10, 206) claims that, in Gellius 2.12, the section *et absurdum admodum est* and so on is Gellius speaking, not Labeo – flagrantly a special plea and simply untenable considering Gellius's customary manner of presenting his material. Even if it were Gellius speaking, he must draw on a juristic treatise since, as already indicated, the idea reappears in D.21.1.11. Beseler condemns this text as interpolated, unjustly in my view. Anyhow, whether genuine or interpolated, it ultimately derives from the same early classical legal source as Gellius's account.

[1] It may be retorted that war is conducted for the sake of a principle, not for advantage; that it need not lead to the hydrogen bomb; that if it should, it will be time enough to desist; that even a nuclear war could not destroy us; etc.

[2] *Microcosmographia Academica*, 1908.

Reductio ad Absurdum

results. And whereas in lay reasoning any consequences would do, the jurists, concerned with the building up of a system, a coherent or coherent-appearing body of rules, inclined to think of the consequences threatening from a rigorous extension of the inferior decision; or to put it differently, it was consonant with sound juristic technique to base the rejection of the alternative on its own internal 'logic', on what would happen if one kept going on in that direction.

The second-best character of *reductio ad absurdum* (I mean the fact that the ancients judged it second-best) comes out in a further way: the argument is apt actually to figure as a second one, added to another principal one, to tip the balance where the first one alone may not be quite sufficient. No doubt once you do have another argument as well, the assignment of second place to *reductio* has also to do with the general rule for a forensic address, that you should put your positive considerations first, and the demolition of your opponent's case after.[1] But the phenomenon of *reductio* as a makeweight extends far beyond legal texts. I remember no instance where *reductio* leads, to be followed by another argument.[2]

I mentioned above that one of the characters in Cicero's *de Officiis* defends by means of *reductio ad absurdum* the right of the seller of a house to keep quiet about its pestilential condition. The *reductio* is preceded by several other arguments. There is no coercion on the buyer. The buyer knows that the seller dislikes his house. Now an argument *a fortiori*: a seller

---

[1] E.g. *ad Herennium*, 1.3.4, Cicero, *de Inv.* 1.14.19, 2.40.116ff., *de Part. Orat.* 38.133. *Confutatio* in *ad Herennium* does not, as suggested by Caplan (Loeb Classical Library, 1954, 32 n. b), correspond to *elegchos* in *Rhetorica ad Alexandrum* 7 and 13. The latter serves both to build up your own case and to demolish your adversary's; it is one of seven kinds of proof, several if not all of which are destined for both purposes. It is indeed the *tekmeria*, 7 and 9, which seem to be used by way of refutation only.

[2] In my writings, this would not mean the same – I am in the habit of putting my strongest point last; the ancients, and particularly the jurists, were not.

is not accountable for certain express misstatements, puffery, such as 'well-built villa for sale' when it is not so well-built, *a fortiori* he must not be condemned for silence. It is only after all this, by way of termination, that the speaker turns to the absurdity of your auctioneer shouting 'Come and buy an unsanitary place'.[1] Similarly, Labeo, in dealing with the lack of a tooth, begins by urging that this is not *morbus*, not an abnormal state, seeing that most people find themselves in it. Apparently he feels that this consideration might not be enough to overthrow Servius's verdict, so he adds the *reductio*: if *morbus* covers even normal disabilities, humans are born ill.[2]

In the quarries case, the first argument against the vendor's claim to a quarry discovered after the contract is from analogy plus definition. I cannot sell non-existent things[3] and, simi-

---

[1] As usual, the ought reasonings are very precarious. In fact Cicero himself comes down on the other side: whatever the law, at least from the moral point of view he definitely disapproves of a vendor who does not disclose defects. See Stein, *Fault in the Formation of Contract in Roman and Scots Law*, 1958, 9, 33.

[2] To which one could reply, for instance, that to subsume under *morbus* some normal disabilities need not mean to subsume all. In D.21.1.11, incidentally, Paul *XI ad Sabinum*, the babies serve as material for an argument from analogy and the *reductio* refers to old men. There are now three arguments. The first is that lack of a tooth is not *morbus*, is not an abnormal disability, since many people are minus some tooth. The second, from analogy, is that though we are born without any teeth, we are not therefore suffering from *morbus* till the teeth appear: it is a normal stage. Third, the *reductio*: otherwise – i.e. if *morbus* were to cover normal disabilities – no *senex* would be sound (*esset*, imperfect subjunctive). Why the miserable normal no longer is preferred for the *reductio* to the hopeful normal not yet I am not going to discuss. As stated above, Beseler assumes interpolation. Among his main objections to the text is this, that some old men do have all their teeth. I suppose, according to him Paul ought to have written: disregarding an exceptional case here and there, no *senex* would be sound. But, then, there are infants born with teeth: Merlin and Richard III, for example.

[3] D.18.1.8 pr., Pomponius *IX ad Sabinum*: *Nec emptio nec venditio sine re quae veneat potest intellegi*. Buckland, *Text-Book*, 482, prominently quotes D.45.1.97 pr., Celsus *XXV digestorum*. That text is about stipulation and not here relevant. As a matter of fact, there is nothing against a stipulation without a physical object: I may, for example, promise you a

Reductio ad Absurdum

larly, cannot reserve such things in a sale (analogy), and quarries not known are non-existent (definition). The *reductio ad absurdum*, taking the form of a *deductio* to the extreme, where all the land finally turns out to rest on stone, comes second.[1] Again, take the decision that the *edictum Carbonianum* is to cover the allegation that a person under age set up as heir is a slave. As first argument we are given an *a fortiori:* if the law sees to it that nobody should be unfairly denied his status as child, it must all the more see to it that nobody should be unfairly labelled as slave.[2] It is then that the *reductio* is added, pointing to the undesirable consequence of the opposite decision, the premium it would put on the more dangerous allegation.

A good example occurs in the discussion of a *lex commissoria*,[3] an agreement between the seller and buyer of a farm that if payment is not made by a certain date, the farm *inemptus sit*, literally, should be unbought. Obviously, the seller may cry off if not paid in time. The problem arises whether the buyer may avail himself of this term against the seller's will: may the buyer say, I have not paid in time, in which event our pact provides for automatic lapse of the contract, so I regard it as off?

The answer is, No. It is supported by two arguments. First, a reasoning from the purpose, meaning, of the agreement: it is entered into for the seller's sake, designed to strengthen his position. Then a *reductio ad absurdum*, with that typical introduction of a hypothetical extreme: otherwise, if the farmhouse

---

service. D.45.1.97 pr. turns on impossibility. I promise you a possible service (a service!) and, should I fail to perform it, a hippocentaur. The decision is that the first part of the stipulation stands as if the second were not there at all.

[1] I have already pointed out that it is deemed far from conclusive by English lawyers; they wonder whether Tubero was not right after all.

[2] This consideration was presumably helped by the fact that the edict spoke of a controversy whether the person was *inter liberos*, 'among the *liberi*' (Lenel, *Edictum*, 348). Though *liberi* here primarily denoted 'children', it could be easily pressed to denote 'free children'. The *a fortiori* argument, then, to some extent included an argument from definition, interpretation of an ambiguous term.

[3] D.18.3.2, Pomponius *XXXV ad Sabinum*.

burned down, the buyer could not only get out of the contract but also, by so doing, shift the risk normally on him. Normally, from the moment of sale, destruction or deterioration of the object is the buyer's loss (unless the seller is at fault). Hence, in the absence of a *lex commissoria*, or even in its presence if he paid in time as he undertook to do, there would be no question of relief for him because the house burned down. It would be monstrous, the *reductio* implies, if he did not pay in time, to reward him by conceding that the sale was automatically cancelled so that he could save his money.[1]

We have before us a neat illustration of the use of *reductio* in a fairly balanced case. To present-day civilians the rule of this text as to the effect of the pact may seem self-evident. But it was far from self-evident in the period of Sabinus, from whom in essence the fragment may be considered as deriving. No doubt the pact – a usual one long before him – had from the outset been conceived in the exclusive interest of the vendor. The firm phrasing *ut fundus inemptus sit*, 'the land should be unbought', was to be a threat to the buyer; when it became customary, it did not occur to people that it might be invoked by the buyer contrary to the vendor's wishes. However, there came a moment when it was, and it must have been hard indeed to frustrate this manoeuvre. The words of the pact – automatic lapse – were against the seller; and as he himself had formulated it, his request for a very loose interpretation was further weakened.[2] Accordingly, the first argument, from purpose, though highly important, was not by itself conclusive. Nor would even a reference to the result of a verdict against the seller in a simple case have been quite sufficient. It would not have been sufficient, that is, to point out that it

---

[1] One might, of course, retort that he relied on the phrasing which, so long as the seller did not actually sue him for payment, enabled him to keep his options open. My friend from English law does incline to reject the *reductio*. The latter, by the way, uses the future tense, *futurum*: 'it would be in the buyer's power'.

[2] See D.18.1.21, Paul *V ad Sabinum*, 50.17.172 pr., Paul *V ad Plautium*. This consideration may indeed have been a factor in Labeo's decision against the vendor in the quarries case, D.18.1.77: above, pp. 176, 186f., 190f.

Reductio ad Absurdum

would be unfair, generally, to allow a buyer who did not pay in time to treat the contract as null. That in itself would not have been a crying iniquity (though in modern expositions this is how the *reductio* always appears[1] – understandably, from a modern point of view, as the argument from the spirit of the agreement is now dominating and accepted as fully adequate). It is the *reductio*, or *deductio*, revealing where the alternative course might 'logically' lead to which supplies the additional push needed, the picture of a fire in which the house on the land perishes and a non-paying or slow-paying buyer backs out unscathed, leaving the seller with the ground and the ruins. That, Sabinus argues, would surely be intolerable. Beseler declares the *reductio* superfluous, even annoyingly so, coming as it does on the heels of what he deems an absolutely cogent argument – that the *lex commissoria* is intended to help the vendor.[2] This is an unhistorical approach, it is to base early first-century law on presuppositions not current till some hundred-and-twenty years later.

My impression is that the *reductio ad absurdum* had its heyday in the early classical era. Naturally, it did go on afterwards, but not, it looks to me, in the same degree. There are many reasons. One of them may be that the early classics were nearer to rhetorical thought; which means that they had a sound schooling in, and a heightened sense for, the variety of possible reasonings and their respective appropriateness for different uses. Another point to consider is that the *reductio ad absurdum* more than other arguments, such as *a fortiori* or analogy, has something of an antithetical, combative flavour. It is always against, and that rather suits the early classics. Their predecessors, the late Republican jurists, had produced some general order and *Übersicht* in the law; they had done the most urgent analysis and synthesis, definition of concepts and

---

[1] E.g. Buckland, *Text-Book*, 496: 'It was not void *ipso iure*, as this would enable the buyer to cry off, if he did not like his bargain, by not paying the price.'

[2] *Tijdschrift*, 8, 293: *Nach dem durchschlagenden Argumente des quia-Satzes, ist nam rell. überflüssig und ärgerlich.*

classification. The ground-work was thus laid for further systematic, thorough development. The early classics availed themselves of the opportunity; and – again, maybe, to some extent under the influence of rhetoric – they proceeded to work out right and wrong often by establishing where they differed from those who had gone before and from one another. There was a certain polarization of positions, as shown by the setting up and keeping up of the two well-known schools. In this climate not surprisingly the *reductio* flourished. In course of time, jurisprudence flowed in a more unified stream of broad consensus, with a corresponding recession of the adversative argument.

Some years ago, when Alcatraz was given up as a prison, I hoped that All Souls would buy it to have a *dépendance* in that beautiful bay. I am glad now this did not happen, for I hear that one of the theological Colleges at Cambridge is up for sale. . . .

INDEX

Compiled by H. McN. Henderson, MA, LLB, *to whom the author wishes to express his thanks for his help.*

INDEX OF ANCIENT SOURCES

1. Legal Sources

A. Corpus Iuris Civilis

Code		Digest	
2.57 rubric	35	1.1.4	42
3.33.16 pr.	37	1.3.1	24
3.43.2.2	36	1.3.2	25
4.16.5	33	1.5.15	95
4.16.6	33	1.5.16	95
4.54.7	32	1.6.2	37
5.3.1	110, 111	1.6.3	86
5.4.1	115, 116	1.6.9	84
5.4.20	116	1.7.39	38
5.5.8	9	2.13.1.2	51
5.17.1	104	4.4.3.4	41
5.23.1	20	4.6.15.3	35
5.58.3	33	5.1.18.1	91
6.4.3	96, 118	5.1.32	42
6.23.18	38	5.2.7	43
6.30.19.1	23	5.8.7 pr.	20
6.30.22.9	33	6.1.23.5	16
6.50.14	33	6.1.57	31
6.61.6	83	7.1.9.3	176
7.14.5	37	7.4.10.4	14
7.31.3	35	8.1.16	35
7.39.3	39	8.6.15	32
7.39.8.1	35	9.2.4 pr.	66
7.62.31 pr.	34	9.2.5 pr.	66
7.72.7	33	9.2.27.14	15
8.33 rubric	36	9.2.27.17	67
8.42.9	32	9.2.27.20	15
8.55.30.1	38	9.2.27.24	68
9.13.1.2	103	9.2.30.4	70
10.2.5 pr.	9	9.2.31	143, 153
10.26.1.1	37	9.2.41 pr.	38
10.68 rubric	46	9.2.45.1	67
10.70 rubric	46	9.2.52.1	155
11.6.5.1	43	9.2.52.4	143, 153
11.6.6	34	9.3.5.12	69
11.59.14	38	10.3.26	143
11.62.6.1	9	12.1.2.1	41
		12.1.2.2	41

Index of Ancient Sources

Digest

12.1.2.4	*41*	23.3.9.1	*106*
12.1.3	*181*	23.3.9.3	*15*
12.1.8	*41*	23.3.23	*41*
12.1.17	*91*	23.3.24	*107*
12.1.20	*109, 111*	23.3.85	*109*
12.1.27	*41*	23.4.30	*31*
12.4.8	*106*	24.1.3.8	*21*
12.4.10	*32*	24.1.32.1	*38*
12.6.18	*94, 122, 123*	24.1.34	*41*
14.5.8	*27*	24.3.1	*107*
14.6.1.3	*89*	24.3.20	*109*
14.6.3.3	*41*	24.3.22.8	*36*
14.6.3.4	*90*	24.3.66 pr.	*154, 155*
14.6.6	*90*	24.3.66.2	*107*
14.6.7.3	*41*	25.1.5 pr.	*35*
14.6.9.1	*21*	25.1.9	*15*
15.1.7.5	*83*	26.7.39.6	*47*
15.1.8	*41*	27.1.13	*33*
15.1.47.6	*41*	27.9.3.1 f.	*20*
15.2.1.5 f.	*20*	28.1.25	*31*
16.1.2.1	*27, 41*	28.2.3. pr.	*80*
16.1.8 pr.	*41, 42, 43*	28.5.6.4	*42*
18.1.8 pr.	*190*	28.5.9.8	*80*
18.1.21	*192*	28.5.49.1	*80*
18.1.36	*96*	29.1.1 pr.	*77*
18.1.67	*20*	29.1.11 pr.	*79*
18.1.77	*176, 192*	29.1.17 pr.	*77*
18.3.2	*191*	29.1.17.3	*77*
19.1.13.3	*49*	29.1.24	*79*
19.2.15.3 ff.	*30*	29.1.40 pr.	*78*
19.2.24 pr.	*34*	29.2.74.1	*41*
19.2.60.3	*34*	29.5.1.21	*7*
20.1.16.9	*42*	29.7.14 pr.	*42*
21.1.1.7	*187*	30.39.7	*21*
21.1.11	*187, 188, 190*	30.54 pr.	*80*
21.1.21 pr.	*43*	30.116.4	*33*
21.1.40	*158*	31.21	*109*
21.1.42	*158*	32.37.2	*80*
21.2.22.1	*104, 105*	32.49.6	*15*
21.2.24	*104, 105*	33.4.1.8	*108*
21.2.60	*31*	33.4.6	*108*
22.3.18.2	*34*	33.5.9.2	*42*
23.2.19	*105*	33.6.9.4	*181*
23.3.2	*106, 107*	33.6.10	*181*
		33.6.11	*181*

Index of Ancient Sources

Digest		44.4	17
33.6.12	181	45.1.2.1	41
34.2.19.13	16	45.1.5.2	30, 31
34.2.39 pr.	176	45.1.21	108
34.3.28 pr.	27	45.1.97 pr.	190, 191
34.3.31	42	45.2.2	32
34.4.3.8	42	45.5.18	107
34.4.9	42	46.1.8.7	123
34.4.14.1	42	46.1.69	26
34.4.26 pr.	42	46.2.9.1	123
34.5.10 pr.	42	46.3.54	29
34.5.10.1	95	46.3.34.1	5
35.1.37	95, 120	46.3.67	93
35.1.57	41	46.3.68	41, 42
35.1.82	41, 42	46.3.93.2	33
36.1.2	41	46.3.94.2 f.	27
36.1.32.2	41	46.3.95.3	27
36.1.32.3	42	47.8.2.24	38
36.1.52	91	47.9.9	161
37.9.1.1	42	47.10.43	37
37.10.1.5	186	48.3.7	7
37.12.5	83	48.8.7	154
38.2.47.2	118	48.8.12	21
38.2.47.1	118	48.8.41	167
39.5.33.1	109, 111	48.14.1 pr.	47
40.7.2.2	42	49.16.6.8	7
40.7.29.1	20, 29	49.17.4 pr.	80
40.9.14.6	20	49.17.11	78
40.9.20	42	49.17.17.1	77
41.1.9.3	31	49.17.20	77
41.1.48 pr.	15	49.19.28.12	161
41.2.1 pr.	58	50.16.28 pr.	20
42.4.7.4	46	50.17.23	41
42.4.7.5,7,9	46	50.17.172 pr.	192
42.5.18	107	Institutes	
42.6.3 pr.	27	1.5 pr.	42
42.8.6.5	20	1.9.2	86
42.8.12	21	2.1.27	16
43.25.1.5	35	2.1.40	31
44.3.6.1	16	2.11.1	79
44.3.15.1	16	2.12 pr.	76
44.6.3	37	2.20.15	108
44.7.1.2	41	2.25 pr.	100
44.7.13	91	4.3.5	143
44.7.44 pr.	17		

Institutes
- 4.4 pr. — *145, 156*
- 4.9.1 — *158*

Novels
- N. Just., 22.24 — *35*
- Jul. Epit., 7.5 — *35*

B. PRE-JUSTINIAN SOURCES

(a)

Collatio legum Mosaicarum et Romanorum
- 1.11.1 — *167*
- 2.4.1 — *67, 161*
- 2.5.1 — *145, 156*
- 3.3.1 — *37*
- 5.1.2 — *161*
- 12.2.1 — *161*
- 12.5.1 f. — *161*
- 12.6.1 — *161*

Gaius

Epitome, 2.7.8 — *79*

Institutes
- 1.13 — *121*
- 1.46 — *94, 95*
- 1.55 — *86*
- 1.93 f. — *86*
- 1.122 — *123*
- 1.159 ff. — *130*
- 1.189 — *86*
- 1.195 — *79*
- 2.71 — *16*
- 2.74 — *69*
- 2.84 — *21*
- 2.114 — *77*
- 2.226 — *97*
- 2.228 — *121*
- 2.243 — *42*
- 2.274 — *99*
- 2.285 — *100, 101*
- 2.286 — *101*
- 2.286a — *101*
- 3.44 — *121*
- 3.90 — *41*
- 3.91 — *41*
- 3.110 ff. — *28*
- 3.122 — *123*
- 3.124 — *121, 123*
- 3.126 — *17, 123*
- 3.141 — *183*
- 3.210 — *69*
- 3.212 — *68, 70*
- 3.216 — *68*
- 3.218 — *69*
- 4.13 — *29*
- 4.22 — *25*
- 4.151 — *16*

Paul, Sentences
- 4.6.1 f. — *32*
- 5.20.1 ff. — *161*
- 5.23.12 — *154*

Ulpian, *Liber singularis regularum*
- 19 rubric — *17*
- 19.3 — *21*
- 19.7 — *21*
- 19.9 — *21*
- 29.3 — *121*

Fragmenta Vaticana
- 50 — *22*
- 102 — *41*
- 121 — *155*
- 256a — *38*
- 259 — *38*
- 294 — *38*
- 318 — *42*
- 329 — *32*

(b)

Twelve Tables
- V 4 — *72*
- VI 1 — *45*
- VI 3 — *39*
- VII 12 — *20*
- VIII 1 — *43*
- X 6 — *128*
- X 8 — *43*

Miscellaneous Laws
- lex
  - agraria — *30, 43, 46, 57, 58*
  - Apuleia — *123*

Index of Ancient Sources

Miscellaneous Laws—*contd.*
  lex
    Aquilia   65–71, 146, 153, 155
    Acilia repetundarum   45
    Canuleia   113, 114
    Cincia   38, 109–10, 111
    Cornelia   121, 122, 123, 124, 154
    Fannia   125
    Fufia Caninia   94, 95, 119
    Furia   25
    Julia de adulteriis   20
    Julia de ambitu   47
    Licinia   125
    Malacitana   40
    Oppia   87, 125
    Romana Visigothorum   27
    Rubria, 1.15   30
    tabellariae   47
    Voconia   96, 97, 99
  Senatusconsulta
    de Bacchanalibus   40, 45, 57
    5   34
    Macedonianum   89–90
    Pegasianum   98
Theodosian Code
  1.10.1   33
  2.3 rubric   35
  4.4.4   38
  4.14.1   39
  5.3.1   38
  5.13   27
  5.16.30   35
  6.22.8.1   33
  10.16.3   9
  11.14.1   37
  11.20.3   35
  11.30.67   34
  13.5.32   34
  13.9.6   43
  16.2.37   38

Bruns, *Fontes Iuris Romani Antiqui*
  23   72
  25   29, 31, 39, 45
  28   20
  29   43
  37   43
  40   39
  59   45
  75   30, 58
  76   58
  78   43
  80   43
  82 f.   30, 46
  88   58
  97   30
  108   45, 94
  150 f.   40
  165   34
  200 f.   17
  271   35
  323   17

2. Non-Legal Sources

A. Latin

Aelius Spartianus
  Hadrian, 22.10   100
Apicius
  de Re Coquinaria, 8.7.12   81
Appuleius
  Apol., 18   103
  82   39

Auctor ad Herennium
  1.3.4   189
  2.16.23 ff.   153
Augustine
  Civ. Dei, 11.21   34
Augustus
  Mon. Anc., 3.7 ff. ch. 15   82

Index of Ancient Sources

A. LATIN—contd.

Ausonius
  Ludus Sept. Sap.   95
Caesar
  Bell. Gall., 1.39   75
Cicero
  Epistulae
    ad Atticum, 12.14.2   122
                12.17   122
                12.19.2   25, 122
    ad Fam., 7.18.1   57–8
            7.21   56
    ad Quintum Fratrem,
      1.2.10   93
  Orationes
    in Catil., 4.6.13   30
    pro Caecina, 14.40   186
                 26.74   23
    pro Fonteio, 8.17   34
    pro Murena, 34.7   122
    pro Plancio, 6.14   40
                27.66   73
    pro Roscio Amerino   88
                14.39   90
    in Verrem, 2.1.23.61   85
            2.1.47.123 f.   97
  Philosophica
    de Amicitia, 10.35 ff.   92
    de Finibus   97
              2.17.55   96
              2.31.99   119
              5.22.62   34
    de Inventione
              1.14.19   189
              2.4.116 ff.   189
              2.31.94 ff.   153
              2.40.117 f.   182
    de Legibus   48
              1.18.48   119
              1.21.55   23
              2.7.18   48
              2.59   128
              2.60   128
              3.3.10   47
              3.48   18

    de Officiis   189
              1.10.33   180
              1.14.44   120
              3.6.30   13
              3.10.43   97
              3.10.43 f.   92
              3.13.55   185
    Tusc. Disp., 1.14.31   74
  Rhetorica
    Orator ad Brutum, 144   18
    de Oratore, 1.38.173   15
                1.38.174   28
                1.55.234   103
    de Part. Orat., 38.133   189
    Top., 5.28   18, 23
          8.37   31
          50   56
Columella, 1 prael. 10   126
Festus, 164   41
       165   56
       229   43
       233   58
       241   58
       242   43
Gellius, Aulus
  Attic Nights, 2.12   188
                 4.2.3   187
                 4.2.12   187
                 4.4.2   25, 28
                 13.10.3   188
                 14.2.7   31
                 15.8   125
                 20.1.23   99
Horace
  Epist., 1.17.46   103
  Sat., 1.2.1 ff.   124
       2.6.23 ff.   122
Isidore of Seville
  Differentiarum appendix
    162   29
  Dedicatio historiarum ad Sisenandum   37
Jerome
  Against Rufinus, 1.17   78
                     3.6   29, 33

Index of Ancient Sources

Jerome—contd.
 Commentary on Isaiah,
  ch. 12 praef. — 78
Juvenal
 Sat., 16.51 ff. — 77
Livy, 2.32.4 — 115
 3.39.6 — 185
 3.52.3 — 115
 3.56.13 — 185
 4.9 — 112, 115
 7.15.13 — 126
 33.28 — 39, 59
 34.4.12 f. — 125
 34.7.5 f. — 87
 34.7.11 — 87
 39.19.5 — 21, 40, 45
Macrobius
 Sat., 3.17.7 — 125
Martial
 Epigrams
  7.10.14 — 103
Persius
 Sat., 3.115 — 79
Phaedrus
 Fables, 1.16.1 — 25
Plautus
 Asin., 203 — 30, 50
  257 — 46
  307 — 50
  874 — 57
 Au., 486 — 50
 Bacch., 4.9.52 — 30
  843 — 56
 Captives, 1030 f. — 49
 Curculio, 30 — 74
  621 — 74
  695 — 74
 Miles Glor., 485 — 50
  1417 — 74
 Most., 5.2.47 — 30
  6 — 49
 Poenulus, 925 — 50
  1297 — 50
 Pseudolus, 852 — 80
  1245 — 50
 Rudens, 502 — 50
  525 — 50
  1371 — 56
 Stichus, 228 — 50
 Trin., 2.2.58 f. — 43
  709 — 49
 Truc., 148 f. — 57
  149 — 57
  258 — 49
  685 — 50
Pliny, the Elder
 Hist. Nat., 18.20.93 — 79
Pliny, the Younger
 Epist., 8.18 — 75
  10.72 — 51-2
 Paneg., 25 — 82
Quintilian
 Inst. Or., 5.10.45 — 46
  7.2.46 — 46
Rufinus
 Hist., 5.2.7 — 33
Seneca, L. Annaeus
 de Beneficiis, 5.10.1 — 19, 24
 de Clementia, 1.15.2 — 88
  1.23 — 88, 90
 Epist., 105.4 — 118
Sidonius Apollinaris
 Epist., 8.6 — 39
Suetonius
 Augustus, 33 — 88
  40.3 — 121
  56.1 — 99
  66.4 — 99
 Claudius, 34 — 88, 90
 Domitian, 9 — 99
 Nero, 32.2 — 99
 Tiberius, 15.2 — 83
Symmachus
 Relationes ad principes,
  10.41.3 — 28
Tacitus
 Agricola, 43 — 99
 Annals, 2.48 — 99
  3.76 — 99
  6.38 — 99

A. LATIN—contd.

Tacitus
  Annals,
    14.31.11 — *99*
    14.43 — *185*
    16.11.2 — *99*
    19.19.5 — *99*

Terence
  Adelphoi, 874 — *88*
  Heaut., 3.1.70 — *43*
  Hecyra, 650 — *48*
  Phormio — *88, 89*

Tertullian
  Apol., 9, p.150 — *34*

Valerius Maximus
  Facta et Dicta memorabilia, 4.4.10 — *103*

Varro
  de Re Rustica, 2.6.3 — *23, 43*
    3.16.2 — *103*
  de Lingua Latina, 6.69 — *5*
    6.71 — *25*

B. GREEK

Antiphon
  Choreutes, 4 — *171*
  Second Tetralogy, 1.2 — *170*
    2.2 — *169*
    2.9 — *170*
    3.6 — *143*
    3.7 — *170*
    3.8 — *149, 171*
    3.9 — *170*
    4.9 — *171*

Apollodorus, 2.4.4 — *175*

Appian
  Bella Civilia, 1.3.26 — *154*

Aristotle
  Ath. Pol., 57.4 — *168*
  Nicomachean Ethics
    3.1.13 ff., 1110b, 18 ff. — *134*
    14 ff., 1110, 25 ff. — *136*
    21 ff., 1111a, 22 ff. — *136*
    3.5.7 ff., 1113b, 21 ff. — *137*
    9, 1114a, 1 — *142*
    9, 1114a, 3 — *145*
    5.8.1 ff., 1135a, 15 ff. — *140*
    3, 1135a, 30 — *141*
    6, 1135b, 11 ff. — *141, 142, 143*
    6, 1135b, 15 — *141*
    8, 1135b, 20 ff. — *142*
    8, 1135b, 23 — *146*
  Poetics, 11, 1452a, 29 f. — *150*
    13, 1453a, 7 ff. — *150*
    14, 1453b, 30 f. — *150*
    14, 1454a, 3 f. — *150*
  Politics, 7.14, 1134b, 31 — *151*
  Rhetoric
    1.5.7 — *84*
    1.13.15 f., 1374b, 1 ff. — *133*
    2.22.7, 1396a — *146*
    2.23.8, 1398a — *179*
    3.18.1, 1418b, 1 ff., 1419a, 1 ff. — *178*
  Topics, 8.2, 157b, 34 ff. — *178*

Clement of Alexandria
  Stromateis, 14 f., 60 — *144*
    15, 62 — *144*

Demosthenes
  Against Aristocrates
    53.637 — *132*
    76 — *168*

Dio Cassius, 56.33 — *121*
    58.26 — *99*

Dionysius of Halicarnassus
  4.24 — *86, 120, 121*

Hesiod
  Fr. 144 (Rzach) — *165*

Homer
  Iliad, 1.153 — *171*
  Odyssey, 22.1 ff. — *166*

Josephus
  Jewish Antiquities
    4.8.38.285 — *163*

Lucian
  Nigrinus, 30 — *99*

Philo		22.6 ff.	*162*
de Leg. Spec., 3.71	*103*	22.9 ff.	*162*
4.6.26 ff.	*159*	Leviticus, 5.18	*135*
de Posteritate Caini,		Numbers, 35	*136*
13.48	*146*	35.16	*164*
Plato		Deuteronomy, 5.21	*163*
Apology, 15.27 B ff.	*179*	32.18	*140*
15.27 D f.	*179*	32.20	*140*
Laws, 8.873 E f.	*168*	Joshua, 20	*136*
843 C ff.	*160, 162*	I Samuel, 17.34 f.	*162*
928 B	*151*	II Samuel, 4.10	*148*
Plutarch		I Kings, 3.16 ff.	*175*
Cato Maior, 9.6	*73*	Jonah, 4.11	*148-9*
17.7	*73*	Psalms, 35.19	*54*
C. Gracchus, 17.5	*154*	69.4	*54*
Marius, 46.1	*130*	121.4	*163*
de Comm. Not., 39	*184*	New Testament	
Rhetoric to Alexander		Luke, 15.29	*84*
4, 1427a, 23 ff.	*131*	John, 7.30	*34*
Sophocles		Galatians, 3.28	*129*
Fragm., 354 (ed. Pearson)		Hebrews, 11.22	*54*
	179		
		D. RABBINICA	
C. THE BIBLE		*Bab. Shabbath*, 32b	*54*
Old Testament		*Bab. Yoma*, 9b	*54*
Genesis, 1.4.31	*34*	*Bab. Ketuboth*, 8b	*128*
18.25	*184*	39b	*103*
29.15	*119*	*Mekhilta* on *Exodus*	
Exodus, 20.17	*163*	22.5	*158*
21.2	*119*	22.6 ff.	*162*
21.11	*119*	*Mishnah Baba Q.*, 1.1	*158*
21.12	*164*	6.4 ff.	*158*
21.36	*160*	*Prayer Book*, p.5 f.	*129*
22.5	*158-9*	p.261	*54*